COLLECTING

RARE BOOKS

COLLECTING
RARE BOOKS

FOR PLEASURE AND PROFIT

BY
JACK MATTHEWS

G. P. PUTNAM'S SONS

NEW YORK

The author and publisher express deepest thanks to The House of El Dieff, to Sotheby Parke Bernet, Inc., and to Mr. Anthony Fair for generous cooperation in providing many of the illustrations reproduced in this volume.

SBN: 399–11775–X

Library of Congress Cataloging in Publication Data

Matthews, Jack.
Collecting rare books for pleasure and profit

Bibliography
Includes index.
1. Book collecting. 2. Bibliography—Rare books.
I. Title.
Z987.M37 1977   020'.75   76-21863

PRINTED IN THE UNITED STATES OF AMERICA

For Za, Wyman, Jed, Barbie, Smith,
and John with all cheers and blessings.

ACKNOWLEDGMENTS

D irectly and indirectly, many people have helped in the writing of this book. The antiquarian book dealers and collectors referred to in the text have been of great assistance, taking the time and trouble to answer—often at great length—my inquiries concerning this vast and complex subject, and their testimony has proved valuable indeed. I would like to list them individually, but their number is too great. And yet, I would hope that specific reference to them by name in the text might be considered tantamount to thanks. The Library Associates of Wichita State University—a vital, generous, and dedicated group of people—deserve special thanks for allowing me to adapt a paper I read before them on March 5, 1971, for use in writing the introduction of the present work. I am also grateful to the Guggenheim Foundation for their assistance in the form of a grant, during the term of which some of the work for this book was done.

In researching my subject, I leaned heavily on the bibliographical resources of the special collections division of Ohio University, whose head, Richard W. Ryan, and his assistant, Doris N. Zahn, have been most cooperative. My editor, William Targ, whose bibliophilic productions I enjoyed and admired long before he became "my" editor, deserves special thanks for his attentive wisdom and expertise in the great subject. Dr. Stanley W. Lindberg and Dr. Frank B.

Fieler—both of the English faculty of Ohio University—read the manuscript and made useful suggestions; William F. Rogers, Associate Director of the Ohio University Libraries, and Dr. Richard Weatherford at our little sister institution to the northwest—Ohio State University in Columbus—did the same, providing valuable criticism. It is conventional to say, at times like this, that these people must share in the virtues of the book; but the faults I claim as my very own. As is often the case, the convention is perfectly just and true. It is also conventional to thank one's wife not only for enduring sullen mumblings and spectacular fits of strong language while one was in travail, but also for bringing the gifts of insight and judgment to the evolving task. The principle regarding conventions still obtains.

All these, and many, many more. Thus, my acknowledgment begins and ends in that spirit essential to all acknowledgments—gratitude.

J. M.

CONTENTS

PREFACE

are books afford an exciting and valid alternative to conventional investments. The fact that their prices appreciate sturdily and relatively steadily is an indication that they present an investment opportunity. The ceremonies, ways, and means of their selection, sale, and dispersal are fascinating and unique to the world of rare books. In one way or another, I will be repeating this point throughout the pages that follow; but even if I were to repeat it verbatim, it would mean significantly different things in different contexts.

The principles of rare-book collecting are threefold. The first is that rare books *can* be collected realistically for investment purposes. The second is the axiom that investment in rare books is valid only for those who really love rare books. The last principle states that viewing rare books with regard to their investment potential is in no way incompatible with that fervent love of books that has graced humankind for centuries with its beautiful madness. This principle needs repetition most often, because it attacks the passionate prejudice of a sizable group of people who will not easily believe that their ideal of bibliophily will lie down with the highest bidder in the bed of the market. For all their silliness, these people have my sympathy, for I am a booklover first and an investor second. But that second factor demands its place, and it will have its say.

I.

INTRODUCTION:

or, Book Collecting as Investment

and Search for Reality

The collecting of first editions, Americana, illustrated editions, and other rare books is one of the most enlightened forms of play—much too intelligent a passion to be stigmatized by the words "hobby" or "pastime." The way to be happy, an unhappy man once claimed, lies in being occupied with the perfectly trivial. Happiness is itself not at all trivial, however, even though its poor cousins pleasure and entertainment may be considered so. What explains the mania some people have for collecting such objects as rocks, empty whiskey bottles, noncirculating coins, carnival glass, butterfly corpses, and old dueling pistols? Quite independent of any aesthetic value, and independent of any negotiable value they might acquire because of the similar passions of others, there is a simple joy in collecting them. This joy to collect seems intrinsic, for very young children possess it and soon extend the simple delights of touching and owning to include those more sophisticated delights of building and ordering.

It is difficult to discriminate closely between play and nonplay. The problem of arriving at a clear judgment of the relative moral or social value of the "trivial" preoccupation of the rock collector and the grimly serious activity of the brain surgeon is not easy. After all, the man whose life is saved by the brain surgeon might be a rock collector or maybe even a collector of butterflies; therefore, it is delusive to think of the surgeon as a man of uncommon importance simply because he perpetuates human life: he perpetuates rock and butterfly collectors, and he saves the lives of policemen and firemen who help protect and ensure the safety of rock and butterfly collectors, and so it goes.

It is axiomatic that one best expresses himself in the things he does when he is not forced to do anything particular. The moral and intellectual character of a man watching television is different from that of one who is talking with friends or reading. Emerson claimed that a man *is* what he thinks about all day long—so sobering a thought we might think about it all day. Although it would be folly to grade people in terms of some rigid code of cultural priorities, it is equally foolish to pretend that all actions equally encourage the growth of human values or that all actions are equally satisfying. Some pleasures that can be difficult to acquire prove the most enduring, the deepest, the most satisfying. Scholastic courses in such subjects as literature, art history, and music appreciation have as one of their premises this truth.

Every collector is engaged in creating a personal environment out of objects that interest him. In this sense, collecting is an act of self-realization. It is also in this sense that the collector of books manifests his great superiority over all other collectors, for his is the greatest freedom to select—his is the richest material environment from which to create his personal one, his library. Books possess individual personalities; they possess interiors much like the interiors of human beings, and every bit as varied. The collecting of whiskey bottles and coins is an accumulation of surfaces which, no matter how historically resonant or aesthetically attractive, have nothing inside. In contrast, a book is a symbolically intensified object—one that is so intensified, indeed, that it often contains, by implication and symbol, the sense of an entire world. Multiply this inner amplitude by the thousand and more volumes that are required for the modest beginning of a personal library, and you can see what rich cacophonies and babbles, or what splendid symphonies and chamber music, can result.

The intellectual's personal library is his garden, whose cultivation is a continuous act of dedication and growth. It is his proper personal task; and his immersion in it during his leisure—no matter how hysterical and fatiguing his "means of livelihood"—will confer upon him that exemption from the natural fear of mortality that Pindar says is the reward of occupying oneself with one's own proper work—or play.

14

The library is itself an enlarged book, written by the collector; for what is writing a book but the collecting of information into a unique and telling pattern, in order to create new insights and revelations? This is one's task in library building, of course; although it is never finished, and only receives the ultimate imprimatur if it goes to the printer to be fixed permanently in type because the collection has become famous as a personal creation.

The idea of a library as an expanded book is no trivial or whimsical metaphor, for as a created environment it becomes a microcosm of the ideal world. "The world is a great volume," John Donne wrote in one of his sermons, "and Man the Index of that Book." The only comment this splendid figure requires is that one's personal library is an intermediate map of that largest conceivable world, so that book, library, and world exist in a connected, interrelated series, reflecting one another, and presided over by the mind that conceives them.

One collects books and builds his library in order to create a personally satisfying, intensified environment for himself. The impulse to accumulate meaningful objects, order them in lucid and reasonable patterns, and accept the covenant and responsibility of ownership for them—simply put, the impulse to create a personal environment, with all its commitments—is a deep and natural one. It is also a philosophical statement insofar as the environment created is a microcosm of one's sense of the world that transcends it. *Stylus virum arguit*—style reveals the man—and the building of a personal collection is an act of style and thus an expression of what we are; at the same time, it is important feedback for the use of modifying, correcting, amplifying, restricting, and "creating" ourselves in terms of the cultural judgment we are forced to make on the basis of the eloquent and abiding evidence contained in our choice of books.

Whatever our definition of reality, this definition must be a symbolic expression, conveying a sense of the vast and intangible by means of words. And since our need for meaning is essentially a symbolic need, the physical presence of books—containing in stable symbolic configurations of print virtually all that can be conceived of as having happened, as happening, or as about to happen—is the clearest epiphany of all these elusive glories and terrors.

But one should not philosophize about book collecting until it seems to be a moral obligation, and therefore a drag. This is like getting serious about humor and arguing about the necessity for our

15

celebration of the comic to keep us sane. Nor should one ignore the exciting investment possibilities rare books afford, in spite of the fact that so much of the tremendous fascination in collecting rare books derives from its being the existential creation of a symbolic environment. One collects books to surround oneself with the most commodious vessels of meaning one can find, believing in the act that meaning and reality are one.

Here reality is construed in its broadest sense as expressing whatever we can most depend upon to satisfy our need for certainty—therefore it is always at least half ourselves. Beyond that, it is nothing. It is no more a fact, for example, than it is a place. Reality is the essential condition in which we find ourselves. And since we can never fully escape the value structures of the world about us, these must be considered part of that essential condition. It is impossible to conceive of reality without some sort of cultural reinforcement. Therefore, while it might be perversely heroic to collect something that no one else would even *think* of collecting—say used gauze, discarded sheets of carbon paper, or empty Michelob beer cans—it would surely be mad. Reality is always to some extent a human convention, a consensus. Part of the charm of collecting lies in the hope that your books are socially or culturally worthwhile, or will someday be acknowledged worthwhile, and will appreciate in negotiable value correspondingly.

It is simpleminded to claim, as some otherwise intelligent people do, that to "collect rare books" is to ignore their true literary or spiritual value. No matter how much you revere the accomplishments of Jonathan Swift or Herman Melville, the incarnations of their glories have always been printed words, which DeBury called "the sacred vessels of wisdom." It is a similar silliness to pretend that buying books "as an investment" is incompatible with scholarship or the true love of literature. Quite the contrary: it is the man who divides his love of literature from his material life who is the true heretic, using only the public library or the niggardly functional paperback for the leavening of his sensibility, and investing his money in Ford Motor Company and AT&T stock. What a dreary divarication is this, and how schizoid and truly mercenary is the man who plays such a nasty game against himself! To invest in books does not imply that the collector intends to sell them; he merely buys them with the conviction that his taste in honoring them will be validated by posterity and that—with effort and know-how comparable to those of other investors—this validation will have a dimension of financial profit.

16

The investment aspect of collecting is utterly fascinating, for it carries with it the excitement of competition in skill, expertise, and taste. Often, too, there is the added excitement of the chase, in the auction room, the book fair, and in the "field," tracking down literary manuscripts, letters, or rare titles.

Ideally, one should not buy books solely as an investment, for "content" is the great and obvious advantage a rare-book collection has over stocks and other negotiables: books are beautiful and interesting in themselves. Like antiques generally, their value is twofold, consisting of appreciation on the market, as well as the uniqueness, historical presence, and beauty of the thing possessed. Also, there are all those symbolic worlds referred to—those "interior landscapes"—that books contain. To collect them solely for financial gain, without consideration for their marvelous and varied excellences as desirable and uniquely meaningful *things*, would be a pity, indeed; one may as well go to the Big Board and be done with it. In book collecting, appreciation should always be of two kinds: in our private possession of them we should appreciate them at least as much as we expect them to appreciate on the market.

As with all other kinds of investment, the instability of rare book prices can prove sobering. Fifty years ago, some collectors invested heavily in first editions and signed editions of books by James Branch Cabell and Christopher Morley. Some of the auction prices of these authors were extraordinarily high, but today the dollar worth of most—not *all* of their titles—has fallen. As with all market fluctuations, this deflation of value is not an unmixed curse: it may represent an opportunity for today's collector to stock up on Cabell and Morley first editions, association copies (books inscribed or autographed by the author, or otherwise bearing unmistakable evidence of his personal use), perhaps even an occasional manuscript or letter that did not find its way into institutional libraries during those heady inflationary Cabell-Morley days. The fact that such authors are not avidly collected today should not discourage anyone who honestly *likes* their books and is willing to invest a few dollars. Because of the oscillations of fashion, these deflated stocks may yet prove to be handsomely productive. (Morley's *The Eighth Sin,* for example, is still a highly desirable—and an expensive—item.)

The course of literary judgment and the swing of fashion constantly affect rare book prices. This effect is obviously less pronounced in the realm of classics of science, philosophy, or historical works—such as Americana—whose values are cultural and historical, than in literature. While literary and bibliophilic values tend to be positively related, this relationship is not consistent. However, it is more likely that a book of high literary worth will have corresponding collector's value than that a collectable book will necessarily be of high literary merit—as shown by the recently appreciated prices of first editions of Horatio Alger, Edgar Rice Burroughs, and Zane Grey—along with such nostalgic items as comic books and even the Big Little Books from the 1930s.

In any discussion of the relative safety of investing in rare books, one should consider the case of Jerome Kern, one of the most famous of modern collectors, who sold his rare-book collection for $1,700,000 and invested the money in stock. This was in 1929, right before the great stock market crash. If he had sold his books four years later, in the depth of the Depression, he conceivably would have lost something of his investment; but undoubtedly he would have been better off than he was after converting to stock.

I have heard people say that books are the greatest investment of all, and they just might be; but, of course, this depends upon a number of factors, including what and how you buy (not to mention, how you define "investment"), and what you are after. One of the problems with the rare book market, like the antique market generally, is its lack of definition. If a book happens to sell at auction for one hundred dollars, it doesn't necessarily become "a hundred-dollar item." First edition copies of *Huckleberry Finn* have within a decade had auction records ranging from $10 to $1,500. The first was described as a damaged copy, and I believe it. The second was a mint copy with the rare blue binding. A book selling at one auction might go for half the estimated price; at another, the price may be three times the expected amount. What is a price? What is a book? When asked how many hours' walk it was to the next town, that folklore philosopher Til Eulenspiegel answered, "Walk."

But there are indications all about, and if you are shrewd you can interpret them. As a 1930s Depression investment, the book might serve well. For example, think of what a collector might have done in those years if he had been sufficiently judicious or lucky to predict literary reputations. He could have bought first editions by F. Scott Fitzgerald at a nickel or dime apiece; and undoubtedly there were plenty of first editions by William Faulkner, Nathanael West, Wallace Stevens, and the early titles of Edward Dahlberg available for a dime or a quarter. These were all writers whose qualities were as yet undiscovered by the larger literary public at the time, who were reading *Anthony Adverse* and *The Sun Is My Undoing*; but a sharp reader—undeceived by the hysterical relevance of the period—might well have known that these neglected writers would soon have to fare better and that "their stock would rise."

Buying first editions of contemporary, or temporarily neglected, writers with the conviction their work will appreciate is an exciting game; but it is only part of the fun. The average antique, used furniture, or junk dealer is not likely to know very much about book values, and their establishments are fair game to the energetic collector. Do not feel sorry for these dealers, for they are willing to play for keeps or they would not be in the business; and if they are gullible and ignorant in negotiating with you, they will get even in another context, buying crystal goblets at the cost of Orange Crush bottles and fine china for the price of Dixie cups. They are not likely to resent your outsmarting them, providing you have the minimal grace of not gloating over some bargain you have gotten through their ignorance. And in spite of all the fine bargains I have gotten through the years, I think it is certain that the seller has seldom, if ever, taken much of a loss.

Needless to say, book dealers themselves—all of them—occasionally miss great opportunities, for no one can know enough about books, about their prices, their points, the pen names of authors, the desiderata of countless anonymous collectors throughout the world. Several years ago, in an antique and book shop in New Bedford, Massachusetts, I was informed by the proprietor that "ten New York dealers" had gone through his lofts recently and that no real finds could possibly remain. I thanked him for his courtesy, but climbed up into the lofts anyway, to descend some two hours later with a stack of dirty books in my dirty hands. Included in the stack was the first printing of Thomas Bailey Aldrich's *The Story of a Bad Boy*, (1870) which I purchased for three dollars. Next month, Goodspeed's of Boston advertised a copy of this book for five hundred dollars, although the Goodspeed copy was described as mint, whereas mine was only good. Still, I traded my copy to another dealer for some Mark Twain first editions, along with several other more desirable books (in my opinion), adding up to at least fifty or sixty, or perhaps one hundred, times the money I had invested in the Aldrich volume.

Every collector has such stories to tell, and it is a happy and relatively innocent form of boasting to tell them, bringing back to the teller himself the memory of that unique thrill of seeing a rare and highly desirable book stuck unknowingly on the twenty-five or fifty-cent shelf, along with the despised and musty detritus from past years. The joy is complete when you reach for it and discover that it has the right points, that it is indeed the real thing. I picked up such a book in a junk store in Zanesville, Ohio, once; it was a first edition of F. Scott Fitzgerald's *Tender Is the Night,* and I paid forty cents for it. At a similar store in Columbus, I came upon the first edition of William Butler Yeats' *Fairy and Folk Tales of the Irish Peasantry,* which I paid thirty-five cents for. The Yeats volume is rare, for it is only his second published book; it is also a beautiful and desirable copy (with the spine only slightly faded) that I found lying at the bottom of a cardboard box, with junk of all sorts piled on top. Later, in checking the book out, I found that a similar copy had sold at auction in 1965 for $225.

Unlike that of corn and wheat, the harvest of good books is gratifyingly consistent to anyone who cares enough about them simply to keep looking. Years ago, I tried my hand at various kinds of door-to-door selling, and it was an axiom common to all that if you knock on enough doors, you'll be sure to make a sale. Maybe you'd have to knock on fifteen doors, maybe twenty, but, as the saying went, that sale had to be getting closer. Generally, I've found this a more valid principle in book scouting than in selling during those hard old days. But, of course, one is often discouraged, and one can often hear the voice of the Devil whispering in his ear, "What in the hell are you doing wasting all this *time?*"

As a matter of fact, that voice was becoming more and more audible to me recently on a cold Saturday morning, when I drove to a moving sale held by some hardy movers in an open, unheated garage. The temperature was five above zero, and after shuffling through several boxes of some twenty or thirty books each, my bare hands were so cold they were beginning to feel like big wooden spoons. The books were a dreary lot—drab school texts, mostly—and stuffed under various tables and behind dusty picture frames along with an old lawn mower for the sake of maximum inconvenience. The owner, obviously insensitive to most human values, was jovial, and asked me a question of some sort (I couldn't hear, because the Devil's voice was too loud by now). I think he was asking what sort of books I collected, and I think I answered evasively, not particularly interested in starting up a conversation. He then told me he had a complete set of Shakespeare that was very old—published way back around 1918, which made me feel worse, because that wasn't a hell of a long time before I was born. I was about to point out that his index of age in books was a trifle screwed up, when I saw what might have appeared to be a geography text lying there among the school books. It was titled *Geography and Plays*. It had been printed in Boston, at the Four Seas Company; the single date on the copyright page was 1922; and the author was Gertrude Stein. In excellent condition, this copy was nevertheless in a basket of books that were being sold for a nickel apiece. Five cents, or half a dime.

By the time I left with my prize, I was pumping this insensitive fellow's hand most heartily, and blessing him in all his future dwellings. Returning home and warming myself I consulted a catalogue I had gotten only two days before, and saw a copy of this very book (like mine in excellent condition but lacking the dust jacket) advertised for $95. Not really a bad price even at that, for the book is very rare and very important, representing the work of a genuinely significant modern author. It is in this book that Ms. Stein delivered herself of the Rose is a Rose is a Rose sermon.

These stories are of course the good stories, the successes. I will remain silent about all the errors I have made in judgment, trading more expensive books for less valuable ones (which is always defensible, of course, if one knows what he's doing and simply desires the less expensive one), paying too much, or buying books that were not what I thought they were. I don't regret these lapses, however, any more than I resent those who knew more than I; if I was not deliberately lied to or misled, I have no justifiable complaint. When you enter the arena, for *this* contest, you're sure to get hit sooner or later. And indeed this is part of the game, part of the adventure.

Often people quite reasonably ask why a collector should covet first editions, and—as in trying to define any passion—the answer is not easy. And yet, there are several important qualities inherent in the first edition of a rare book that can be explained. First of all, it is simply human to want to possess what others desire. If that sounds too ugly, let me suggest that the desire to possess is not necessarily conversely a desire to deprive others: it is to own that which is acknowledged to be worth owning. There is, of course, a certain arbitrariness in this, and indeed if great numbers of people—for whatever inscrutable reason—started to collect jelly glasses or empty cereal boxes, many of us would be tempted to join in the madness. This is really not so strange, nor is it a particularly grubby human quality. Possibly half the people in a football stadium don't really have a clear idea of what's happening on the field, but their enjoyment is genuine, for they are participating in a ceremony of enthusiasm. In very much the same way, a collector of first editions—whose hearing is preternaturally acute in such matters—can hear the cheering when he makes a great play and buys a first edition of *Innocents Abroad* or *The Spoils of Poynton* for only five dollars.

But there is more than this, of course. It is almost an understatement to remind ourselves that a book is a visible act of communication and not just a thing. To read a novel by Anthony Trollope, for example, is to gain familiarity with a remarkable man and to understand through the words he wrote something of the world as he uniquely experienced and conceived of it; it is to "see things through his eyes" and to take on some of the shrewdness and wisdom that were the particular signature of this fascinating writer. But if one can read his novel in the first edition, he is given a still closer access to his world, for the style of Trollope's time, as well as that of the man himself, is expressed in the physical book—the paper, the binding, the illustrations, the type. The first edition possesses its own signature; it is the book as Trollope first knew it, and it thus possesses a validity that later editions—even skillfully produced facsimiles, and even those that followed almost immediately—do not possess symbolically. For the collector of Trollope, a complete collection of his first editions is not a shrine, but an abiding statement of the man, symbolically and—in the form of these symbols—tangibly present.

But this still does not exhaust the matter. Like all first editions, that of *Huckleberry Finn* (which in only fair to good condition is not extraordinarily expensive in view of its stature as a classic) carries with it the signature of the time, the author, and the occasion. But also it is *original* and possesses the singular appeal of the original. There is something in our human need for truth that wants to know the origin of a thing in order to understand its nature. In fact, the world *nature* originally (QED) signified the birth or origin of something as the key to what it "naturally" is. And so it is with the word *genuine*, having to do with the original form of something, that which is not vitiated or changed and thus of a pristine worth. The collector of first editions is

22

therefore concerned with the genuine and natural state, in both these old-fashioned conceptions, of the books he honors and desires to own. This is one aspect of the reality he desires.

In addition to the virtues of collecting that I have already discussed—the cultivation of one's library as his personal environment, the promise of financial appreciation, the game of competing with other collectors, the mystique of the first edition as symbolically presenting a deeper access into the mind and spirit of the book—there is another that increases the adventure in a unique way. I am speaking of the serendipity of book collecting, which affords two sorts of adventure to the alert and willing "mental traveler." The first is simply the glorious unexpectedness of the occasional splendid find, the total and marvelous unpredictability of what will turn up when you scout around in junk stores, secondhand bookstores, garage sales, auctions—and most often, of course—in the stacks of rare-book dealers. The second is the occasional discovery that the book or author you've stumbled upon possesses a unique signature and interest, which you probably would not have learned about in any other way.

My own chance discoveries have verged at times upon the amazing. For example, there is the first edition of Frank Harris' biography of Oscar Wilde that I bought at a small country auction, inscribed by Harris. While it is true that the rascally Edwardian inscribed copies liberally, I'll never know how this copy got to this place. The fact that I consider Harris a greatly underrated writer and "collect him" makes this chance discovery all the sweeter. At another auction, some ten miles and three years away, I came across a rare, fine-binding reprint of Barclay's *Ship of Fools*. In a small city some hundred miles away I bought Grose's *Antiquities of Ireland*, two volumes in mint condition, printed in 1791, and containing the bookplate of Lord Cornwallis, who was Governor General of Ireland at that time. A splendid association copy! Speculation as to how these books got to such places leads one very quickly into the sense of the mystery of contingency which everywhere and always seems to guide human events.

Of course, the rare find is indeed rare, and if one is intent upon scouting for his finds, he must be willing to spend a lot of time and energy, often with negligible or invisible results, for the occasional kiss of luck. But like the prospectors for gold in the Old West, the true book

23

collector is never defeated or discouraged; and failure only goads him on to more passionate efforts and to more intense visions of the Great Reward.

Just as the collector who doesn't read his acquisitions mocks the very things he professes to admire, so does the bibliophilic serendipper fail grievously if he does not respond fully to the accidents that befall him. A book is, after all, part of a message: it is the transmitting part that does not become a full message until it is received or read. Consider a used-book store, with shelves crowded to groaning under their thousands of books; then consider how many of these books are being read now, or have been read within the past year, or even the past decade, by anyone.

In short, it can be an adventure and an excitement to read from an old, forgotten book and thus receive a message no one else today is taking in, or no one else remembers clearly. It is an act of liberation, of freedom, to pick up a volume on impulse, give it a few minutes and listen to the message it is sending out. No doubt most of the books you pick up will prove worthless to you at that time; still you have given them another chance, and you haven't *really* wasted your time.

But of course it is possible to discover gold in the unknown book: to read authors who are not read today—who are not even remembered. Surely some of these are worth our attention! Several years ago, I went into an antique shop in Parkersburg, West Virginia, and bought two things that were wonderfully unexpected. The first was a framed letter in Henry George's handwriting whose first sentence reads: "I think Count Tolstoy has never read my book, though I am inclined to think one has been sent to him." The letterhead is that of George's paper, *The Standard*, and the date is April 2, 1888. When I asked the price, the lady proprietor asked how much I would be willing to give. I told her five dollars, and she consented willingly. This letter still hangs on the wall of my study.

My other purchase from this shop was a book I had not heard of, and it was priced two dollars, a price I promptly and happily paid, for the book was an 1870 edition (a first, probably, since this was also the copyright date) of *Belden, The White Chief. Or,* as the title page goes on in that gabbiness of old-fashioned title pages, *Twelve Years Among the Wild Indians of the Plains. From the Diaries and Manuscripts of George P. Belden, the Adventurous White Chief, Soldier, Hunter, Trapper, and Guide. Edited by Gen. James S. Brisbin, U.S.A.*

Who could resist a book with such a title? Never mind the fact that almost *any* book of this date, having to do with the western Indians or the frontier (and in decent condition) is going to prove a nifty bargain at two dollars. Wright Howes' *U.S.-iana*—possibly the most dependable price index for books about America's past, even though the prices are almost all far too cheap, since the second and last edition was published in 1962—lists the first edition of Belden as an "a" item, which is Howes' code for books in the ten-to twenty-five-dollar class.

But the Belden volume was not simply a good find in terms of its resale value, should I choose to dispose of it (which I won't). When I started reading it, I was immediately fascinated. Belden was a natural egotist, a natural braggart, a natural adventurer, a natural writer. He had a clear, vivid, focused mind; and his brief life was filled with extraordinary events. His flamboyant style, along with a habit of being somewhat casual with regard to historical fact, quickly earned him the distrust and even disdain of historians. As Colton Storm, in his monumental compilation of the *Catalogue of the Everett D. Graff Collection of Western Americana*, says with austere and understated disapproval: "Belden's veracity has often been questioned."

Nevertheless, the book itself is so lively and so informative in regard to the folkways, mentality, and daily life of the Sioux (among whom Belden lived for several years) that it is immensely readable, interesting, and valuable. My enthusiasm proved irresistible, in fact, and eventually I edited and wrote the introduction for a facsimile edition published by the Ohio University Press in 1974, a few parts of which introduction I have just now repeated and paraphrased.

I have come upon many other interesting and powerful writers in this way—writers who may not all be "unknown," but certainly people who are not found in today's canon of important or even worthwhile writers. Elias Canetti, Mason Weems, Jake Falstaff, O. E. Rölvaag, John Cowper Powys, Janet Lewis, H. M. Brackenridge, and Norman Douglas (still a famous name in England, but almost unknown to the large American reading public), are only a few of the writers whose work, in the form of old or first editions or rare bindings, I came upon via the antiquarian book dealer or one dusty used-book pile; and the richness and diversity of their testaments is, although only a sample, nothing short of marvelous. To receive a message that all other people conspire tacitly in ignoring is to focus one more area of the infinite human spectrum, one of whose names is "reality."

Man finds and creates maps for this reality everywhere. His games, whether of book collecting, poker, or chess, are microcosmic, for they present symbolically those varieties of occasion for skill, along with those disruptions of chance, that characterize the macrocosm, or the world beyond. The game of collecting shares this symbolic intensification. Who knows what book I will come on tomorrow, and how it may broaden the horizon of my mind, or introduce an enzymic idea into the compounds of my emotions, and enrich my sense of life! Whatever it is, if I feel its power, I will want to own it and let it find its place in that little world of my library, whose cultivation is a human and vital act.

By now it must be firmly established that the collecting of books—particularly first editions—is the most reasonable, moral, and spiritually therapeutic activity in all the world; it may in addition—with the help of shrewdness, passion, industry, and good breath—prove to be financially profitable. But it must also be admitted that to become a true book collector it helps if you are benignly and a little—*just* a little—mad.

Still, as history teaches us, again and again, and with tireless patience, today's sanity is tomorrow's madness, and vice versa. And of all ways to be crazy, the best is unquestionably to be crazy like a fox. Which, in this context, means that all of us constantly find ourselves surrounded by a multiplicity of books for sale, a few of which, within a few years, might well prove to be worth ten or a hundred or even a thousand times what we are now required to pay for them.*

These are some of the books, and some of the ways, I want to talk about in the pages that follow.

---

*For those whom the smells of the marketplace offend, I have this secret to divulge, which I hope they will take to their minds and hearts: Remember, *price is a metaphor!*

II.

WHAT AND WHY

IS A RARE BOOK?

I n Henry James' masterful short story, "The Abasement of the Northmores," a widow—frustrated by the world's indifference to, and ignorance of, her dead husband's gifts—gathers up all of his intimate letters to her, takes them to a printer, and pays to have them set in type. Then she sees that only one copy is run off, and stands watch as the plates are destroyed. After her death, she fancies, a book will be printed from this single copy—the "first edition"—that will prove to the indifferent world the greatness of the man she had loved and married. With characteristic irony, James has named this woman "Mrs. Hope."

Like all his best work, this story is strangely moving, subtle, perceptive, and even though pathetic, a little cool. The reader knows that there is small chance that Mrs. Hope's single-copy first edition will ever have a second printing. Whether the world is insensitive and wrong, or whether she is a foolish and deluded woman is, in terms of the story, a pointless question; it is the enormous difference between an inner pride and the terrible machinery of the world that matters; it is this powerful tension which James celebrates.

Mrs. Hope's sad little volume represents the ultimate bibliophilic scarcity: that of a single copy. There are relatively many such one-of-a-kind copies in the world's libraries. Most of them are the sole survivors of the years; and since printing has been an important part of our his-

27

tory for over half a millenium, and often first printings have numbered only in the hundreds, rather than thousands, it is not surprising that this should be so.

The question may be asked: is poor Mrs. Hope's single-copy first edition a rare book? One might think so, for it was indeed the only extant copy. The point of the story, however, requires that we understand that it was not a rare book at all, it was merely scarce.* To be rare, it would have to be valued by more than the author's pathetic widow. It would, in fact, have to be somewhat generally conceded to be worth having. It would have to be desired at the level of affluence (what if a single copy of an unknown book by James himself were discovered!); it would have to be sought after, as well as scarce, to be properly classified as *rare*.

This is nothing more than one application of the old law of supply and demand, of course; and no matter how this law may be complicated and qualified in the worlds of international finance and macroeconomics, it still prevails relatively uncorrupted in the rare-book market, as it does in the realm of art and antiques generally.

A book is rare if the demand for it exceeds the supply. If a Hawthorne or Emerson first edition appears in a box of drab old hymnals and odd copies of the standard English classics at a country auction, and you are lucky enough to be the only one there who knows it for what it is, then in the microcosm of the world formed by that event, the book has no competitive worth, and is not, in that particular situation, rare at all. There is no *forced* demand relative to that supply. However, if two of you know the value of the book in question, then there are two bidders (demand) for one value (supply), and the price for the book will be forced to something like its "true" (i.e., general predictable maximum) value.

To understand all that constitutes, or may constitute, desirability in a book would be to understand all of fashion, and possibly all of aesthetics and "truth" as well. Like other manufactured things, books reflect the time and place of their making. The great bibliographer, Seymour de Ricci, claimed that any English binding may be dated within thirty years, independently of other evidence. And this is probably the case

*The distinction, surely, is natural, for the word *rare* is honorific in a way that *scarce* is not. According to his famous epitaph, for example, Ben Jonson was *rare*, not *scarce*.

with even less knowledgeable booklovers: it is impressive how subtle the hand and eye become in identifying books, without any conscious intent to train them. The heft of a book, the style of the binding, the materials used all conspire to distinguish one book as a product of the 1890s, for example, and another of the next decade. In some respects you can indeed judge a book by its cover.*

Scarcity of supply is, of course, essential to rarity; and there are a number of factors at work to determine this scarcity in the history of any book. Some of these factors are natural, and some are contrived. One of the natural factors is the limitation that the publisher must set upon the first printing of a book, according to his prediction of the market, of demand. If the demand proves to be less than or (after several months or a year) merely equal to this first supply, then the book will die a quiet and natural death. Such is the fate of the overwhelming majority of books; Charles Lamb, who was a wise and passionate bibliophile, observed that first editions were not so rare as tenth. (Of course, he meant not so *scarce*.) So far as posterity is concerned, most books might just as well be printed in vanishing ink upon newspaper pulp as stamped in imperishable dyes upon fine paper. The flourishing of paperback publishing is theoretically an acknowledgment of this fact.

Things are never this simple, of course: public and publishers both are fallible. Every book published may be said to be either over-printed or under-printed. Since so few go into a second printing, it's evident that most are over-printed. This would seem to be a clear and simple distinction; however, the world of books cannot be easily mapped. What might obviously be overproduction in one context, is underproduction in another, because of the coexistence of two more or less distinguishable publics—the popular reading public (which accounts for the vast majority of sales) and the class of collectors. It is very interest-

*The range of book design is not so closely reflected in type designs, for some reason. Perhaps the conventions and proprieties of legibility restrict design possibilities; and perhaps the old Baskerville and Caslon and Roman styles represent "inevitable" types for western European languages, upon which only minor variations can be attempted. Whatever the reason, a book cannot be as closely dated by means of its type alone as by other means, with the one possible exception of the title page, which is often splendidly evocative of a period, a time, a temper. General distinctions on the basis of print are naturally available—the most obvious, in English, being that between the long and the modern *S*—this change of fashion taking place conveniently in the year 1800, with very few exceptions.

ing, and at times amazing, to contemplate how often these two publics are not in anything like communication with each other.

Thus it is that a recently published book, which has (according to the most sophisticated extrapolations of the publisher) traveled to the far slope of its sales arc, convincing all but the author and his agent that there's little hope for sufficient sales to keep the book in print (much less to run off another printing), this recently published book will, at such a time, be remaindered—which is to say, the remaining copies will be sold as a lot to one of a number of firms specializing in the sale of remaindered books, either by mail-order catalogues or to bookstores for sale on the familiar discount or publishers' overstock table. The remainder houses often buy their stock at slightly more than the cost of the paper in the books, thus purchasing the physical remains, from which the spirit (commercially speaking) has presumably fled.

Usually, these remainder catalogues and discount tables consist of third and fourth printings of yesterday's best-sellers, intermixed with first printings of the worst; characteristically, they are of a particular vintage, published from one to six or seven years previously, and while some are still familiar to the larger reading public, others are as fresh to the casual browser as if they had been printed just that morning.

Shortly after John Berryman's death, I found a small stack of his volume, *Love & Fame*, on the remainder table of a new- (rather than used-) book store. All the copies were absolutely "new" (with dust jackets, of course) and priced $1.95. Each was also quite clearly marked "First Edition" on the copyright page. I bought five or six copies, for myself, and for trading with friends and dealers, knowing that this had to be a bargain.

Which of course it proved to be. Two recent catalogues listed this identical volume, one at $10, the other at $12.50. Did they have the book overpriced? Of course not. Berryman is a vivid and unforgettable poet, which is to say, eminently collectable. A volume of *Love & Fame* in good condition is well worth twelve dollars, by almost any standard of poetic or bibliophilic taste. My getting those copies so cheaply is simply my good luck, not an indication of overpricing on the part of dealers. Does this way of operating convert the book collector into a book scout or quasi-dealer? It may or may not, depending upon one's definitions.

Personally, I can't see that it makes any difference. The collector who goes out and looks for bargains demonstrates his love for books in a

way that the cool and august wealthy collector who orders from catalogues by phone and refuses to enter the arena does not. The latter
may be able to build a more handsome or expensive collection faster
and with greater ease than the collector who labors in the fields, but he
certainly misses out on a lot of the fun, even if all the titles he wants
eventually do end up on his shelves. He also misses a lot of opportunities for coming upon the unexpected title or author and learning to appreciate or understand something he didn't even know he was missing.

So far as it explains the rare-book market, the law of supply and demand requires a very strong emphasis upon the demand for there are
no more demanding people in the world than collectors. This is especially, dramatically the case with those specialized collectors, who collect
not only for all those good reasons expressive of personal taste and
creativity, but with a view of assembling a working, scholarly collection.

One such collector is the Detroit businessman, editor, and collector,
C. E. Frazer Clark, Jr.—a man who is, by this or any other standard,
clearly one of today's great bookmen. Clark's special interest is Hawthorne, and he is editor of the *Nathaniel Hawthorne Journal.* His bibliomania is classic, for it is the collecting that comes first; but, as he explains in the following pronunciamento, the scholarly value is never far
behind:

> I seek anything by or about Hawthorne and collect both as a
> scholar and a bibliophile. That is, I chase not only rare, in-
> scribed, first editions and manuscripts, but pursue with equal
> vigor examples of later printings, reprintings, ephemera, and
> such other material which may have textual or bibliographical
> significance.
> The appeal in such collecting comes first from the hunt—
> that is, there's excitement in the chase and capture of elusive
> trophies, however trifling. In fact, scrounging in attics and
> finding "sleepers" of minor rarities can be even more exciting
> than a successful bid at auction for a well-known treasure. Most
> exciting of all is to chase down an item which may have been
> sold at auction fifty years ago and dropped from sight—track-
> ing it, finding it, and acquiring it from the barest of clues is
> most satisfying. In this respect, the collector is the "literary de-
> tective."
> Secondary aspects of appeal come from the scholarly use that
> can be made of the material. Finding a rare letter is something

31

in and of itself; finding that the content of the letter holds new and unsuspected research value makes the appeal all that much more meaningful.

Finally, there are inevitably aspects of appeal which are at best personal—something known and appreciated only by the collector involved, a matter of taste and collecting temperament.

That natural scarcity of books that is first determined by the size of the first printing helps explain the appeal of first editions (which, to most bibliophiles, in most cases, means "first printing"). Such books continue to decrease in number and "become rare by the process of the suns" (in Holbrook Jackson's good phrase).

But there are artificial rarities—books whose first and only printings are austerely and calculatedly limited and numbered for the sake of establishing a recorded scarcity. These are limited editions; and their appeal is enhanced by several devices: usually they are numbered, thus giving an individuality to a product of the printing press, which is the prototype of mass production with the infinite and anonymous duplication that characterizes such production. Also, limited editions are often signed by the author, or by the illustrator, or even the designer. And last, limited editions are likely to be opulently and beautifully made, composed of rich binding and paper and splendidly wrought. These frills and extras (in terms of the minimal pragmatics of reading) are nothing more than Veblen's "conspicuous consumption"—which becomes, for the bibliophile, conspicuous possession.

The economics of limited-edition publishing is often classically pure: an edition of 225 copies represents a market appraisal of at least 226 interested buyers with enough money to prove that interest. If the appraisal were 251 or 252, you can be certain the "limited" edition would be 250. (In bygone days, editions were limited by the prediction of how many good copies could be printed from the plates, particularly regarding illustrations; and in some cases this is still true.)

Since the printing of limited editions is aimed at the rare-book market alone, ignoring the mass commercial market, the natural depletion of such books is inhibited. They are, after all, purchased by people who care for them as books, as objects. They are not simply means toward the end of reading, but ends and means combined. From the beginning, they are marked "collectable," whereas the first edition of, say, *The Red Badge of Courage,* or Sherwood Anderson's *Windy McPherson's*

Son, was not. Copies of the first editions of the latter books were often read, loaned to others, marked in, cast aside, stored in the attic or shed, lost, thrown away, used to start fires in the old grate, and forced to make their exit from this world of things in a thousand ways, constituting a grim list of indignities to the mind of a booklover. Or they were bought by public libraries, stamped, circulated, and read to death by palpable mutilation.

The perishability of the first editions of great books (not many were known to be great when they were published) is an important factor in their value. But limited editions do not acquire scarcity in the same way; they are less likely to be sold or disposed of by people ignorant of their worth, and they are of course less likely to be lost or destroyed.

And yet, such things do happen, in spite of all logic. Occasionally, people will buy a limited edition for someone as a gift, knowing he is "bookish," and knowing that any book that is opulently made, splendidly decorated and boxed—and expensive—must constitute a handsome gift. Such a purchase may then become the exceptional rarity in that "bookish person's" otherwise worthless accumulation of book-club editions; and will eventually, years later, find its way to the shelves of the local Salvation Army, Goodwill, or used-furniture store. Where, you may be sure, some knowledgeable browser will soon pluck it from its place, delighted to pay a quarter or fifty cents or a dollar for it.

There is a kind of "limited edition" that is not, strictly speaking, contrived; and it approaches that absolute rarity of Mrs. Hope's single-copy first edition of her husband's letters. This is the association copy—a copy signed, or better yet, inscribed by the author (or illustrator or book designer—again, depending upon the emphasis of rarity in the book).

The ideal association copy is one presented, with full inscription and autograph to a member of the author's family or to a literary notable or other famous public figure. If the inscription is dated at about the time of the books' publication, that copy is preferable to one with a much later date. And if that copy is a first edition of Poe, with the following message inscribed on the front flyleaf: "To Janet in memory of a wonderful night in 1842, spent in the Lavender Cat Motel, Love, Eddie," why, you've stumbled upon something well worth possessing.

Limited-reprint and facsimile-edition publishing is a flourishing business. The Cooper Square Publishers in New York brought out a 996-copy, two-volume edition of the Gutenberg Bible, priced at $750,

33

along with a complete set of the 167 volumes of the Library of Congress Catalog for $1,500. Facsimile reprints of the original *Encyclopaedia Britannica,* Johnson's *Dictionary,* Shakespeare's First Folio and the Kelmscott Chaucer are only a few recent additions to this ever-growing and most collectable species of fine books.

Many limited editions are in truth splendid. They constitute part of the glory of modern-day collecting. There is no reason that a book—vessel of wisdom and facts, magic and beauty—cannot have this magnificent office celebrated by as noble an artistry man is capable of. But of course such books are made not solely for the celebration of the genius within but to make money as well. Their manufactured, calculated scarcity, along with the conspicuous display of their adornment, are meant to serve mammon and the goddess of beauty both. And in this somewhat less than perfect world, such a state of affairs is neither surprising nor in most cases reprehensible.

Nevertheless, it is judicious for the collector to take a long cool look at this flourishing industry devoted to the manufacture of calculated rarities before investing in one of their products. It is not always the case that "flourishing industries" flourish at the expense of others, but the fact that there are gullible people in the world is not entirely unknown, nor is the fact that whatever form their gullibility takes, there will surely rise up an entrepreneur to satisfy it. More about limited editions and press books later.

While James' short story serves to demonstrate the underlying factors that create rarity in a book, a story by a contemporary writer celebrates the insidious power of bibliomania. This is Louis Auchincloss's "The Collector," whose protagonist is named Grenville Thorne. Mellowed in years, patrician, wealthy, whimsically learned, he is the popular image of the collector of rare books. Thorne's private library was both inherited from his grandfather and embellished by himself.

Thorne liked to believe that, if he had given his grandfather's hobby a contemporary suit, he had still retained its essence. He congratulated himself on having preserved from the past the only passion that could burn as brightly in the nineteen sixties as in the eighteen sixties. God and progress were dead, and love was mechanical; peace and salvation were pipe dreams, but whatever else he had missed, Grenville Thorne would be able to say, at the moment of his extinction, "Ah, but I owned the manuscript of 'Endymion'!" During the students' strike at Columbia, which as a trustee he had had to observe, he had felt only a faintly contemptuous pity for those shouting youths. "Collect, you fools, collect!" he had wanted to tell them. And he had smiled at the thought of what their stupified reaction would have been.*

Auchincloss has created an interesting study of an insidious corruption in Grenville Thorne—that of valuing objects more than human relationships, and lusting to possess the rare books that inflame his passion "in fee simple absolute." Of course, anything we care strongly about has the power to corrupt us; furthermore, the moral character of a habit or undertaking is a matter of nuance, tone, and implicativeness, rather than a literal, pharisaic programming of act or possession.

Be that as it may, Thorne's fantasy of telling those protesting students to collect books conveys the "faintly contemptuous pity" bibliophiles sometimes feel for the noncollector; and the imagined "stupified reaction" of the students surely represents the obtuseness of the great world when confronted with a collector's passion for rare books.

At the heart of this incommunicativeness lies a mystery—one that many have tried to clear away, but most have ended with the tacit assumption that there is, after all, no way to explain the appeal rare books have for a collector. But as with all mysteries, such a difficulty of explanation is an invitation to try.

Louis Armstrong's famous nondefinition of jazz—"If you gotta ask what it is, you ain't got it."—is all right for musicians and mystics upon other quests; but book collectors are by vocation people of words, and their testimony is a rich harvest of gabble about the elusive but hypnotic power inherent in Elzivirs, first editions, illustrated books, and Americana.

Books are, after all, created to be read. Most of the collectors I know are readers. They are lovers of the spirit, first, and the body second. Wealthy philistines who speculate in rare books *solely* for the profit there might be in them are not true collectors; and more importantly, their number is pathetically—and deservedly—small. "Behind all the paraphernalia of bibliography," A. J. A. Symons writes, "behind the bookshops, auctions, exhibitions, catalogues, collations and research

*Second Chance, Boston, 1970, p. 176. Auchincloss himself is a collector and says he considers rare books a good investment . . . "*until* the thieves catch on, as they now have in paintings."

which define the collector's efforts, is the single fact of the love of books."*

The praise of books and reading is an old and venerable *genre,* extending from Plutarch and Richard de Bury to references embedded like jewels in the works of contemporaries like Borges and Edward Dahlberg. Such literature has an inevitability about it, for it represents self-selective process, in which no one but those who believe strongly, if not passionately, in the majesty of the printed word will bother either to write or read; therefore, praise of books and reading is the communication of like unto like.

The mystery still remains, however: why do people covet books so passionately that they want to collect them? Modern collectors are no less eloquent than those of the past. Gary Lepper, a collector of modern first editions, is a lawyer now with the district attorney's office in a California city. He writes, "Last week I was engaged in the tracking down of a particularly endearing thug who stole five cars, robbed four people (shooting one and stabbing another) and murdered two others in two days. And people ask me why I collect books. . . ."

Like all good rhetorical questions, this testament from Lepper communicates by implication; but the implication here is a deeper, more important one, for Lepper's lyric defense of his bibliomania signifies that the book is a "stay against confusion," as Frost said of poetry, and is thus by nature a kind of poem. Which of course it is, being the permanent dwelling house, not only of the written word, which ever abides, but through and in the written word, of passion, fact, beauty, and wisdom.

To turn to your books for solace is to turn inward, for the populations of your library have their spiritual home in the mind. Ownership of books is a personal testament, a fine and private place, but there lovers *do* embrace and become joyous and fecund. To be sure, there are records of people going into their books and never coming out—but there's no certain evidence to indicate whether they've gotten lost, or simply escaped.

Other dangers lurk in that forest of words. Ownership—especially of the passionate sort—is classically dangerous. There is the pitfall of pride, as Richard Eberhart explains in his *Chicago Review* essay, "A Haphazard Poetry Collecting" (pp. 57–70, Vol. 24, Spring 1973), in

*Holbrook Jackson, *The Anatomy of Bibliomania*, London, 1930.

reference to collecting first editions: "Of course there is a snobbery about all this, but the fact remains that a first edition of a book of poems bought in the twenties or thirties seems infinitely preferable to a second or *nth* edition of the same words. It is the splendor of the newness that counts."

And then there is that related sin of selfishness lying in wait. In *A Primer of Book Collecting,* by John T. Winterich and David A. Randall (Third Revised Edition, New York, 1966), the following is written:

> Book collecting is essentially a selfish pursuit, and the man or woman who collects books on that matter-of-fact basis ought to get the most fun out of the business. In a day when, however wretchedly it may be practiced, the principle of the Golden Rule is preached as never so vehemently before, let us be grateful that at least one oasis of self-interest remains wherein the individual of some cultivation and less ready cash may partake of intellectual sustenance without even having to yield up the core to a fainting fellow creature.

Obviously, the writer of such a passage is vulnerable to charges of insensitivity, opacity, and even depravity. But there is, in spite of everything, something healthful and exuberant in such an attitude, providing we understand that it is not intended for projection as a social program but as sane and honest relief from the sickening cant and hypocrisy that jam the communication lines all about us, and that the joy is positively focused upon the pleasures of collecting, not negatively focused on the deprivation of others.

Every collector, in every state of his collecting—whether dreaming into a catalogue or hacking a slow progress along the aisles between bookshelves, is looking for *the* book—scarcely conceivable, only dimly apprehended, unnameable as well as uncollated—which will ease his passion for a moment, and satisfy his mind with a totally committed and clarified possession for that moment. If this state of atonement and grace proves ephemeral, and if its occasion is bewilderingly varied, who cares? The pragmatics of ecstasy have never been mastered or programmed; and the true believer agrees that this is, after all, for the best.

I read someplace, years ago, the assertion that writers, themselves, were seldom book collectors. This statement is foolish for two reasons: first, it is not sufficiently true to warrant the generalization; second, the extent to which it *may* be true is largely explicable by the fact that, until very recent times, collecting has been a passion almost exclusively reserved for the wealthy, and writers have seldom belonged to the class of the wealthy.

Certainly, the percentage of "writers" (however one might define that term) who do not simply accumulate them, but collect books with the *idea* of collecting them, and with some sense of them as rarities or physical objects of great attraction (my definition of "bibliophile"), is vastly greater than almost any other class of people. Some of the great, near-great, and just plain worthy writers of the past who have been in one sense or other "collectors" are Petrarch, Anatole France, Sir Walter Scott, William Hazlitt, Andrew Lang, Montaigne, Charles Lamb, Horace Walpole, Eugene Field, George Gissing, Wallace Stevens, Edmund Gosse, Samuel Pepys, Flaubert, Walter de la Mare, Thomas Jefferson, George Moore, James Russell Lowell, Leigh Hunt, and Robert Southey. Many of these, being poor throughout their lives (e.g., Lamb), collected at great sacrifice, but collected nonetheless. Others, such as Walpole, may be considered collectors who wrote, rather than writers who collected, but such narrow jesuitical distinctions are hardly profitable in the present context.

One of the great benefits of democracy is the relative affluence which enables writers and professors, generally, to collect rare books in a way that was hardly possible before 1900. Years ago, when I asked a distinguished and scholarly friend if he collected books, he answered, "No, I can't afford it." This was, of course, nonsense. He may not have been able to afford an immediate purchase of all the first editions of the Victorians he admired and was so admirably read in; but he could have collected intelligently and effectively by putting aside cigarette or beer money, letting it accumulate for a month or two; and then he could have indulged in the luxury of sitting down and poring over a dozen or so catalogues, choosing an early first of Dickens or a first of Carlyle or George Eliot, or . . . But this man, an old-fashioned scholar, was still possessed of the idea that book collectors must be wealthy.

In the past, a disproportionately large number of physicians and attorneys seem to have been collectors. Such men were, of course, affluent; conversely, however, as they were successful, their time was usually severely limited; therefore, they were forced to collect "from afar," ordering through their secretaries or by mail or phone, stealing a half hour here and there to unwrap packages of recently purchased treasures, or to browse in their libraries for a moment's peace.

Today, the situation is different. Just as arc welders and beer salesmen hold stock in major corporations, while housewives collect eighteenth-century porcelain and old silver, so do people from every part of society enlist in the ranks of bibliophiles. I have known active collectors of rare books who make their livings as auto mechanics, farmers, chemists, printers, art directors, professors, teachers, secretaries, publicists, editors, commercial artists, bankers, scholarship students, administrators of various kinds, and, of course, there are still many physicians and attorneys.

I have never yet known anyone on welfare who collects actively, but I don't for an instant doubt that there are such people. In the list above, one of the most interesting classes is that of "scholarship students." In my years of teaching at a university, I have known many students who were becoming interested in the idea of collecting rare books, some of whom were already bona fide collectors. There is no happier or more encouraging sign than this for the future.

There is a vividness, a focused energy, a *passion* evident in collectors of rare books that is perhaps evident in all interesting people, but seems to be almost an integral part of the *idea* of building a personal collection.

One of the finest collectors around is a young poet and professor of English at SUNY in Brockport, named William Heyen. In college, Heyen was twice all-American at soccer. At six feet five inches tall, he stays in good physical condition. He is a fine poet, whose works are becoming more and more obviously collectable with each new publication. His own bibliophile's testament? Let him give it himself:

> I've always loved books, remember running home from school when I was a kid to finish reading *Heidi* and *Swiss Family Robinson*. Got sidetracked for some years, but even as a jock in college I used to haunt one particular junkshop in Brockport and their 3-for-25c books. Just to read. Maybe I first entered that other dimension of craziness when my wife, Han, bought me, when I was thinking of doing a dissertation on Wallace Stevens, a first edition of *Harmonium*. This was about 1963, and she paid $35. It's worth considerably more now. It turns out, indeed, to be one of the first 500, according to points in the

39

Edelstein bibliography. (And, parenthetically, certainly, one of the marks of our mania is this love of reading bibliographies. Have you seen Ernest Stefanik's wonderful bibliography of Berryman?) There were times in graduate school when we didn't have a quarter for a quart of milk and I thought of selling that book, but didn't. Well, I started collecting, scrounging shops indiscriminately, ignorant about first editions and book club editions and such.

I suppose I'm a kind of investor, but one who never plans to sell any books—I'd like my whole collection kept intact, and I'm vain enough (and sly enough) to know that it will be important enough—I guess I have about 2,000 signed volumes now, not to mention manuscripts and letters, etc.—to be kept together. I'm an investor insofar as I know that the books I get signed become more valuable, that my collection as a whole, the wider it gets, will become more valuable. I've bought many, many books at face value (that must have come from the days before my coin collecting dilletantism gave way to a more durable love), list price, that have just leapt up like Wordsworth's heart. And I'm not above buying a double of a book that seems a steal for me, as when I find a beautiful first (hardback and dustjacket, of course) of James Wright's *Saint Judas* for six bucks, or of a book that is going to go right out of sight and be impossible to find, so I've paid $15 for a second copy of the lovely Perishable Press edition of Galway Kinnell's *The Shoes of Wandering*, limited to "100 copies or less." I know that to some *real* book collectors my collecting of contemporaries especially will cause snickers and cries of delusion. But I must collect the people I admire and believe in, for one thing. And I am not in this thing for the money. I love to hold and read from a book signed by the writer. At the same time, I certainly do consider my library a sort of insurance policy for Han and the kids, and right now (hell, I hope to collect for another four decades) any bookseller dealing in modern firsts could put out one beautiful catalogue with my collection, if Han needed money and I were up in the old bookshop in the sky.

And I must say I *learn* from my books, they help me teach, help me feel comfortable because I can feel the contours of a career because of my collections of various poets. Well, this is all corn. I am sentimentally attached to my books, and so enthusiastic about collecting that five, count 'em, friends have become as crazy-sane as I am. A few people are even beginning to collect *my* things now.

Heyen's library of more than 2,000 association copies of contemporary poets must be one of the finest private collections of its kind around; and, of course, he is still adding to it with all the energy, vision, and determination that are essential to the building of any good library.

There is a group of bibliophiles in Wichita, Kansas, who meet once every month. Several years ago , when I was there on a year's teaching assignment, I was privileged to join these good fellows informally at their meetings, and it was at one such meeting that I met a handsome, white-haired banker named Harold Null, who had traveled well over 200 miles from his home in Nebraska to attend this meeting.

During our conversation after the evening's talk on early printing, Harold mentioned that his special collecting interest was incunabula, and that it was getting so hard to find incunabula anywhere in Europe that he was thinking of going behind the Iron Curtain, to try his luck there. What an adventure!

But in a recent letter, he doesn't even mention his plans to search behind the Iron Curtain. He does, however, reveal that he has branched out—wise and prudent strategy for a collector who suddenly finds himself confronted by a diminished market. Null's letter was written shortly after he'd returned from a sixty-day trip to various places in South Europe, Turkey, Israel, and North and West Africa. He writes:

On this trip, we did not succeed in buying any incunabula—couldn't even find any available. In European Turkey I tried to buy manuscripts, especially of the Koran, but could get none worth having—or equal to previous purchases because it is now against Turkish law to allow the marketing of any manuscript older than 200 years. A smart move for Turkey, and it makes my 1620 Koran manuscript worth probably $500.00 more than I paid for it, due to scarcity. Unfortunately, I had in 1969 bought a beauty in vellum at $300.00, but generously let a passenger on our cruise ship have it at my cost—anticipating, of course, that I could get another—maybe better, at a lesser price, later. A huge mistake. This time I saw only items from

41

about 1800 and at $100.00 to $150.00, and on paper, and not illuminated.

Last September I went around South America again, and while in Buenos Aires, I had the good fortune to find a two-volume *exact* reproduction of *Don Quixote* of the 1605 and 1615 first editions. The reprint was dated 1905 and was authorized by the Spanish Government as a celebration of the 300th Anniversary of the First Edition. I am delighted with them.

When I served on the University of Kansas Library Development Committee, we authorized the purchase of the famous Sterling-Maxwell Collection out of Scotland, and among the books that we received for our $75,000 were two First Editions of *Don Quixote*. My 1905 reprints are exact reproductions except for the paper and cover, and my two copies were $75.00.

What I like about this brief report are its resiliency and honesty. No doubt but what the Turkish government was judicious in outlawing the sale of manuscripts two hundred years and older—but, of course, that killed Null's plan to buy; still, it increased the value and generally enhanced the manuscript Null had purchased a few years earlier. And the resiliency is further manifest in Null's joyous acceptance of the facsimile *Don Quixote*. That for many collectors this is not a mere eccentricity, much less a base compromise, is evident in the fact that good facsimile editions are much sought after, and can be splendid and *in themselves* as valid a collecting interest as incunabula, modern firsts, Elzevirs, or what have you. They are part of the expanding market in the world of rare books. About which, more later.

One would think that the charm and interest of incunabula would have been evident to everyone, quite independent of their "content" . . . and that this interest would have been obvious from the earliest years of book collecting as we know it. In the eighteenth century, people began to feel the thrill of antiquity and were charmed by the idea of things ancient. But for some odd reason, this love of the antique did not translate into a coordinate passion for fifteenth-century books. A hundred years later, the Victorians jauntily referred to incunabula as "fifteeners"; and the term "inkies" was part of bookmen's slang up until the modern era. Inexplicably, this neglect lasted until recently. Speaking of the incredibly low prices paid by a bidder at auction for a library of incunabula, David Magee writes, "But one must remember he was buying in the '40s and '50s when 15th-century books were going begging. No on seemed to want them and their cost was ridiculously low compared, say, to that of Americana or modern first editions."*

Like most interesting human actions, book collecting is compounded of various portions of proprieties and vagaries. As a matter of fact, *Proprieties and Vagaries* is the title of a book which I bought at a trashy little book shop in a nearby city. This book, by John Hammond, is subtitled: "A Philosophical Thesis from Science, Horse Racing, Sexual Customs, Religion, and Politics." (If that list doesn't command just about everybody's interest, I don't know how it could be improved . . . unless maybe book collecting were added.)

The author of this 264-page book was a professor of philosophy at Johns Hopkins University; and the book was published by the Johns Hopkins Press (1961). I had never head of the author, but the title of the book intrigued me, so I bought it for one dollar, took it home, and read the essays included therein, some of whose titles were "Thinking Ways," "Good Use and the Use of Good," "Proprieties and the Motion of the Earth," and "A Defense of Horse Racing."

This book must have seemed a little quirky at the time; but today, it would seem to be exactly the sort of book a professor of Philosophy should write if he had Hammond's free spirit and intellectual muscle.

Essentially, the book is about the interplay of these two seemingly contradictory forces—propriety and vagary—in the formation of human events. It is an insightful and rewarding book, which I would not likely have come upon if I hadn't put myself in the posture of "wasting time" scouting in a back room that was poorly lighted, sagging in the floors, and cluttered with boxes of dusty old books.

The force of chance, of vagary, in collecting is one of the most profound attractions it manifests. In entering a miscellany of books, one is confronted with a constant bombardment of chance signals that evoke intense and varied reactions, and challenge his memory and connecting powers in intricate and fascinating ways. In such moments, the collector is living in a symbolically intensified universe of discourse—a microcosm. The forces of vagary and propriety are excellently called upon.

Why propriety? Well, because it is at the heart of book collecting. Why should one collect *first editions* except that there are significant numbers of others who agree, both tacitly and explicitly, that such edi-

*Infinite Riches, (New York 1963), p. 179.

tions are worth having? There is more than this, but even that "more" is largely a matter of propriety—propriety at a deeper level, perhaps, but propriety, nevertheless. Because, why should we assume that the origin of something is more clearly indicative of its "nature" than any subsequent transformation? Why should the first edition have an "authenticity," a "validity," an "integrity" that later editions do not? The answer is many of them *don't*. And yet, they are coveted for reasons that are connected with such assumptions; and our proprieties are such, that we agree upon their being more valuable. The first edition is the nearest, public approach to the private, personal manuscript . . . which is the nearest approach to the mind in which such ideas or images—such powers and excellences—dwell in their native state. It is in our largely unarticulated system of proprieties that we assume such things; and they are neither right nor wrong but merely *there*: active, valid, assumed, and to that extent, "proper."

It would be incorrect, however, to give undue emphasis to the arbitrary character of book collecting. Since all scholarship as we know it requires bibliography, a carefully gathered collection of books will prove to have a usefulness in research. And of course, the role of the first edition may well prove to be crucial. Consider the following statement by Frazer Clark, which concerns not only the validity in collecting the first edition, but the critical problem of condition, as well:

> Collectors have different reasons for collecting, which affect the criteria they use to measure the desirability of an offered item. Generally, you want the item in the original form in which it was first published. That is, the original binding, wrappers (if a magazine or pamphlet), or unbound newspaper. There are important reasons for this, both investment and scholarly reasons. First, if future resale is a consideration, you want the item in the best condition since this contributes materially to value and saleability. A battered copy of the first of *The Scarlet Letter* is regularly listed in catalogues for $75.00 to $100.00. A pristine copy, seldom seen, commands a price upwards of $1,000.00. The only difference is condition. It doesn't matter that people scoff at this, it is simply a market fact. And the principle holds just as firmly for Hemingway as it does for Hawthorne. And, there are important reasons why being close to original published form is crucial in scholarly terms. You can only collate with certainty a volume which is in its original cov-

ers. Dust jackets often carry important information about the book, the author, the publishing facts, etc. The same might be said about wrappers—e.g., we know that Hawthorne was a contributor to the *Monthly Miscellany of Religion and Letters* only because his name appears among the contributors printed on the wrappers; the contributions are unsigned (only one copy of this item in wrappers exists, and thus, it is only through this copy that we can extend Hawthorne's authorship to that periodical). All of which is to say again that there are important reasons for insisting on material in as close to original condition as possible.

In many cases it makes no more sense to accord value to a first edition than it does to agree that gold should serve as a standard of currency. The more traditional and more deeply settled a propriety is, the more it pretends to be some kind of law. And of course, people do take their games seriously, especially these more venerable sorts that have become so integral a part of our thinking. And throughout history men have been known to kill for gold, which, one would think, is carrying the game a bit too far, but evidently is not. Also, if we are to believe two or three of the gaudier fictions that surround the subject of bibliophily, men are capable of killing (and, indeed, perhaps have done so) for the sake of a rare book.

Testaments to the charm of book collecting are, as I said earlier, a *genre* in themselves. This is not the place to quote them at length; their witnessings are available in other books and well worth going to for nourishment and vindication in one's inspired belief that his bibliophrenesis is a benign affliction that, like the madness of prophets and poets, reveals not error and delusion, but truth.

But I will quote from three such testaments: only the first may be said to belong to the canon of bookish enthusiasm, because the second is obscure, and the third is from a recently published book and has not yet had time to be celebrated in the way of being liberally reprinted.

The first is taken from the introduction of John Carter's learned and authoritative *Taste and Technique in Book Collecting;* it delineates those features which Carter believes to be essential to the ideal collector; but in this delineation, his object, as well, is figured forth:

> The book collector, then, is not just an eccentric who prefers one edition to another for some ritually compulsive reason. He

45

is not a man who says simply, "the old is better" or who thinks that rarity is an objective in itself. It is not even enough to say that he is a man who is not as well satisfied with a photographic reproduction of the original, or a roll of microfilm, or a well-edited verbatim reprint, as with the genuine article. He is rather a man (or of course a woman, though bibliophily, like dandyism is less common among women [?!]) who has a reverence for, and a desire to possess, the original or some other specifically admirable, curious or interesting edition of a book he loves or respects or one which has a special place among his intellectual interests. And the book must be either in its original state or in some contemporary, associate or otherwise appropriate condition. Furthermore, he enjoys, with a degree of intensity which will vary according to his temperament, his training and the standards of his fellow-bibliophiles, that exercise of his natural and intellectual faculties which is involved in the application of knowledge, observation, ingenuity, foresight, enterprise and persistence to the pursuit of his quarry, its description when secured. But above all and pervading all is the element recognised in the second half of the very word bibliophile. Indeed, the Greeks might almost have been justified in invoking $\Sigma\rho\omega s$ to describe the feeling which animates the true book collector; that kind of love which demands the physical possession of its object, which consumes the collector with passionate longings, chills him with fear of his rivals, tortures him with envy. Bibliophily is on the whole a civilised pursuit, yet its votaries know the heights and the depths.

The objects of book collectors' attention have always been of an infinite variety. Their own attitude, and that of the public, towards their collections has changed with changing tastes and conventions. The degree and direction of the connoisseurship applied to book collecting—that is, method and skill as distinct from motive—have developed and will continue to develop.

The next quotation is from a book I bought in an antique shop. (Question: Don't I ever buy from rare-book dealers? Answer: I do! I do!) The proprietor of this shop has always reminded me a little of the Ancient Mariner, not because he, like the fabulously inept short stop, "stoppeth one of three," but because he stops me every time, fixes his bony finger at my chest, and informs me in a sepulchral voice about the exact velocity at which the world is going to hell in a bucket. This old fellow has eyes that are dark and sunken, and he looks somewhat like an extra in an old horror film. His name for me is simply, "Mister" (although he knows my other name well); and I sometimes suspect that, for him, I represent the world, or at least that part of it which should be *told before it's too late.*

The book under question is a rather austerely bound edition, with the mutilated title, *Ex Libris Antiq,* on the spine, with *Pilcher / 1918* beneath. It is an annotated bibliography of the antiquarian books collected by the once-famous surgeon, Lewis Stephen Pilcher. Published in 1918, in Brooklyn, the volume's title page reads:

> *A List of Books by Some*
> *of the Old Masters*
> *Of Medicine and Sur-*
> *gery Together with*
> *Books on the His-*
> *tory of Medicine*
> *and on Medical*
> *Biography in*
> *the Posses-*
> *sion of*
> *Lewis Stephen Pilcher*

and then it continues: *with Biographical and Bibliographical Notes and Reproductions of Some Title Pages and Captions.*

Such bibliographies as this also constitute a *genre* beloved to collectors, for they celebrate the book by both occasion and detail, and they almost always prove to be wonderfully informative.

The present volume is no exception. It is number 111 in a limited edition of 250 copies. It is unpretentious but thorough and rich with arcane facts, featuring whole sections on "Hippocrates, Galen, Celsus," "Mundinus and the Prevesalian Anatomists," "Vesalius and Vesaliana Diversa," and so on. What do you know of Ambroise Paré? Well, he was a famous sixteenth-century surgeon ("*Conseiller et premier chirurgien du roy*"), and in Pilcher's book, there is a whole section on him, containing titles and annotations of books in French, Latin, German, Dutch, and English, and two reproductions of old portraits, showing a dour and grim old fellow, glowering out at the world from behind a blunt and massive nose, a typical sixteenth-century goatee and mustache, and a neck-choking collar.

In his Foreword, Pilcher very modestly and unassumingly states the rationale behind the collection, as well as the book representing it. The tone is somewhat wistful, but in spite of this, the statement is an idealistic one, asseverative of the collecting spirit (the "he" referred to is himself):

> As he himself has constantly profited by the breaking up of other collections of books in making his own collection, he is not sanguine as to the permanence of any collection, but nevertheless he hopes that, when he himself has had to leave his own, some way may be found whereby it may be kept together, or at least that such groups as the editions of Vesalius, of Paré or of Harvey, which it contains, may not be broken up. The slow accretion of a collection of such books is like the growth of a child, and one who has cherished it, until finally it has been brought to some degree of importance, cannot help but have for it a feeling akin to that which a parent has for the child which he has reared. It is somewhat with such a spirit of affection that the writer has been influenced to compile this list of the titles of the books by which he is now surrounded; books which have been the companions of many years, with whom he has shared so many pleasant hours, and who have presented to him models upon which he has endeavored to construct the ideals of his own life.

The last quotation in this section consists of the very opening words of the Introduction to Eric Quayle's *The Collector's Book of Books* (New York: Clarkson N. Potter, Inc., 1971):

> I am a bibliophile; an otherwise rational member of the community consumed by a love of books. It gives me pleasure to handle any printed work that has something important to say; but most of all I cherish rare editions, finely printed texts, beautifully illustrated books, and volumes scarce and unprocurable except by knowledgeable means.

". . . scarce and unprocurable except by knowledgeable means." Yes, I think that comes close; that's almost got it.

But like many of the enduring mysteries, bibliophily is best known not directly or descriptively, but reflectively and from its effects upon our lives.

A week ago, I was sitting in the office of a friend, and he was telling me at great length about a collector who lives in a large city several hundred miles away. He told me about this man's distinguished collection of miscellaneous first-class items, about his huge and beautiful home with its specific appointments for the housing of his various period collections, etc. Not unnaturally, I became curious about the man himself, and asked what he did for a living.

"Well, he's retired," my friend said. "But he made his money in real estate. Although I think he has a law degree, and maybe even practiced for a while."

"How old is he?"

"Oh, he's in his mid-seventies. His health's really gone. He's had a couple of heart attacks and strokes, and has diabetes bad; hell, he can hardly get around the house anymore. These things just came upon him without warning a couple of years ago. He's really in bad shape."

We were quiet and thoughtful a moment, and then my friend frowned, slapped his palms on his desk, and said, "The trouble with him is . . . well, dammit, *he paid too much for his books.*"

III.

RARE BOOKS

AS INVESTMENTS

eriodically, a familiar story will break in the paper. This may be a very short notice of how much a recently discovered letter by Mark Twain sold for at auction, or it may be "a featured news story," showing a picture of the old woman who found the letter lying at the bottom of a trunk in the attic (she is always photographed holding a small dog that looks like an intelligent rat), or it is an article or book, ranging from the soberly thoughtful (such as this one) to a jazzy bit of ephemera titled something like: "A Fortune Could Be Buried in Your Old Tomes" or "Take a Leaf from Book Collectors: You May Be Rich and Not Know It!"

Here is a recent notice published in the PENewsletter of May 1975:

> The rare-book trade is experiencing a boom. A first edition of *The Marionettes,* a one-act play by William Faulkner,* was sold to the Univ. of Virginia Library for $34,000 by the heirs of

---

*This was interesting for another reason: I had never heard of this title—which is perhaps not so strange—but apparently James B. Meriwether, in his *Faulkner Check List* (Princeton, 1957) had not heard of it, either, for I couldn't find it listed there. I wrote to J. St. C. Crane, curator of the American literature collection at the University of Virginia, however, and she explained that this play was an unpublished 55-page manuscript, six copies of which Faulkner had hand-lettered, illustrated, and hand-bound for friends.

the woman who had purchased the copy in 1940 for $125. . . . A copy of the "open fly" edition of Mark Twain's *Huckleberry Finn* is likely to fetch a starting bid of $5,000. The "open fly" edition is the work of a pressman who, in a moment of creative abandon during the making of one of the editions in 1884, altered an engraving so that the fly of an old man's pants was open . . . (Have we thus missed the significance of Erica Jong's *Fear of Flying?* Is her title perhaps an arcane reference to open flies on men's pants in nineteenth-century midwest America?) . . . The Gotham Book Mart, one of New York's literary landmarks, and rich in first editions, recently sold about 65 percent of its stock to New Mexico State Univ. at Las Cruces for $485,000. The sale is believed to be one of the largest retail sales in bookstore history. Current owner Andreas Brown (Frances Steloff founded the store and still minds it daily) said the sale was dictated by the exorbitant premiums for fire insurance. Brown hopes to relocate the store in the same general area . . . Not a rare edition, but a luxury one, is the new $450 (trade price) edition of Melville's *Moby Dick.* Even at this whale of a price, the publishers, A. Colish of Mount Vernon, N.Y., expect to sell out the limited 1,500-copy edition. Jacques-Yves Cousteau has written an introduction and signed all copies. . . .

Reading a notice like this is enough to make a body think. (That's why it was written.) Especially those references to the Faulkner and Twain books. And what a body thinks is "My God!" The next thought this body thinks is, "I wonder why anybody would pay that kind of money for a *book!*" The third thought, reflecting upon the fact that old books are seen all over the place, encountered everywhere, given away, not returned when borrowed, and sold for a quarter apiece, is: "I wonder if I've ever come across any books like that, and haven't known it!" And the fourth thought is: "I wonder how you can tell if a book is valuable like that."

Such will likely prove to be this body's last thought on the subject, until it is prodded once again by a similar article's appearance, introducing once again that vague uneasiness that one has been *missing out on a good thing.* But there's another possibility. Before he sees the next article, he may happen upon a book that reminds him of the article and its astonishing information. The book before him seems to him to be very old. Maybe somewhere he'll find a date on it that is impressive, perhaps even an inscription: "To Samuel Brown from his Aunt Florence, June 12, 1887." Almost a hundred years old. Even though this body may be a dealer in antiques, he may still consider this to be a very old book, not realizing that books generally constitute the second oldest of American antiquities (prehistoric Indian relics being the oldest), and that a book printed in 1887 has no more claim to be considered an antique than a rocking chair manufactured during the First World War.

Let us suppose this book is a copy of *Robinson Crusoe,* and the finder remembers reading about it once, and even has the prudence and industry to go seek out the article, or perhaps go to the local library in search of some information about its value. After a brief search, he finds a reference to the first edition having been sold at auction for $1,200 several years ago. Armed with this information, he goes to the nearest bookstore that is listed in the Yellow Pages under "Books: Used and Rare," walks in and lays his prize on the counter before the proprietor.

Here, a series of frustrations is invited. First, the book in question will prove to be an Arlington Reprint (circa 1880); and even if it were in good condition (which it is not), even if it had been reasonably well printed, on decent paper and with good type and a heavy binding (none of which is the case, in a manner of speaking), it would not—at this late date—have any particular value. Unless, that is, it had been signed by Ulysses S. Grant or Teddy Roosevelt, or reprinted as a work of art, with some ostentatious concern given to the quality of materials and workmanship, in which case. . . .

But by now, our body has drifted off, if not actually, in his mind, suffering from disillusion. ("Hell, I knew there wouldn't be anything that good come my way!" or "I should have known that damned article was just another con!")

If this example seems familiar, but a little farfetched, it is nevertheless substantially true. A successful antique dealer of my acquaintance once told me she had a book worth a thousand dollars, and when I asked to see it, she invited me back into her office and headed toward a huge safe, on the top of which resided a single book—a copy of the Arlington edition of *Robinson Crusoe,* whose cheap dull binding and browned pulp pages I recognized (as any collector of any experience would) from a distance of fifteen feet. Fortunately, this lady was not interested in selling the book, or even being confirmed in her judgment (she *knew* this was the valuable first edition). All that was required of me was polite envy and a token humble worship before the shrine; but she was really a very nice woman, and this wasn't required for long.

The point of all this is not simply that the general public tend to be incredibly ignorant of books, but that under the pressure of some sort of business transaction, or in the event of an appraisal or evaluation (which imply a business transaction, and thereby represent a hypothetical one), people very often reveal a strange and complex attitude toward books. The uneasiness, suspicion, and defensiveness of someone *who doesn't know,* when he is confronted by someone *who does,* are surely not surprising: these are common reactions in any contest. But with regard to books, these reactions are subtly altered by the admixture of a certain guilt. Books are not simply objects, but highly symbolic objects, whose power can radiate through insulating layers of contempt and neglect. Even the ignoramus who refers patronizingly to "just a bunch of old books lying out there in the shed," may shift nervously, if only for a moment, when you bring a stack you've selected for pricing. That this is basically financial, I don't doubt; that there is an added fear of his being "taken" by selling his wares too low, I don't doubt. But often, and in surprising ways, there is this other truth manifest: the book radiates a power that affects the mind and spirit, whose actions, in turn, cannot readily be seen. In short, the book is an object that often, and in many different situations, verges upon being both hieratic and taboo.

Such superstitious hangups can even be observed in more sophisticated people; they are to some extent essential to the unique passion of the collector, and probably to almost any human scale of values. De Quincy called superstition "sympathy with the Invisible"—a good and kind definition; accordingly, this bibliophilic sort of superstition is not all bad; but obviously it can be excessive. Books represent those "thoughts in the concrete" that William James said "are made of the same stuff things are." But an exaggerated, *ignorant* exaltation of the book—while somewhat defensible in the semiliterate—is ridiculous in those who should know better. As ideal and idea, books are splendid; as objects, individual books exist in the world, and belong to the class of things that can and must be handled, worn out, cherished and preserved, thrown aside, discarded, sold, bought, traded, forgotten, shelved, boxed, marked in, dog-eared, whispered to, ripped and torn, prayed over, preyed upon, borrowed, and occasionally loaned.

Even the finest, most beautiful, most desirable books have cost money; they have been paid for at sometime, by someone; even if they were lovingly constructed by one man, from the papermaking to the designing and casting of the type, and then bestowed upon others as gifts, somebody had to pay for the raw materials and previous workmanship. We live in that kind of world. It is, among other things, an economic world, and any object that possesses—or is considered to possess—value is likely to wear some kind of price tag. Whatever has a price tag shows some character and potential as an investment.

There are occasions, however, when one would think such obvious facts were unthinkable. Recently, when I consulted a variety of collectors, librarians, and dealers in rare books for testimony they might give in view of their particular experiences, most of them responded warmly, sympathetically, and with obvious interest in the matter at hand.

And yet, a few were not at all sympathetic; in fact, one must assume that they were quite hostile to the idea. It was as if I had mentioned something profane, if not downright obscene, in inquiring about rare books as a unique and exciting form of investment in today's world. Part of their silliness and cant was no doubt caused by a blind reaction to the pejorative connotation of the word "invest." "I do not 'invest,'" an attorney-collector wrote, "though I do expect a certain percentage of my purchases to rise in value." How high would this expected percentage have to be before he would acknowledge that he is, in fact, "investing"? Does this "certain percentage" represent a portion of books that he *does* invest in, only "collecting" the others he buys? If so, let's talk about those investments. Do they glow with the additional charm of monetary gain, thereby allowing him to buy more good books, knowing that they will likely prove negotiable, should he someday be forced to sell them, or should they become part of his estate after death? If so, let's *call* them investments.

Many people would agree with a banker-collector, who says he prefers to think of buying rare books as a speculation, rather than an investment—which in the lexicon of most people would mean they belong somewhere between treasury bills on the one hand and 1919 Ontario gold bonds and pari-mutuel betting on the other. The distinction seems valid in times that we have learned to think of as "normal" (i.e., good and bullish). Speculation belongs to chaps who wax their mustaches, wear tooled pigskin boots and gold plaid jackets—and love the thrill of increased risk coupled with giddy rewards.

However, in less certain times, traditionally conservative investments tend more and more to be speculative. Think of how many unasked-for thrills the recent financial tremors of New York City have afforded holders of municipal bonds; maybe you could have traded some of your Aldines or Doves Press volumes for a small packet, maybe even for Detroit or St. Louis bonds. Maybe you still can.

People who view the rare-book market as speculative are to be listened to, however, for most of them are sensible folks whose thinking is almost 180 degrees off from the hysteria of those canting asses who profess a sort of ethical/aesthetic horror at the mere thought of buying or selling a book with an eye on its future negotiability.

The representative of a prominent firm in England responded to my inquiry with cold dignity, saying that the subject of investing in books was one which did not interest them. (He assumed the monarchical first-person plural, which had a certain felicity in terms of his diction.) On this side of the Atlantic, the eponym of a renowned Boston firm wrote, "I am sorry to have to say that I cannot consider rare books as a form of investment. Accordingly I doubt very much that any comments I might make would be of use to you." This is a pity. I distinctly remember selling, on behalf of an old lady in Findlay, Ohio, a 1492 German Psalter (missing a few pages, alas) to this Prince of Pomposity a number of years ago, and he showed great interest in the matter of price at the time; in fact, I got the impression that he might conceivably have paid less for this incunable than he did, if I had not been so earnest in demanding a slightly higher price than he'd first offered.

Even otherwise sensible and admirable folks share in the mummery of dismay that the inamorata of their dreams could be so whorishly fickle as to go to the highest bidder. I consulted a splendid collector, famous for his superlative collection of eighteenth-century literature, asking what he thought about investing in rare books. "I deplore it," he answered. That was all. I wrote back a single-world letter: "Why?" hoping he would answer, "Because"; in which case, I could have answered, "Oh." But this laconic exchange has not taken place, and I don't think it will. Infra dig, no doubt.

Larry McMurtry, a popular novelist who has become a dealer in rare books and has opened his own bookstore in Washington, D.C., gave the following testy reply when I wrote asking him about his views on the subject of investing in rare books, along with his feeling about the fact that there are actually some collectors who consider his own novels collectable: "We don't like customers who regard books as investments. Also I don't like being collected, although I like being read." Unquestionably, the rest of us should feel grateful for the existence of such high-minded folks; they make the world just a little better for all of us.

McMurtry's protestation has nothing of the style in James Joyce's angry rhyme inspired by A. S. W. Rosenbach's purchase of the manuscript of *Ulysses,* and his subsequent refusal to consider selling it back to Joyce:

> Rosy Brook he bought a book
> Though he didn't know how to spell it.
> Such is the lure of literature
> To the lad who can buy it and sell it.

But the truth is, Joyce was not really castigating those who invest in books, as the background of this episode reveals; he was merely annoyed, and insulted, by the purchase price of only $1,975.

The greatest, noblest, most principled statement against investing in books occurs in a letter written many years ago by a man whose name has become famous in the history of book collecting. Speaking of "book speculators," he cried:

> What love for their books can such men have! It is desecration for good books to fall into their utterly unsympathetic hands! Why do they not go to Wall Street, and there gamble with the paper that Mr. Morgan has created for their use? They only serve to run up prices, and keep books out of the hands of those who would love them and treasure them!

Note here the distinctive inability to understand that people can be sufficiently complex as to have a twofold motive in collecting. This quotation affords a somewhat dim-witted example of that either/or absolutism that is the despair of all sensible people: that is, you collect books either because you love them, or you collect them because you want to "invest" in them; no combination of motives is possible.

As for the writer of that glowing denunciation, it was none other than Thomas J. Wise [letter to John Henry Wrenn, October 17, 1903; *Letters of Thomas J. Wise to John Henry Wrenn,* Fannie E. Ratchford, ed., NY, 1944] Bibliophilic Con Man Extraordinaire, who committed a series of legendary frauds upon the collectors of his day.

It was Emerson who wrote: "The louder he talked of his honor, the faster we counted our spoons."

There are, to be sure, more responsible doubts concerning the idea of rare books as a form of investment. Some are matters of taste rather than prudence: "I am not an investment counselor," Jake Zeitlin, of Los Angeles' Zeitlin & Ver Brugge, Booksellers, says. "I sell books to people who want books." Another Los Angeles dealer, Glen Dawson, of Dawson's Book Shop, says, "We do not recommend books for financial investment. However if you take a cruise to the West Indies or go to the theater you have only the ticket stubs. With books, you can sell them for something if you need or wish to." Dawson also points out that the book buyer has certain obvious disadvantages in that he "buys at retail and sells at wholesale." He states that some collectors, "with skill or luck, have been able to make a profit, but most collectors do not." Probably, most don't really try, since profit isn't their primary motive in collecting, and that is as it should be.

Matthew Bruccoli, Professor of English at the University of South Carolina, has built what is probably the finest private F. Scott Fitzgerald collection in the world, consisting of all the editions, issues, and states of all Fitzgerald's books, many signed and inscribed copies, manuscripts, letters, and other ephemera. Bruccoli is emphatic: "My advice to someone who wants to collect rare books as an investment is . . . don't. Collect books because you love them; collect books because collecting books gives you pleasure; collect books as a scholarly activity. If you're looking for an investment, put your money in something else. Also, there's the fact that your heirs—your wife and children—will have a much harder time even than you in disposing of your collection. If a collector collects as an investment, then he'd better be sure he disposes of his collection himself before he dies, otherwise he's going to leave his widow and children assets that in most cases they will dispose of badly, reducing the income of the return even more substantially."

Surely this is some of the most important and most often neglected advice for the collector-investor. A man will spend years accumulating, building, *creating* a fine and expensive personal library, whose potential value might run into five or six figures; but if this library is disposed of casually, impatiently, or ignorantly, all his effort—*insofar as it is to be considered an investment*—was for naught. One can only conclude that there are a large number of modestly valuable collections, that might be valued at from one to ten thousand dollars, that are disposed of casually and half-knowingly by heirs that really don't seem to care, or at least don't seem to care enough to take the obvious steps of finding out;

so that such collections are sold at estate sales at fantastically low prices, very much in the same spirit as those same heirs might dispose of a genuine Queen Anne lowboy or a silver castor set for fifty dollars. (The truth of this observation explains the popularity of such sales.) One can only lament the indifference, ignorance, or imprudence of such folks; but if they're determined to sell too low, someone with better sense will surely be found available to profit thereby. Every time you get a great bargain, if you listen hard, you can hear the sound of snoring somewhere.

Some collectors, no matter how much they may love books and no matter how faithful they may remain to their commitment in collecting them, consider them inferior, *as investments,* to other types of rarities. The problem with such people, it seems to me, lies not in their skepticism regarding rare books, but in their truly naive belief in the easy money available in other markets. Don't they think that coin and stamp dealers have to make a profit? Where does that profit come from, if not from the collector-investor? How do they think stockbrokers make their profit? Haven't they heard of people *losing* on the stock market, as well as earning?

Concentrating upon one's own special set of problems is likely to render one powerfully sophisticated in the pitfalls of that landscape, and make all more distant enterprises look simple, well-cultivated, easy, and of an ingratiating opulence. Or, as a wise speculator once said, "The felt is always greener on the other side of the table."

There are other problems, too. A collector of modern first editions who did not do as well as he had hoped when he recently sold part of his collection at auction, had this advice to give to anyone who is thinking of rare books as an investment:

> Instead of assembling a hundred-thousand-dollar library, consisting of a thousand hundred-dollar books, he'd be much better off buying a hundred-thousand-dollar painting in terms of investment sense.

This advice is sobering, indeed; but the comparison between a thousand hundred-dollar books and a one-hundred-thousand-dollar painting is invidious. How would a thousand one-hundred-dollar books compare, as an investment, with a thousand one-hundred-dollar paintings? Or, how would a single hundred-thousand-dollar book—say, Caxton's 1477 edition of *Dictes, or Sayings of the Philosophers*; the first dated book printed in England—compare with a single hundred-thousand-dollar painting? This is all very hypothetical, of course, and the result of an actual test of such a comparison might easily be tipped one way or the other depending upon various factors of shrewdness, opportunity, and simple chance.

Still, dealers generally agree that the more expensive a book is, the better it will prove as an investment. That such may be the case is indicated by the fact that many dealers claim they will pay as high as ninety percent for extreme rarities (in the thousand-dollar-and-up range); whereas they can pay only fifty percent, or even less, for the more modest rarities. The reason for this is fairly obvious: the extraordinary rarities are very likely to have buyers waiting for them, on virtually a "standing order" basis (if this were not so, a dealer would indeed be foolish to cut his profit margin so thin); where as the "more common rarities" will likely have to wait on the shelf for a random buyer, or else be listed on a hit-or-miss basis in the dealer's next catalogue.

As Roderick Brinckman, of Monk Bretton Books in Toronto, sums it up: "I will pay more for an expensive book and more for a book I can sell right away."

Most dealers agree with this policy.

A common warning from those—dealers and collectors alike—who are a little bearish in their view of the rare-book market has to do with the fact that a collector is, as mentioned above, generally at the disadvantage of "buying at retail and selling at wholesale." This is, of course, a disadvantage that is not limited to investments in rare books. For example, diamonds are popularly supposed to be very good investments. Very well; let us suppose you go to the local jewelers and purchase a modest pair of diamond earrings, nicely set, for two hundred dollars. The instant you have bought them, they have depreciated approximately fifty percent. Are diamonds rising in value? They are. Or at least, the dollar is inflating at a high enough rate that diamonds, with their relatively stable value, appreciate relatively.

Assuming that retail diamonds appreciate at the rate of ten percent per year, it will be over seven years before you can go to a retail jeweler and expect to get your money back. Not a good investment at all, so far.

But of course, *if* diamonds continue to appreciate at ten percent per year, and *if* you can afford to hold on to your diamonds, they will tend to prove themselves valid investments, beyond that break-even date, more and more as you keep them. But it will be a long time before that two-hundred-dollar pair of diamond earrings will prove to be as good an investment, on purely financial grounds, as the same sum of money invested in a bank or credit union at six percent.

There are many problems in comparing investments, even when one ignores the very real aesthetic and personal value that antiques, jewelry, coins, stamps, paintings, rare books, and other valuables possess in contrast to stocks and bonds. The greatest problem and simultaneously the greatest opportunity in the rare book market is its lack of definition. It is simplistic to talk of "buying at retail and selling at wholesale" for the very good reason that the whole antiquarian market lacks sufficient definition for establishing a scale of retail and wholesale prices.

How does a dealer price a book? He resorts to several methods, analyzing the book in terms of several marketing criteria: subject, author, edition, demand, his own clientele, the condition of the book, and so on. If the book is unknown to him, he'll go to whatever reference volumes are available and try to find out what features there are to make the book interesting. He will consult auction records, book catalogues of other dealers, various bibliographies, etc. Sometimes, if he is imaginative, he will study the historical background of the book. If there is a past owner's signature, he will go to historical biographical works and look for interesting and meaningful connections this person might have had with the author or, indeed, with anyone else who might lay claim to public interest. If the book in question sold for fifty dollars in 1970, the dealer may extrapolate according to what he considers the rate of appreciation in the field, or with this author, and price the book at, say, seventy-five, or a hundred, or perhaps a hundred and fifty dollars. Here, he will probably be influenced by his knowledge of his clientele—their interests, buying habits, and so on.

This is obviously all very haphazard, very impressionistic. One man's retail is another man's wholesale. If our hypothetical dealer, above, does not have the "right" clientele for the book in question, and doesn't think he could get a just, or high enough, price for it, he will likely peddle it to another dealer, or send it to New York, Chicago, Los Angeles, or possibly England, for auction. This is obviously feasible only for very rare and valuable books; for the smaller fry, it just isn't worth all the trouble.

That there is no clearly defined scale of retail prices for rare books is evident in the fact that dealers more or less consistently buy from one another. Thus they are ostensibly buying at retail prices that are lower than "wholesale"—low enough for them to make a profit in reselling a book. And of course, if *they* can do it, so can the alert collector. No one would think the less of him. The fact is, there is such a marvelous heterogeneity in the "marketing" of rare books that dealers' catalogues are veritable argosies of opportunity if (and this is important) one buys only what he genuinely likes and respects for itself alone and not for its promise of turning a fast buck. It is a rare catalogue indeed that does not contain at least a few bargains in rare books.

There are several reasons for this, the most important being the dealer's "signature." If a dealer specializes in books about the sea, naval history, colonial America, and so forth, this is obviously a likely place to find the superbly elusive rarities that lie in those areas. But it is not where the more astonishing bargains are to be found, for two reasons: first, the dealer will very probably know much more about the maximum or "true," values of the books in his field than the collectors he serves; second, his clientele will be selective in their interests, and therefore more willing to pay top prices for the books he advertises.

Where the alert collector will search most avidly in such a field is along the edge, or indeed over the edge. A dealer in nautical Americana is not likely to place much value on the occasional first edition of Faulkner or Twain that comes his way. Indeed, he may not even take the trouble to research it, thinking that the difference in price between a highly desirable (in other markets) first edition of, say, Faulkner's *Go Down, Moses and Other Stories* and a later edition may be only a matter of ten or fifteen dollars, and not only that, the book may not sell at all, to his market, for that price. So he lists it at three dollars and forgets about it. What he does not know, in this instance, is that *Go Down, Moses* is a somewhat scarce Faulkner item in the first edition, containing the first book appearance of Faulkner's masterpiece, "The Bear"; and a mint copy (in the dust jacket, of course) might well bring a hundred dollars or more if advertised among the right people. (The limited, signed edition fetches a much higher price of course.)

The bargains that can be gotten from dealers are plentiful and various. As a matter of fact, I myself purchased a mint copy of *Go Down, Moses* from a dealer several years ago for three dollars. In dust jacket. An utterly smashing bargain. Other bargains I have gotten from dealers, either through catalogues or in visiting their places of business, include the first edition of *A Classical Dictionary of the Vulgar Tongue,* Capt. Francis Grose's classic of street slang in eighteenth-century England (so rare, I can't even find an auction quotation, although Barnes and Noble reprinted the third edition, with Eric Partridge's annotations, several years back). I paid four dollars for this to a dealer in Americana; similar bargains include a mint copy of Hemingway's *Farewell to Arms,* with DJ of course, for fifty cents; the second (1748) edition of Smollett's *Roderick Random* for four dollars; the first edition of Edward Dahlberg's *The Flea of Sodom,* for $1.50.

I could extend this list, although these are some of the highlights, to be sure. It would be nice to follow each listing with the "(!)" that indicates a superb move in chess; but the fact is, these were not really superb moves on my part. My role in each transaction was simply to manifest the minimal good sense to say yea to each opportunity as it appeared. Also to put myself *in the way* of such opportunities, of course— that is, to seek them out, upon occasion, by visiting dealers and studying catalogues, and of course, learning the points and general range of values for as many books as possible.

All dealers have these careless and hazy price margins in their catalogues; all catalogues have books listed at what must be considered bargain prices for the right people. Undoubtedly, most dealers are perfectly aware of this fact, and perfectly content to pass along an occasional bargain. In fact, they are *happy* to do so: it's good for business. And to repeat what was said much earlier: those bargains I have gotten from dealers are probably bargains that are passed along, rather than created by them. Which is to say, even fifty cents for that perfect Hemingway copy (breathtaking purchase!) undoubtedly represents a quarter profit for my benefactor. And that isn't so bad when you consider that the next "quarter book" he sells may bring him fifty dollars, rather than fifty cents.

Dealers are happily imprudent, sometimes, and occasionally genuinely beneficent in pricing a treasure too low, often casually willing to let a number of books slip by without close scrutiny, but these are dangerous habits, and if they are indulged in too often, a dealer is risking disaster. Because there is another risk in his enterprise, and that is the constant disadvantage of ignorance. Nobody knows enough about books. The most knowledgeable dealer will make mistakes in his own circumscribed area, not just in alien fields. And, being human, he will do foolish and even stupid things upon occasion. We're all vulnerable, and it's a good thing that our follies don't coincide and aren't in phase.

One of the great pitfalls awaiting the dealer when he undertakes to issue a catalogue is that of listing a book in the "wrong" category. A year ago, while rearranging some of my books, I came across an old catalogue put out by a dealer in Connecticut. His name was Turnbull, and for the life of me, I couldn't remember having ever seen this catalogue. Naturally, I couldn't resist looking through it, and my idle curiosity was very quickly transformed into a sort of feverish, if half-skeptical, excitement. The prices listed were incredible: a second edition of Sir Thomas Browne's *Urn Burial* for fifty dollars; an early copy of Howell's *Epistolae Ho-Elianae* for thirty; a slightly imperfect first edition of *The Vicar of Wakefield* for thirty-five. As this sample indicates, the offerings were particularly rich in early literature. I looked the catalogue over carefully, and my anxiety grew when I realized there was no date on it and no possible way of dating it.

In view of the prices, it might have been issued in the 1920s, I thought. In fact, the prices seemed compatible with those in an old Maggs catalogue I had around somewhere. But then, Turnbull's catalogue couldn't have been *too* old, because there was a scattering of contemporary authors. I studied the pages carefully, and began to check off items. I checked off twelve, and then thirteen—far more than I could afford; but my idea was that most of these were surely sold.

Then it was that something caught my eye. (All such accounts must bear this line; and I have gotten so much pleasure through reading it all these years that I happily pass it on to the reader.) There were two listings under "Lady Charlotte Bury." These listings featured Lady Bury's autograph. Very well, only I wasn't quite sure who she was, or why I should be interested. There was, however, a brief reminder (for the learned) of her claim to fame; but this information did not move me particularly; what *did* move me particularly was the almost off-hand reference in one of these listings to the fact that Lady Bury's autograph was on the first printed page of an undated Italian emblem book. Unfortunately, the notice stated, the title page of this emblem book was missing. However, be that as it may, the price was twenty dollars. Sold "waf," with all faults.

Did my heart beat faster then? No, it did not. But I was very interested. In fact, I was more pleased than if my heart *had* beaten faster, for I was not thinking of myself, but of that "Italian emblem book." Emblem books were generally creatures of the sixteenth century, I knew; and I did not have one. I now wanted one. And it seemed to me that this book might, indeed, be most interesting, that there was a very good chance it was quite valuable, with or without a title page, and of course, with or without a trace from Lady Charlotte Bury's hand. Oh, yes: it was stated that the book was bound in old vellum—a very good sign, indeed.

By this time, I had marked nearly twenty books in Turnbull's catalogue that had to be excellent bargains—if their descriptions were accurate—as well as personally attractive to me in terms of my collecting interests.

Although the catalogue was undated, there was, of course, a postal address at some small town in Connecticut, along with a phone number. I dialed this number, but the buzzing on the other end was soon interrupted by the familiar recorded voice, saying that what I had dialed was "not a working number." (Mild sinkage of the heart.)

I then phoned the area-code operator for directory assistance. When I told her my story, she looked for the name Turnbull, and finally (even reluctantly) told me that no such name was listed in the directory. Pause. Mild cursing. Then I said, "Operator, do you have a listing of nearby towns? This is very, very important."

She paused, and then said, yes, she did.

"Would you please look for my party's name in one of those other listings you have?"

I don't think this dear person was supposed to do what she did, then; however, I think she must have responded to some sense of urgency in my voice, and she just took it upon herself to shuffle through those few extra pages, after a minute or two of which she told me that there was a party of the name I had mentioned in a small nearby town.

"What is the number?" I asked.

When she told me, I immediately dialed that number, and after a few rings, a woman with a very cultivated English accent answered.

"Is this the number of the Turnbull who deals in books?" I asked.

"Yes, it is," she said.

"I'm calling about your catalogue number eleven. I'd like to order a few things from it."

Of all the pauses I have recorded in this account, the pause that now ensued was beyond all doubt the longest. For an instant, I was afraid Mrs. Turnbull (for I knew it had to be she) had mocked me by disappearing into some dark and distant room, leaving a telephone receiver dangling from its cord.

But this was not so. In a voice whose surprise was most exquisitely modulated, Mrs. Turnbull (*Lady* Turnbull, I now thought of her) said: "Oh, my, that *is* an old one, isn't it!"

Her comment seemed almost a private one. But she excused herself, saying she would try to find a copy, if any still lay about.

Of course, I waited several minutes; and then when she returned, she settled down (I could *hear* her doing this), and said, "Now, what books are we interested in?"

Of all those I read off, only one remained. This was the "Italian emblem book," with Lady Charlotte Bury's signature on it. I asked Mrs. Turnbull to hold it, awaiting my check.

"No," she said. "We'll post it to you immediately, and you can pay after you receive it."

With which, we both said good-bye.

A few days later, my book arrived; and as I had dared to hope, it was in excellent condition, printed in Lyons in 1559; and consisted of three separate titles (bound together), by Paolo Giovio, Gabriello Symeoni, and Ludovico Domenichi. The emblems were utterly fascinating, populated (as emblems should be) with the whole bestiary of the world's traits and characters, done with all the skill and wisdom of those early cartoonists of the soul's travail and victory both.

Although this is not an extraordinary book, as the world goes—and certainly not extraordinarily rare or valuable, it is in my view a handsome and desirable thing to own. As for its monetary value, this is hard to nail down, but, in view of its age, general condition, and the auction records of similar volumes, I would guess it is worth close to ten times what I paid for it.

Like book collecting generally, reading a catalogue is an art that makes demands upon one's general knowledge, scholarship, and imagination. It is also, almost always, a very profitable learning experience. Acting upon what one finds is, I suppose, a test of one's industry, and—as in any other business coups—possibly even something of a test of character, as well.

That Charles Hamilton, the dealer in rare manuscripts and autographs, can lay some claim to having mastered the art is evident in the following quotation from his book, *Scribblers and Scoundrels:* the quotation also gives in every one of its details, sound advice for collectors of rare books:

> During the past twenty years I have made more than half a million dollars by buying from other dealer's catalogues. I follow these simple principles, here set down for the first time:
>
> —*Read catalogues the moment they arrive.* Even seconds are precious when you seek desirable items. A man who understood the science of ordering was the late Dr. Max Thorek. I once had a hurried—and successful—order from Dr. Thorek, who had read my catalogue while walking down the hospital corridor from one room to another in each of which he was scheduled to perform a major operation; and even as he phoned, his second patient was being anesthetized.
>
> —*Order instantly by phone or telegram.* Important and interesting catalogues are often out-of-date within twenty-four hours after they are issued. Try to get them sent to you by airmail.
>
> —*Never assume any item is sold; always order it.* A few years ago I ordered a pair of letters of Conan Doyle about Sherlock Holmes from a French catalogue so ancient that the paper was already turning brown. I had no idea of the age of the catalogue, only that it had taken three weeks to reach me from Southern France. The price for the two letters was just thirty-five dollars, a ridiculously low sum, and although I was certain some alert collector had long ago snapped them up, I cabled to Nice for them. The letters came to me by airmail and I sold them at once for somewhat more than ten times what I had paid.
>
> —*Get catalogues from as many dealers as possible.* By examining the catalogues of half-a-dozen or more dealers, you will soon learn which dealers are reasonable and which are expensive. Never, however, refuse to buy a really significant and desirable autograph merely because the price is high. How many "high" prices of yesterday now look like incredible bargains.

Hamilton's anecdote concerning the Conan Doyle letters, might sound a bit familiar; and indeed it should, for it is a common experience with collectors and dealers alike. A good catalogue is an argosy of surprise and opportunity; and sometimes it is years before its adventurous voyage is over.

Considered as an investment, how do rare books compare with more traditional investments such as stocks, bonds, real estate, and even savings accounts? What are the signs?

Gordon N. Ray, in his essay, "The World of Rare Books Reexamined," writes: "For the past ten years surveys in the *Wall Street Journal* and by independent investment advisory services have placed rare books and manuscripts among the properties that are appreciating most rapidly in value."*

Professor Ray is not only a distinguished scholar and book collector, but president of the John Simon Guggenheim Foundation, as well; therefore his testimony deserves close attention in its claim to expertise in bibliophilic and intellectual as well as pragmatic affairs. Furthermore, in view of the fact that the market of any commodity rests finally upon the attitudes of a great number of people, he sent inquiries to a number of collectors, dealers, and librarians of rare books, receiving seventy-five replies. His long piece that appeared in *The Yale University Library Gazette* is recommended for anyone who is seriously interested in rare books as an investment. Some of its cautionary gospel is already familiar, but it will be judicious to quote at considerable length from Professor Ray's article, in a section where the question about speculation in rare books rises:

> In an effort to find out how knowledgeable people really regard this topic I asked my respondents (except for the librarians): "Have you noted among collectors and dealers of your acquaintance more emphasis on buying for investment, even a tendency to speculative buying that parallels playing the stock market? Can you cite examples?" As far as collectors were concerned, the answers to this question usually began, "No, but . . ."; that is, they knew of no clear-cut cases, but they sensed that the idea was in the air. One respondent, with a particularly wide circle of collecting friends, reported as "frequently heard remarks: Good investment, don't you think? Better than stocks and bonds. My children can sell this if they want, it's better than stocks." A professor-collector admitted that the investment element "often plays some role" in his own collecting. "After all," he explained, "collecting in what one regards as an unjustly neglected field is a form of speculative

The Yale University Library Gazette, July, 1974, Vol. 49, No. 1.

buying, even if monetary gain is not uppermost in one's mind."
He added the subacid comment that "some academic people
are beginning to be interested in books, now that they see that
money is involved." But some of them are undoubtedly empha-
sizing their investment possibilities as a sort of smoke-screen.
When pressed to sell, they say: "Books do better (by far) than
my stocks." And so these collectors hold on until things get
"very rough." Perhaps another collector's comment best sums
up the whole situation, that "while there is regret for higher
prices, there is not resentment," since the appreciation in value
of one's library is a substantial consolation, even if the general
price rise has clipped one's collecting wings.

The increase in collecting for investment, Ray argues, is not necessarily an argument in favor of its wisdom:

> For the average collector rare books and manuscripts remain
> a dubious speculation. Before he embarks on such an invest-
> ment program, he should study the rules of the game, which
> are to a certain extent stacked against him. Not all rare books
> rise in value. Those which do appreciate, often do so only mod-
> estly. Moreover, the prices recorded at auction and the prices
> asked in booksellers' catalogues are sellers' prices, not the
> prices at which the collector's books will be bought. Unless a
> dealer is offered a small collection of immediatcly disposable
> "high spots," he may not want to buy a library at all, and even if
> he does want to buy it, he rarely can afford to offer more than
> 50 per cent of its resale value.

Sobering, yes. But the last word? Of course not: it is not intended to
be. In the study of such a market as this, there *is* no last word; if there
were, this would not be a market, but a machine.

It is a truism that there is no single adequate calculus for investment
analysis. What stands as a good investment today, in the context of one
market, would be a weak investment tomorrow, in the context of
another. But there are signs, always. One sign is the negative one: not
how high and how quickly will my investment appreciate, but how stable is it in a fluctuating economy? Most dealers, even those who refuse
to advise their customers in the way of rare-book investments, agree
that in bad times, rare books tend to keep their value.

David Magee, the San Francisco dealer, claims that books held up

69

well during the Great Depression. "One would have thought that in bad times collectors would sell their libraries, but that was not the case in the early thirties. I cannot remember a single instance when a collector parted with his books on account of financial reverses."*

"People rarely lose money buying good books or paintings," Harvey Tucker of Black Sun Books says. And during inflationary times, he believes, "they increase at a faster rate than the dollar declines in value, and are therefore good investments."

Their value is of course increased by the natural and steady acquisitions of collectors and collecting institutions. John F. Fleming, the New York dealer (he is Rosenbach's successor) sees this shrinkage of the market as an important factor in the appreciation of rare books: "They seem to be the last to fall off during a recession and are a wonderful hedge during inflation. Their value rises far faster than other commodities. Institutions rarely ever sell and private buyers usually love their literary or historical possessions and they are rarely sold before the collector's death."

Roderick Brinckman, of Monk Bretton Books in Toronto, well expresses the necessary caveat, as well as the profound and uneasy ambivalence that many students of the subject feel: "I would say that book prices, generally, have held up very well during the last two years, and *good* books have shown themselves to be a sound investment. But collecting books is a very specialized pursuit and can hardly be recommended as an investment activity. However, it is true that *knowledgeable* collectors seldom have reason to regret their investment."

Such advice is prudential and sound, no doubt; but the higher one goes in the rare-book market, the less relevant it seems. One reason for this is that the dollar-as-index possesses an identity in the domestic market that it does not possess internationally. Translated, this means that there are foreign investors who are showing greater interest in buying—not just American books, but books in America—than ever before. A dealer recently told me two things that are intimately related: foreign (i.e., English, French, and German) dealers are now buying rare books out of America; and he (the aforementioned dealer) is now finding it hard-to-impossible to buy good books out of Brussels, which has served him as a steady and faithful source of supply for years.

For every boy, the old pop songs tell us, there is a girl. And for every

* *Infinite Riches* (New York, 1973), p. 92.

bear, there is a bull. One of the most palpably bullish dealers around is Ben Weinreb, an antiquarian bookseller in London. In writing about his special love, old illustrated editions, he becomes lyrical:

> William Daniell's *Voyage Round Great Britain,* first published in parts between 1814 and 1826 and collected into 8 volumes with over 300 fine aquatint views—we have a set in stock at 5,500,* last year we had a set for 3,500, ten years ago copies were bringing about 350.
> Gould's *Birds of Great Britain*—now 12,000 (think we have one at 12,500) but four years ago it was 1,000 and ten years ago 200 to 300 and so on.
> What a bonanza—why bother about land values, stocks and shares and such-like?

Weinreb is far from being alone in his optimism for the future of the rare-book market. In inflationary times, art objects, antiques, furs, and jewelry, all seem to compete in the race skyward. Perhaps it is a healthy human instinct to take thoughtful pause when currency is insecure, stocks are volatile, and the world generally gives pretty clear evidence that it is going to hell on a turnpike, and look for security in the near, fine, and tangible—like a sterling silver tea set, a sketch by Rouault, or a first edition of *Tristram Shandy.*

During inflationary times, Roderick Brinckman feels that rare books compare very well with other investments. "But I don't think many people really *invest* in rare books," he says. "The investment aspect is nearly always a distant second to the normal collecting mania which makes people want to form collections of stamps, coins, old bottles, books, or whatever."

Richard M. Weatherford, of Argus Books, in Columbus, Ohio, has studied the market carefully over the past few years, and concludes simply and categorically that, "Books are a much better investment than stocks." (Of course, the books he is speaking of are those that are rare and in good condition, the blue-chip collectables.) Not only are they better than stocks, Weatherford argues, but they are better than paintings, because they are not so vulnerable to those periodic changes in taste that sweep across the buying public.

A number of Weatherford's customers are banks, insurance compa-

---

*Pounds sterling, of course.

nies, and foundations that buy rare books as an investment. They ask him, "How much can we count on these books appreciating?" In answer, Weatherford guarantees to buy back any book in a year's time for the purchase price, plus ten percent, providing he, Weatherford, can select the titles. Not only does he make such a guarantee, but he does so with the conviction that he will not only retrieve the surplus ten percent over the book's original sale price, but make a significant, additional profit. This is very much what in vulgar terms is called putting your money where your mouth is.

Weatherford claims that more and more institutions are buying rare books purely as investments. Among these are a few oil, chemical, auto, and retail corporations. One is a well-known reprint publisher in New York, whose representatives admit privately to investing in the "big ticket" items among rare books. One thing that just about all of these organizations have in common is an instinct for secrecy in their activities. They want to build quietly, rationally, and regularly, without that fanfare which would immediately jack prices up.

Although actual motives are harder to uncover than even the quietest investment activity, it seems likely that when institutional investors buy rare books, they do so with the idea of providing a hedge against losses among their more volatile conventional speculations. If you invest exclusively in one kind of market, you are totally susceptible to the folks that control it, and—in this sense—trapped. In view of this fact, institutional investors tend to buy only the greatest (i.e., "proved") rarities, and buy only under the guidance of a trusted dealer.

Can the private collector of limited means hope to compete in such a market? Of course he can, a lot better than he might hope to compete in the realm of conventional investments—especially if Richard Ney (an investment counselor and one-time film star) is correct in his belief that "more than 99 percent of those who invest in the [stock] market . . . buy *high* and sell *low*."* Ney's argument is that the stock market is manipulated by "forces which are part of the Stock Exchange itself"—which is to say, it is rigged against the small, independent investor. If the rare-book market were exclusively an investment market, the possibility of manipulation would be more tangible; but it is essentially *not* an investment market—there are variables of taste and fashion, as

*"A Controversial View on the Stock Market," *Family Weekly,* February 22, 1976.

well as variables in the books themselves (e.g., condition, binding, state, issue, provenance, association, and so on) that render the rare-book market a very unlikely one for mass manipulation. Books are *not* stocks and bonds; they are *not* integers, vouchers, or counters of any sort.

How good a chance, then, does the private collector-investor have, if there is growing institutional interest in rare books? It is excellent. Heavy buying creates as many rarities as it liquidates—only the definitions change, which is inevitable anyway in view of the march of time and the general population increase. There are only a finite number of copies of a Caxton Chaucer or a William Blake first edition, but people keep coming and coming, generation after generation, and they get to be more and more.

Often, bookmen and others will caution the young collector-investor with some such caveat as, "Yes, books can be a good investment, but you have to know what you are doing." Strange advice, indeed! Do such people think that profits are available in the stock market for anyone who doesn't know what he is doing? Real estate? Banking? Possibly such advice is necessary because there seems to be a certain impurity in the act of buying books with a view towards speculation: namely, one is in danger of buying not rationally, but emotionally. If you want a book badly enough, its status as an investment dissolves into nothing. Like poker, diet, marriage, and a lot of other good things, collecting books with a view to their investment potential is a lesson in self-knowledge. I would hope that there will be books you will want, independently of their investment value; but I also hope that you are aware of this fact as you buy them, and are willing to "pay the price" in both ways.

It is interesting to note that many of those who advise the small investor to consider antiques generally, and rare books particularly, are not themselves dealers, librarians, or otherwise professionally experienced in the world of rare books. Whether they are collectors or not is often hard to find out; but this probably doesn't make much difference, since the collector-investor is, like all private investors, an amateur by definition. Still, it's always smart to observe the successful amateur.

And it's always smart to listen to advice, no matter where it comes from. If a lot of the advice to invest in rare books comes from people who don't obviously possess the credentials for giving such advice, does it mean they're out of their tree? Not necessarily; for some of these people are sophisticated in other kinds of investment activity in a way that the average, intelligent, and informed rare-book dealer is not.

It is classically easy to simplify the unfamiliar and to minimize the problems it carries. One modern collector spent years, money, and hard work building a handsome and complete Stephen Crane collection. In addition to manuscript materials, there were copies of every known edition of Crane's books. It would have made a splendid bulk acquisition for any university library with strength in Crane's work or period to build upon. Unfortunately, no one happened—at this time—to be willing to pay the price. Since this collector was determined to sell immediately, rather than bide his time, his painstakingly gathered collection suddenly became nothing more than a large group of books, some of which were valuable, and some not. Outside of the *gestalt* of an author collection, an nth edition of Crane's *The Open Boat,* or the Modern Library edition of *The Red Badge of Courage,* have no bibliophilic worth whatsoever. All of the scholarship, vision, and effort were dissipated the instant these books were put up for auction singly and in small lots. Therefore, in spite of predictably high prices for the major rarities, as a collection the books brought a disappointingly small price.

The owner was embittered by the experience, and concluded that "rare books simply are not liquid"—which, like antiques and art objects generally, they are not. "On the other hand," the collector continued, "if you own stocks, you can dispose of them simply by picking up the phone." Well, that's true also, of course. However, immediate disposal will often be at considerable loss. Which pretty much puts us back right where we started in comparing these two radically different kinds of investment.

In his delightful and chatty *The Adventures of a Treasure Hunter,* Charles Everitt claims that throughout his sixty years as a rare bookman, he had known "fewer than a dozen" real collectors. Furthermore, he confessed that he wasn't much interested in collectors, anyway. He considered the overwhelming majority of his customers speculators, whether they admitted it or not.

As in all speculations, this kind requires brains, guts, skill, patience, and a willingness to be lucky. Or, in the words of Gerald M. Loeb, "It requires Knowledge, Experience, and Flair." In fact, that is the title of the second chapter of Loeb's *The Battle For Investment Survival* (the twenty-fourth printing!), and of course the author is not referring to rare books at all, but to conventional investments in stocks and bonds. The first two sentences of the chapter read: "Nothing is more difficult,

I truly believe, than consistently and fairly profiting in Wall Street. I know of nothing harder to learn."

It is curious that many people seem to be perfectly willing to believe that attentiveness, hard study, and insight (or "knowlege, experience, and flair") are required for success in stocks and bonds, but not in rare-book speculations; but there do seem to be people who feel this way, or think of such requirements as being a hardship and unfair disadvantage.

Loeb, who, the dust jacket says, "has been referred to as 'the dean of Wall Street,'" is well schooled in the complexities, perfidies, and impetuosities of the money market, and takes the challenge for granted. So should the collector-investor in rare books, no matter where his emphasis might lie (it really is not unliterary or unscholarly to buy wisely). As one dealer summed it up, the rare-book market compares excellently with other kinds of investments, but to be successful, collectors should "know their subject as well as a Wall Street broker knows his."

IV.

THE POINT OF POINTS

One of the more diverting features of book collecting is the premium given to "points" in the evaluation of a book. The idea is fascinating, for the values attached to points are arbitrary and in many cases textually unimportant, if not irrelevant. Why, then, should "otherwise" intelligent people attach so much importance to them?

The question may prove crucial in defending one's passion for book collecting against the scorn or indifference of an obtuse world. The fact that points are arbitrary is not disturbing at all, for the bibliophile is simply more aware than most people of the sportive premises that underlie his serious actions. Such sportiveness gives to collecting a freedom and intellectual order that are seldom possible in those actions whose sportiveness is more insidiously concealed so that one is "duty bound" or "pragmatically obligated" to do this thing or that.

Similarly, the fact that collectors tacitly agree to celebrate and honor books according to the dictates of a complex and Mandarin symbolism of points is simply one aspect of their celebrating and honoring the book as a thing of this world. That so much is made of so little might give rise to the suspicion that the point which beguiles and fascinates the book collector is ridiculous and insubstantial, thereby approaching the mathematical idea of a point as having no property but location, that location being in the fevered projections of a bibliophile's brain.

Before the suspense proves too great, these mysterious "points" should be defined. Easy: points are the physical properties of a book that distinguish one phase of its printing history from another. Therefore, points constitute a basis for the classification of books according to the order in which they are printed—a sort of bibliographical taxonomy.

Since the first edition of an important, generally admired book excites the interest, even passion, of a great number of collectors, "points" often mean "first-edition points"—those visible signs in a book that mark it as the first product of that work to be printed and bound.

Usually first-edition collectors want the utmost, the very first, the Ur-book of their frenetic dreams. This, of course, means first printing, as well as first edition. "Printings," or "impressions,"* as such, are invisible, however, since they normally refer only to a particular press run of a book. Let us say a book is about to be published. Those who decide such things decide that the first printing should comprise 5,000 copies. Voilà, it happens. Let us then suppose that the book sells at a fast-enough rate to encourage those who preside over these matters, and they meet in solemn deliberation and decide that another printing of 2,500 copies is called for. So this second printing is run off, identical to the first in every way, except for the words "second printing" or some other sign, usually on the copyright page. This "other sign" is a sort of code, and it takes different forms, sometimes the letter "b"; sometimes an altered publisher's device; sometimes the omission of the words "first printing" or "first edition," or omission of the symbol that indicates this, such as the capital letter "A" on the copyright page (as with Scribner's) or the omission of the date on the title page (as with Houghton Mifflin), and so on.

Something very interesting has happened here. The second printing is invisible, in itself. If, in the example given above, there is some

*Like many others, I consider these terms as synonymous; still other perfectly lucid and reasonable people do not. "Impression" seems to be the more traditional term, still somewhat favored (or "favoured") in England, for a single press run, here termed "printing." The reader should now be warned that the following discussion will necessarily be somewhat arbitrary and impressionistic, for the terminology of publishers (like their practices), dealers, and even (alas!) bibliographers is inconsistent. Furthermore, terminology, like practice, changes with time and place. My course is to define these terms as I think they are most often used today.

change of type before those extra 2,500 copies are run off, then that press run becomes not simply a second printing, but a second issue.

This all seems very clear, until you realize that in a copy designated in any form whatsoever as a second printing, that designation itself is expressed by a change in type; therefore if a book is typographically labeled a "second printing," it is by that fact alone rendered a second issue, as well.

As if this were not enough, consider the following: I have a copy of Borges's *The Aleph and Other Stories: 1933–1969,* a book whose value is somewhat lessened by the fact that it is not only a "foreign" edition of an author's work but a translation as well. (The old slogan among collectors is, "follow the flag," which means collect the first editions of an author's country. Still, some authors are worth collecting under just about any circumstance, if you like them enough; and for me, Borges is such an author.)

On the copyright page of *The Aleph and Other Stories,* the publisher has very conveniently indicated "First Edition." However, the dust jacket, just as conveniently, and just as unequivocally, says, "Second Printing." If I were to lose the dust jacket, the book could, in the sight of all but God, pass for a first printing. But of course, it would lack the dust jacket, which is always important to the value of a book, and in this case, and insofar as this book may become valuable, could become a matter of great importance. But what if someone were to take a "first printing" dust jacket and put it on a "second printing" book? Who would ever know? In fact, maybe *my* copy is such a hybrid, inverted.

These enthusiasms, rampant on a field of confusion, form the escutcheon of an old-fashioned sort of crank, who flourished more liberally in the past, but can still be seen among us, upon occasion, a figure from another world with an iridescent mold on its clothes and a vagueness in its stare, caused by the burden of crazy information. This funny human being (it comes equally in both genders) is called an "Issue Monger" by John Carter, and described as follows:

> The issue-monger is one of the worst pests of the collecting world, and the more dangerous because many humble and well-intentioned collectors think him a hero to whom they should be grateful. He may be a bibliographer (usually the self-styled type), or a bookseller, or a collector, and his power for harm may be rated in that order. He is an honours graduate of

79

what Lanthrop Harper called "the fly-spot school of bibliography." He is the man who, if he cannot construct a bogus *point* out of some minute variation he himself has discovered between two copies of a book, will pervert the observations of others to the same purpose. Show him a *misprint* or a *dropped numeral,* and he will whip you up an "issue point" in no time. Show him a difference of a month between two sets of inserted publisher's catalogues and he will be good for a whole paragraph of dubious inferences. Show him a wrappered *proof* copy of a book which he happens not to have seen in that state before, and his cry of *"trial issue"* of *"pre-first edition"* will turn Pollard or McKerrow in the grave.

No doubt this *does* seem madness; but if it is, it is a colorful madness. It can, in fact, be an *interesting* madness. William James said that something is important to the extent people think it's important. (This does not, of course, apply to sports and television.) But such a concession doesn't always need to be made. If the printed word is a matter of consequence to all that we deem civilized (it is), then we must have strategies for protecting and assuring the accuracy of the printed word in its native habitat, the book. Textual points that serve and amuse the bibliophile are an important part of that precise knowledge of the whole book that is essential to scholarship. And there are in fact many instances where information about a seemingly humble point has dramatically altered the significance of a passage or even an entire book. So for all the apparent muddle in this matter of first-edition points— for all the hairsplitting and dancing to the clang of typophonous symbols—the scholarship which they represent is a garden, a veritable suite of sanity compared to most of what goes on in the world.

While the word "issue" designates a press run featuring some deliberate textual change in a book, the word "state" refers to a particular variation within a specific issue; and unlike the issue itself, the state of a book is not always classifiable in terms of priority. In the confederation of bibliographical states there are defective letters due to type having broken down, or defective type having been replaced, sometime during the printing, a binding change, an errata slip, a cancel, and so on. Priority of states is difficult or sometimes impossible to establish because of the character of the variations. A defective letter caused by broken type can indicate either that the type was originally broken, then detected and repaired sometime during the press run; or it can indicate that the type broke down *during* the press run. The two states thus created are impossible to grade according to priority unless the testimony of the printers is available, which is of course pretty much a matter of chance.

When the first state is clearly known, the distinguishing mark constitutes a point. One of the more famous is the last line of page 225 in *The Red Badge of Courage*. The last two lines (I quote both as they appear on the page, for the sake of minimal clarity) read:

> him there. They sat side by side and congratu-
> lated each other.

If this last line is perfect, the book is in the first state. "Later states," as Merle Johnson notes in *American First Editions*, "show the type at this point either broken or repaired with the final letter in *congratulated* out of perpendicular."

The first editions of Mark Twain afford a particularly rich harvest of points. One of the more famous (and clearest) is the simple presence or absence of the portrait of Napoleon III on p. 129 of *Innocents Abroad*. This was only Twain's second book, but already he was becoming famous, and there were 30,000 copies printed the first year, 1869. Most of these 30,000 copies, however, have the portrait of Napoleon III on p. 129, signifying that the copy is a second issue. Without that dumb old picture of Napoleon III (and, of course, with the 1869 date on the title page; and in fine condition), a copy might bring well over one hundred dollars. With the picture, it might bring . . . well, what am I bid? Five . . . ten? . . .

We have yet to clarify what is normally meant by that larger word, "edition." To the collector, a first edition means first printing, first issue, first state, any term to which the word "first" can reasonably, or unreasonably, be attached.

Usually (see Ronald B. McKerrow's *An Introduction to Bibliography for Literary Students*) the term "edition" refers to all the copies of a book from one setting-up of type. Logically, this might also be argued to include copies printed by any other process, including photocopying, offset, and so on. But of course that would be nonsense in view of the book's provenance, not to mention paper, binding, and so on.

"Second edition," then, would refer to the same book, or one clearly and directly deriving from the first edition, printed from a new set of plates. But this is not always the case. If a significant amount of text is added to the printing or printings from the first plates (several chapters, for example), but the type fonts are not changed, and the new material is just added to the previous, or if significant sections of the old text are rewritten, then the book may be considered *edited,* and the product of this editing will be logically considered an edition in itself, or a "second edition." The difference here, generally, is that the change should be deemed substantive, material, and either incremental or variant, thus constituting an edition; whereas in the case of a new issue, the change is of a lesser order of magnitude, extending from matters of copy editing within the general language of the original to deliberative matters of enhancement and clarification, extending to corrections, deletions, substitutions of words, and so on.

With the advent of printing of facsimile editions during the past century, the problem is theoretically complicated still further. Today, facsimile editions are usually printed by offset directly from the pages of a rare book that has been disbound for the purpose. Being "printed from the same plates" as the original edition, albeit indirectly, this new facsimile edition could be logically classified as part of the original edition, but of course, such a printing is not made *directly* from those plates; and here even bibliophiles balk and let the cool light of practicality flood their minds with peace.

Facsimile editions comprise a special kind of collectable, and they are considered a boon by collectors, for they make the supreme rarities available—but not *too* available—to larger numbers of people. There is an ethical problem in the printing of facsimile editions, however, that is not always confronted. Somewhere, in type (perhaps modest to the extent of shyness—but legible and unequivocally *there*) should be a label stating that the book is, in fact, a facsimile edition, and nothing else. This obligation is not always met, so that the buyer has to rely upon his knowledge of paper or binding or other signs that the book is not a fraudulent copy, rather than a facsimile.

It may sound a little romantic, but the fact is, points do somewhat humanize the book. Our faces, bodies, emotions, vocabularies, ideas, and tastes are only alike, not duplicated, and we tend to feel a sterility in contexts that do not tolerate a similar, reflective variation. And we like to think that Nature, God, and Truth—whatever they might prove to be in the final solution—for all their awesome precisions, are secretly on our side, and have been all along.

That the type for the very first letter of the very first word in Mark Twain's *Roughing It* broke down somewhere in the first press run seems to constitute a sly and quiet little homily against man's hubristic confidence that his tools and toys will never fail him. That page 94 of the first edition of Emerson's *Nature* (Boston, 1836) is misnumbered 92 simply confirms that we have long suspected—that printers, as well as Homers, nod. But when a typographical vagary extends to the dropping of three whole lines from the bottom of a page, as was the case with page 396 of Thoreau's first book, *A Week on the Concord and Merrimack Rivers* (Boston and Cambridge, 1849), and when those three lines have been supplied in the author's penciled holograph (as Merle Johnson tells us was often done by Thoreau) why—well, the point of *this* point should be evident to one and all, as should be the reason for the difference in price between the first issue—around $1,000—and the second issue, with the print corrected, which sells in the $200 to $300 range.

Early in this century, many publishers got together (sort of, that is, in their manifold ways); and, either in a spirit of exasperation at the first-edition mania that afflicted so many of their customers, or possibly in perverse joy at being able to enter the game, they short-circuited the divertissement of points entirely. In plain English, they signified their first editions, either by printing the words "first edition" or "first printing" on the copyright page, or by means of a clearly identifiable publisher's symbol indicating that fact.

This was of course intended to simplify the lives of bibliophiles; and basically, this policy succeeded, wherever and whenever it was "implemented," that is. For it appears that publishers are not at all the fuddy-duddies of popular conception, but are a whimsical and irrepressible lot in their way; and by 1928, when H. S. Boutell brought out a slender, 62-page booklet, titled *First Editions of To-day and How to Tell Them,* in which general practices in this regard are codified, publishers were still grievously prone to begin their explanations with such cunning evasions as "Although we have no hard and fast rule, our general practice is. . . ." and "It is our habit to. . . ."

"General practice"? "Habit"? Who needs to be tantalized by such squishy precisions? And yet, contrary to the popular conception, publishing houses tend to be congeries of editors, each doing what used to be called "his thing," rather than the austere and efficient organizations suggested by institutional stationery. Therefore, it would be foolhardy for most publishers to presume to speak for all the books they publish concerning what must seem, from *their* standpoint, to be trivial clues of a trivial fact.

In spite of their own rich confusions in their practices of indicating first editions, there are many interesting points for the collector to study. One may legitimately assume that a book is, after all, a first edition unless there is evidence to the contrary. Sometimes this evidence is hard to find; sometimes not. Many publishers did, and still do, base their practices on this assumption. That is, they list additional printings or editions; if such are not listed, then the book may be assumed to be a first edition. The collector will always make sure, however, that if there is a date on the title page, it and that on the copyright page will coincide within one year; this is only a minimally prudential check, of course. Some publishers, like G. P. Putnam's, usually omit both the date on the title page and the explicit labeling of a book as "First Edition" or "First Printing," but list all subsequent printings on the copyright page.

Many publishers unequivocally state, "First Printing"; but of course this practice varies with the years, and sometimes *within* a period of years—so it's best to be cautious. Other publishers have devised their own codes indicating first editions, and some of these are calculated to appeal to the ciphering mind of the collector. Appleton, for example, used to bypass the copyright page, where one normally looks for such information, and simply put the number of the book's printing in parenthesis at the foot of the last page, thus (1), (2), (3), and so on.* George H. Doran & Co. usually indicated a first by the printing of their colophon, "in which the initials 'GHD' appear and which is always placed directly beneath the copyright line." Scribner's in their beginning years did not have a consistent policy, but about 1930 they instituted their famous capital "A" existing in lonely splendor beneath the copyright, thereby indicating all the first editions of Thomas Wolfe, F. Scott Fitzgerald, and Ernest Hemingway that they published after that date. Later, this capital "A" was obscured, somewhat, by the inclusion of the month and year of the first edition, thus: "A–2.64"—indicating "First printing, February, 1964." Subsequent printings are labeled

---

*But I have a copy of H. Rider Haggard's *Dawn* published by Appleton in 1887, with no such indicator—only the signature numeral, "20," without parenthesis, at the bottom of the last page.

by subsequent letters in the alphabet. Harcourt Brace Jovanovich and other publishers have a similar practice, substituting "First Edition" for the "A," but indicating later printings with the "b,c,d," series.

One of the niftiest clues I seem to remember was that of Coward-McCann (certain Albee and Thornton Wilder titles were published by this firm), whose colophon was a candleholder that always appeared on the copyright page. However, if that candleholder had a candle in it, it was a first edition; without the candle, it was something other. (I don't know what it would have meant if the candle were lighted—probably a high fever.)

In spite of all these codes and the air of confidence with which they are explained, there is something a little refreshing in David McKay's response to Boutell's inquiry. He wrote, "There isn't any way you could identify the first editions of our books." So there, too.

Points are significant not only to the scholar in his need to distinguish one phase of a text's printing history from another, but to the collector-investor, as well. Following is a sample list of collectable American first editions, showing their first-issue points, and in most cases indicating the estimated price differential between copies (in excellent condition, of course) which possess those points and those poor cousins that do not:

LITTLE WOMEN, by Louisa May Alcott. Part One, Boston, 1868. Part One does not have an announcement for "Little Women, Part Two" at the foot of the last page of text; and does not state "Part One" on the spine. Part Two, Boston, 1869—First state does not have a notice regarding "Little Women: Part One" at p.i. First issue, $800–$1,200; second issue, $50–$150.

WINESBURG, OHIO, by Sherwood Anderson. New York, 1919. Top stained yellow, and end paper map at front. Line 4 on page 86 has the word "lay" ("an intense silence seemed to lay over everything"); and the type in the word "the" is broken in line 3, page 251. First issue, in dust jacket, $150–$200; without jacket, $100–$150; second issue (lacking above points), probably under $50.

SHAPES OF CLAY, by Ambrose Bierce. San Francisco, 1903. First state of first issue has lines on p. 71 transposed as follows: "We've nothing better here than bliss./ Walk in. But I must tell you this . . . ." First issue, $150; second issue, $30–$40.

THE TROLL GARDEN, by Willa Cather. New York, 1905. At the foot of spine "McClure Phillips & Co." is listed in first issue. Author's second book. First issue, $100–$150. Second, $20–40.

THE PRINCE AND THE PAUPER, by Mark Twain. Boston, 1882. The first state has the "Franklin Press" imprint on the copyright page. First issue, $100–$200; second issue, $25.

THREE SOLDIERS, by John Dos Passos. New York, 1921. The first state has "signing," instead of "singing," on line 7 of page 213. (Some duplicate signatures appear in the first state, but this is a binder's error that cannot be said to designate a specific phase in the book's printing history, and is therefore not a legitimate point.) First issue (with dust jacket), $50; second issue, $15.

MAY-DAY AND OTHER PIECES, by Ralph Waldo Emerson. Boston, 1867. First issue has "flowers" for "hours" in poem on page 184. First issue, $75–$100; second issue, $15.

AS I LAY DYING, by William Faulkner. New York, 1930. First issue has dropped "I" on page 11; also top edges are stained brown. First issue, with dust jacket: as high as $475 (at auction in 1975); second state, without dropped 'I," but in dust jacket, at most, $50.

THE GREAT GATSBY, by F. Scott Fitzgerald. New York, 1925. First issue has "chatter" instead of "echolalia" in line 16, page 60; "sick in tired" instead of "sickantired" in line 9, page 205 along with three other textual points as listed in Matthew J. Bruccoli's "Collector's Handlist" (published by the Fitzgerald Newsletter, 1964). First issue, in dust jacket, up to $500; second issue, $25–$30.

A BOY'S WILL, by Robert Frost. London, 1913. Bronze or brown pebbled cloth. (Subsequent states, bound in white, cream, or buff wrapper.) First issue, $950 (at 1972 auction) to $1,150 (1975 catalogue listing); second issue, $100–$300.

MEN WITHOUT WOMEN, by Ernest Hemingway. New York, 1927.

First issue weighs between 15 and 15½ ounces; second issue, lighter. First issue, with dust jacket, $50–$100; second issue, $20–$30.

TRANSATLANTIC SKETCHES, by Henry James. Boston, 1875. First issue has Osgood imprint on spine. First issue, $100–$200; second issue, $15–$25.

MEDEA, translated by Robinson Jeffers. New York, 1946. First issue lacks word "least" on page 99. First issue in dust jacket, $30–$50; second issue, $10–$15.

WHAT OF IT! by Ring W. Lardner. New York, 1925. First issue has had pages numbered, "191, 201, 200." Later issues has pagination corrected. First issue in dust jacket, up to $75; second issue, $10–$20.

THE CALL OF THE WILD, by Jack London. New York, 1903. First issue has vertically ribbed cloth. First issue in dust jacket, $100–$200; second issue, $10–$20.

GONE WITH THE WIND, by Margaret Mitchell. New York, 1936. First issue has "Published May, 1936," on copyright page (rather than June). First issue in dust jacket, $100–$150, ($140 at auction in 1974); second issue: $10 to $20.

POEMS, by Edgar Allan Poe. New York, 1831. First issue is marked "Second Edition" on title page. First issue probably around $10,000 whenever another copy appears for sale; this is an excessively rare title of a very difficult writer to collect. A first edition of his 1831 *Poems* appeared at auction in 1966, where it sold for $6,250; this copy was defective—stained and with covers detached.

A QUINZAINE FOR THIS YULE, by Ezra Pound. London, 1908. First state (of 100 copies) with "Pollock" imprint; second state with "Mathews" imprint. First state: up to $500; second, $300 (at auction in 1966).

CUP OF GOLD, by John Steinbeck. New York, 1929. Author's first book. First issue reads, "First Published, August, 1929," on copyright page. First issue in dust jacket, up to $500 (sold for $475 at auction in 1974); second issue, $15–$35.

LOOK HOMEWARD, ANGEL, by Thomas Wolfe. New York, 1929. First issue has Scribner seal on copyright page; first dust jacket has Wolfe's picture on back. First issue, with dust jacket $200–$400; second issue (with later dust jacket); $50–$100.

V.

OLD RARITIES:

INCUNABULA AND THE

EVER-EXPANDING PAST

f any one invention can be said to have revolutionized the mind of man, it is Gutenberg's. Not only did the creation of movable type pave the way for a mass readership, and through it, democracy, but it created a basis upon which the idea of fact, as we know it, might be erected. Contemplating the surprising number of manuscripts that were copied from the first printed books, Curt F. Bühler concluded that the primary impetus in the development of print was not economic, but intellectual. It was accuracy, more than wide distribution of texts, that inspired the early growth of printing. "As learning spread," Bühler writes, "and the scholar in Paris wished to confound and controvert that utter fool in Bologna who pretended to know something to the contrary, he had merely to point triumphantly to a certain page, line so-and-so, of any printed edition available to both in order to establish and confirm the righteousness of his position."*

The year 1500 is a convenient date to mark the end of the infancy of the book, and the beginning of its lusty childhood. The products of this

*Fifteenth Century Books and the Twentieth Century: An Address by Curt F. Bühler, and a Catalogue of an Exhibition of Fifteenth Century Books held at the Grolier Club, April 15–June 1, 1952. New York, The Grolier Club, 1952. p. 12.

From the Gutenberg 42-line Bible
Courtesy of Sotheby Parke Bernet, Inc., New York

infancy are appropriately termed *incunabula*—Latin for "swaddling clothes." When it was invented, the book was naturally thought of as an imitation manuscript, much as the first autos were considered "horse-less carriages" and the first films, "photo plays." But during the half century of the incunabular period, the book gradually proved that it was legitimately a thing-in-itself, and no longer needed to follow a model of any sort.

As previously mentioned, it is hard to believe that there was a time when incunabula were not particularly valued, for these are books from the very cradle of printing, the very first antiquities of antiquities, rarest of the rare. Or should have been thought to be such; but the fact is, they were not. Therefore, at one time, someone had to look at these old books with new eyes, understanding what splendid treasures they were, or should be. The creation of value in this instance was not simply arbitrary; as with many profound innovations, it was really more discovery than creation. There is a little anecdote about Marie Antoinette's maid, who, in altering an old hat for her mistress, said, "Nothing is new except what has been forgotten."

Since about 75 percent of all incunabula are in Latin, and since approximately 72 percent are the work of contemporary writers (relevance is obviously not a modern invention), it is safe to conclude that incunabula are not—except in a few research libraries—collected primarily for content. They have other charms to recommend them, one of which is their being a sort of collective "first edition" of the printed word in its half millenium's authority over the mind of man. As antiquarian documents, they are fascinating, even to the non-Latinist, and marked by subtle differences from their descendants. The very first books were not numbered by page, but generally by leaf; and in some of them, as in manuscripts, the catchword was the only connective required for establishing the correct sequence of leaves. The title page was not a feature of early books; like the monks who patiently and painfully transcribed all those millions of pages, the printer first thought of his duty as a nonostentatious, even subservient one. Therefore, his role was referred to almost as an afterthought, at the end of the book, along with the more important data concerning the date and location of the book's printing. This afterthought is the *colophon,* a word that meant "the finishing touch," or "the end" in classical Greek. But it also, paradoxically, meant "top," thus suggesting the title page in its modern position at the front of a book, a position it was to claim—at

Nuremberg Chronicle
Courtesy of Sotheby Pa
Bernet, Inc., New York

first very tentatively, and then more boldly—near the end of the fifteenth century and retains to this day as an integral part of the book as we know it.

While it is true that incunabula have not, until recently, been collected as actively as their antiquarian significance warrants, they have been collected as "an inexpensive hobby" (according to McMurtrie) since about 1640, then thought to be the bicentennial of printing.* Today, they may rightfully be classed among the most collectable of books. And in spite of their vigorous appreciation in recent years, some incunabula can still be purchased for less than $200—a pretty solid investment in view of their general appreciation.

In Sotheby Parke Bernet's sale of March 5, 1975, two copies of the famous *Nuremberg Chronicle* were auctioned. These were both the first Latin edition of 1493, containing 1809 woodcut illustrations. Both copies were slightly imperfect (some repairs, offsetting, a few mild stains and small tears); one was bound in "17th-century blind tooled pigskin,"

*McMurtrie, Douglas C. *The Golden Book*. Chicago, 1927.

and the other in "19th-century morocco gilt (upper cover detached; spine loose); gilt edges." The first copy sold for $5,500; the second for $7,500—the latter no doubt bringing a higher price because the woodcuts were colored by hand.

A similarly imperfect copy of this same edition of the *Chronicle* had sold on January 18, 1972, for $2,250; another some three months later, at Sotheby's in England, for £2,100 (about $5,040). In William Sallock's 1971 catalogue (#283), a similar, slightly sophisticated copy was offered for only $3,250. The mean of the 1975 sales is $6,500; that of the previous sales $3,513—a difference of $2,987 in about three years, which averages out at slightly less than a 23 percent compounded annual appreciation rate.*

At the same sale, the second edition of *Hortus Sanitatis* ("one of the most influential of early herbals"), printed in Strasbourg about 1497, sold for $5,500; a similar copy had sold at Sotheby's on October 25, 1972, for £1,350 (about $3,240), showing an annual appreciation rate of about 20 percent.

One of the greatest prices received at Sotheby Parke Bernet's March 5 sale, however, was *Le Grant Herbier en François,* a small folio printed in Paris about 1498. Embellished with 306 woodcuts, this title is a superlative rarity, being one of only five copies known. And of course, the book is of great antiquarian interest, containing an index of illnesses, along with a list of plants and herbal remedies. In 1968, a copy whose description was so nearly identical to this it may, in fact, have been the same one, sold for £1,150, or approximately $2,760. Seven years later, in its most recent sale, it sold for $11,500, which figures out at an annual appreciation rate of just under 25 percent.

As impressive as all these are, they are nonetheless eclipsed by a sales record of two copies of St. Augustine's *De Civitate Dei,* printed in Venice in 1470. At auction in 1970, a copy of this brought £900; but only four years later, in 1974, a similar copy, out of the Chatsworth Library, sold at Sotheby's for a breathtaking £22,000!

*Here, and throughout, I am not including the commission of the auction houses in the prices given. Auction house commissions are, of course, an important factor in disposal, but the fact that they vary from 12½ percent to 25 percent (the highest-priced lots being charged at the lowest commission rates) makes accurate computation of the fees impossible, since information about the sizes of lots in which individual books are sold is not available. It should be emphasized, also, that auction sales tend to represent "wholesale" prices.

Curious about the durability of rising incunabula prices, I decided to check slightly older records, bridging a longer interval. Not many dealer and auction catalogues proved helpful, for the obvious reason that with incunabula, as with most of the great rarities, sales of identical or similar copies are not repeated very often. The first I came upon was the record of two sales, exactly ten years apart, (1961–1971) of the Elder Pliny's *Historia Naturalis.* This edition is valuable not only because of its age and content, but because it was printed in Venice, in 1472, by the great Nicholas Jenson. In 1961, a copy sold for £500; ten years later, a similar copy went for £2,400—showing an annual appreciation rate of slightly under 20 percent.

While it is true that due to small printings and the gluttony of the years, relatively few copies of any single title and edition remain, there are nevertheless enough incunabula available that the individual collector need not feel deprived, either if he wants a single incunable for his collection, or he wants to specialize in them. They can still be bought for very little money if one is willing to look hard enough and be patient. Some of these copies will no doubt be defective—incomplete, damaged, or sophisticated. But shortcomings that would prove disastrous in later, more common books, are often winked at in the realm of the earliest. Most—even among the higher-priced books—will have later bindings, for as an art, binding lagged behind papermaking and typography; thus, while much fifteenth- and sixteenth-century paper has survived the centuries with laudable fortitude, the bindings have often come apart, so that the texts have been reclothed in bindings representing the taste of a later time.

Sometimes the low cost of what should in theory be superb rarities is as breathtaking as the astronomical rise in cost of less impressive books. Petrarch, for example, had an enormous influence upon the culture of his time, and through that time, of subsequent ages, for not only did he invent the "Petrarchan sonnet," and inspire generations of poets (as well as help mold several romantic conventions that are still with us), but he single-handedly did much to preserve classical learning; and it is possible that if he had not lived, some of Cicero's and Livy's works would have been lost to the modern world. It is said that his graceful handwriting served as the inspiration for Aldus Manutius's invention of italic type. Petrarch was a passionate man, a humanist, a scholar, and a book collector of majestic attainment. Therefore, it is hard to believe that any of his books printed in the incunabular period would not always command the most exalted prices. But the fact is, they have not. In 1973, a copy of his *De Remediis Utriusque Fortunae,* printed at Cremona in 1492, brought only £262, or $628. That is surprising enough, perhaps; but it is nothing compared to a 1963 sale of his *Canzionere, Sonetto, E Trionfi,* printed in Venice, in 1481. Petrarch's reputation rests upon his *Canzionere,* and it is in this work that the image of his beloved Laura—inspiration of poets for centuries—was born. The sale price in 1963? Only £18, or $43. I have stared at this information with utter dismay, but it will not go away. Apparently, that is actually what a copy of this edition of his *Canzionere* sold for back then.

These brief samplings are not large enough to invite people to cash in all their liquid assets today and invest in incunabula tomorrow. And yet, the facts are there: and they show a very real investment opportunity for people who know something about books and the money market both, and like the idea of an option that is interestingly offbeat—one that provides a kind of risk and stability that are both a little different from standard investments and can therefore be considered a good hedge.

"Yes," the familiar cautionary voice says again, "but you have to know what you're doing." Well, of course you do. Insofar as the collector-investor *is* an investor, he faces the fact that he is engaged in buying low and selling high, which means he is pitting his own experience and insights against those of others who are engaged in similar enterprise, and anyone who buys his books paying attention to price fluctuations is engaged in the market, whether he admits it or not.

In spite of the fact that several years ago, Marshall McLuhan advertised typography as history's first mass-production process, there was, by modern standards, very little that was massive about those first printings. Probably the average "first edition" of an incunable was somewhere around three hundred copies. Konrad Haebler* reckoned that all impressions ranged between 100 and 1,000. Given such age, and such small printings, there is little wonder that incunabula are scarce. Some titles have completely evaporated, of course; and the chief factor of salvation seems to be simply the fact that a great number of individual titles were printed.

Small printings have been the rule until the growth of a mass reading

*In his *Study of Incunabula,* translated by Lucy Eugenia Osborne, New York, Grolier Club, 1933.

public in the nineteenth century, when the potential fertility of the printing process seemed to be fulfilled. Thus it is that not only incunabula, with their glamorous appeal to the collector, but sixteenth-, seventeenth-, and increasingly even eighteenth-century books are becoming more and more scarce with the turning of each year.

Most of the obviously collectable books dating before 1800 are "high spots," whose investment value is probably as secure as anything in this world can be. These titles belong to those genuine rarities that seem never to falter in their appreciation, while the fads of the moment take turns in going up like the proverbial rocket, only to fall like a stick.

As in operating successfully in any kind of market, the shrewd buyer will be wise to observe the principle of relativity constantly at work in the buying and selling of books. One is always of a specific time and place, and they, as well as he, are constantly changing. Where are they headed? What are the trends? How can we use trends and even fads, instead of being used by them?

Related to the fad mentality is the cult of popularity; it is a general rule that popularity is more interesting from without than from within; that is, one can take pleasure in the foolishness of galloping relevance if he is not in its midst, in danger of being trampled to death. A vantage point from outside, whether in space or time, can enable one to see a fashion framed, as it were, by extraneous events and forces that deprive it of its tyranny.

Translated, this means that a collector-investor is always wise to reconsider the long-discarded fashions of the past, as they were manifest in particular kinds of books, and give thought to their possible interest and collectability. It's no secret that fashion and attitudes tend to move in historical cycles; therefore, yesterday's despised books can be tomorrow's fashion, which means today's bargain. This is simply one more application of the principle expressed by the distinguished British bibliophile and scholar Michael Sadleir that in book collecting it isn't simply a matter of the early bird catching the worm, but a matter of "knowing a worm when you see one."

A book need not have been printed before 1500 to be considered old; and obviously most antiquarian books are of a later date. The number and variety of these nonincunabular rarities are staggering, and they comprise most of what most people think of when they think of rare books. Some are especially desirable, beyond the simple fact of age: books featuring early maps of almost any area of the world; old books containing historical information—particularly information that is not well known, or perhaps not known at all; early volumes of poems, plays, essays, memoirs, biographies, letters—all will find their places at goodly cost in rare book collections. Age alone can, beyond a certain date, render a book valuable, especially if it can claim to be the "first" of anything—the first book published on the subject of lenses, the first book printed in Connecticut, or the first containing steel engravings, or bound in linen, and so on.

Among very old books, the first edition is not always required; and occasionally not even necessarily desirable. It is Locke's second edition of the *Essay on Human Understanding* that is the masterpiece we remember; the first, 1690, edition did not bear Locke's name, nor did it include a number of emendations that finished the work as Locke wanted it. This bibliographical feature is evidence of the great philosopher's scrupulous care, still more impressively evident in the fact that even the first edition had to wait some nineteen years before Locke would allow it to be published. (The manuscript, in Locke's handwriting, was preserved, bearing the date 1671.)

Normally, a posthumous book is worth considerably less than one published during the author's lifetime. However, here, too, there are concessions in view of a book's importance and scarcity. One of the great documents of western civilization is Copernicus's *De Revolutionibus Orbium,* first published in 1543. There is a story that this classic just missed being posthumous—that Copernicus was near death when he received the first copy on May 24 and had just enough strength to touch the book with his hand, after which he died.

A copy of a later edition of *De Revolutionibus Orbium* published in "Basle," in 1566, was offered in a dealer's catalogue in 1963 for £325. On June 11, 1974, at the Horblit sale at Sotheby's, in London, a copy of this same edition sold for £7,000, representing a rate of appreciation that is enough to make sober folks pause and take deliberate thought.

Scientific works have been enormously appreciative on the rare-book market. Vesalius's classic *De Humani Corporis Fabrica, Libri Septem* went for $2,250 at auction in 1967; only seven years later, its price had soared to $11,500. William Harvey's *The Anatomical Exercitations,* the first edition in English, printed in London in 1653, brought £240 in 1968; in 1974, it sold for over three times that amount, £900. Sir Isaac Newton's *The Method of Fluxions and Infinite Series* (London, 1736), went at only £45 in 1969; five years later its auction price was £220. Joseph

Jakob Plenck's eight-volume folio edition of Linnaeus's *Icones Planetarum Medicinalium* has brought £16,000 at auction. These were published in Vienna, from 1788 to 1812—late in the time span of antiquarian books; but Linnaeus's groundwork for the classification of plants is so important a scientific milestone that such a price is not really surprising.

Most older books have little to do with science as we know it, of course; and while most of these other kinds of books do not evoke such wild appreciation as those just cited, it is nevertheless true that any which have gained the reputation of being classics, or have some as-yet-undiscovered claim to being so regarded (there is always room for close and scholarly research to uncover such as these) will still show the power to attract strong profits. In 1963, Dawsons of Pall Mall issued a catalogue, in which a copy of the first edition of *The Twoo Bookes of Francis Bacon* (London, 1605) was offered for £110, or $308. Another copy turned up at the auction of the Stockhausen Collection, on November 19 and 20, 1974. This copy sold for $1,700.

Bacon's *Essayes or Counsels, Civill and Morall* (first edition, London, 1625) was listed in John Howell's 1963 catalogue for $150. Eleven years later, at the Stockhausen sale, another copy of the same book brought $1,600, which should make the owner of a similar copy feel good, anywhere and just about anytime.

For years, the bane of the collector of old books has been the subject of theology. Even to the religious, our ancestors's deadly obsession with godly living is too much. How could so many people have been so trapped, so morbid, so *sick?* But there are, after all, religious books (e.g., *Christianity for the Business Man*) and there are *religious* books (e.g., *Religio Medici* and Foxe's *Book of Martyrs*). The distinction is pretty much, although not always, one of age. Generally, the farther one goes back in history, the more interesting theological works are. There are two reasons for this, basically: one, the farther you go back in any subject, the more likely things can be thought of as quaint, colorful, and wonderful evidence concerning the variety and even kookiness of mankind; second, in spite of that whole fog of what most of us now choose to call superstition, theology was often the intellectual battleground of past ages, and in the seventeenth century, for example, pretty much where the brains were.

I have Edward Stillingfleet's *Origines Sacrae,* dated 1662. It is a rebound and trimmed copy; and yet, because of its age alone, I think it is worth keeping. But surely there is more than this to recommend it: Stillingfleet was a bishop and the learned antagonist of no less a man than John Locke. If it is at all true that a man may be measured by the stature of his enemies, then Stillingfleet might well prove to be someone worth reading. Furthermore, each age has its own signature and voice; and those of the seventeenth century are memorable. Their love of argumentation, close reasoning, and the convolutions of an intricate and precise syntax, conjoined with a genius for exploiting the counterpoise of dialectic in their utterances, expressed in words of sharp sense and commodious application . . . well, they thought interesting thoughts, and they wrote well. Most of them, anyway. Perhaps Stillingfleet was one of these. Let us open his book at random, and sample his style:

> Men might still have bewildred themselvs in following the *ignes fatui* of their own imaginations, and hunting up and down the world for a path which leads to heaven, but could have found none, unless God himself taking pity of the wandrings of men had been pleased to hang out a light from heaven to direct them in their way thither, and by this Pharos of Divine Revelation to direct them so to stear their course, as to escape the splitting themselves on the rocks of open impieties, or being swallowed up in the quicksands of terrene delights.

"The quicksands of terrene delights!" Indeed. One might be as bigoted as he likes in scorning the old bishop's theology as a curious bump in the road of progress, but the premises of that superannuated theology evaporate in the fire of his passion, and whoever creates such shining prose might be a backcountry Methodist or a Tlingit shaman for all the reader cares.

As recently as ten years ago, one could find eighteenth-century books of one sort or another on the miscellaneous shelves of many antiquarian bookstores. Today, eighteenth-century books have been put aside, with the price marked up. The age on the title page is sufficient in itself to label an eighteenth-century book as being a notch above the motley of other old volumes. If the book is interesting for other reasons—if it is a first or significant edition of an otherwise important book, or if it contains interesting information, or is a work of literary excellence—so much the better; but now any physically presentable book bearing a date earlier than 1800 has some value simply for that fact alone.

The past is moving up quickly; and there is no doubt that if one has sufficient storage space, he would be wise not only to collect any books printed before 1800, but to begin to accumulate pre-Civil War items, as well. The Civil War was a great division in our national sensibility, and any antebellum volume must be recognized as a document from another world, bearing unmistakable evidence of being so. Consider any kind of book from before that date: a medical text on skin diseases, Fowler's *Phrenology*, Stone's *The Life and Times of Red Jacket*, or *The Lives of Remarkable and Eccentric Characters of All Ages and Countries* (to choose titles in view at this moment as I write). All are interesting for various reasons, plus the single one of documenting some aspects of the human condition in the first half of the nineteenth century.

Age is relative, of course, depending upon the printing histories of various regions. Newly settled regions produce few books, thus assuring a scarcity of titles from their early days. An American book published in 1749 is significantly older in important ways than an English book published in 1633; and a book published in Cincinnati in 1830 is older (and as such, probably rarer) than a book published in Boston thirty years earlier. These observations are no doubt obvious; but their point in the present context is that an alert collector should be sensitive to the scale of rarity, as determined by geography, as well as to the increasing rarity of books resulting simply from the progression of the years, along with the ever-increasing interest in book collecting.

Today, an eighteenth-century book printed in America has acquired a more certain antiquarian status than any European book of that date, and thereby, in the context of age alone, can be considered more valuable. And since the edge of "antiquity" is moving forward relentlessly, actually gaining on the years as more and more people are learning to understand its fascination, the time is upon us when we should start thinking of any American book printed before 1860 as rare, and therefore valuable, simply because of the date and place of its printing.

VI.

AMERICANA

I cannot free my mind," A. Edward Newton wrote, in *This Book-Collecting Game,* * "from the belief that if I had my life to live over again I should take on 'Americana.' There is no element of 'fad' about it, as there may be about Conrad or Stevenson, for instance."

"To take on Americana" would seem to be an effortless undertaking for most people, since as a general subject it is the most widely collected of any kind of book in this country. It is natural that this should be the case, since "Americana" refers to the sum total of factual information in print, relating to the history of the United States, specifically, and the American continents, generally; and nothing is more likely than that we should be interested in our own past—the Who and What we have come from. Because of this, a great deal of Americana is regional Americana; for every collector who collects according to a theme (e.g., transcontinental journeys in the nineteenth century or political biographies) or builds a collection around a man or woman famous in our history, there are probably five who collect regional Americana. Dealers, even some of the most cosmopolitan, will reflect this fact, so that while the Current Company, for example, may deal very actively in general early Americana, and specialize in naval Americana, they will also,

*Boston: Little, Brown, 1928, p. 34.

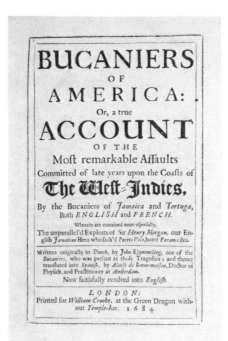

BUCANIERS
OF
AMERICA:
Or, a true
ACCOUNT
OF THE
Moſt remarkable Aſſaults
Committed of late years upon the Coaſts of
The Weſt-Indies,
By the Bucaniers of *Jamaica* and *Tortuga*,
Both *ENGLISH* and *FRENCH.*

Wherein are contained more eſpecially,
The unparallel'd Exploits of Sir *Henry Morgan*, our Engliſh *Jamaican* Hero, who ſack'd *Puerto Velo*, burnt *Panama*, &c.

Written originally in *Dutch*, by *John Eſquemeling*, one of the
Bucaniers, who was preſent at thoſe Tragedies; and thence
tranſlated into *Spaniſh*, by *Alonſo de Bonne-maiſon*, Doctor of
Phyſick, and Practitioner at *Amſterdam.*
Now faithfully rendred into *Engliſh.*

LONDON:
Printed for *William Crooke*, at the Green Dragon without *Temple-bar.* 1 6 8 4.

*Courtesy of Sotheby Parke
Bernet, Inc., New York*

practically as a matter of geographical fact, find a particular interest in books, pamphlets, prints, and letters relating to the history of Rhode Island.

Americana is a collecting area of such prodigious variety, depth, and expanse, that in the contemplation of all this forest of print, one can only conclude that we are the gabbiest race on earth. Truly, there is something for every collector in Americana. If his primary interest is regional, he will likely find himself living in that very place where the titles he seeks are most numerous, and the demand for them most pronounced. If he is smart, he will buy actively from local dealers, but also keep alert for regional titles that appear in the catalogues of dealers from distant places, for they will often be listed at bargain prices, since their clientele will not normally be interested in them.

While some of the most valuable and interesting Americana collections are regional, many are thematic, biographical, or chronological. Anyone who undertakes to build a collection on the subject of Great Lakes shipping, the early fur trade, or slavery is launching forth upon a journey that has neither end nor limit to the variety and fascination of the scenery along the way. Biographical collections tend too much toward the obvious figures—the famous statesmen, generals, and outlaws of our past: how many collectors of Lincolniana are there, today, or how many collectors of Jesse James material?

If someone is interested in Lincoln, but finds the pathways too trampled down (and the books too expensive), he would be prudent to isolate some lesser-known aspect of Lincoln's career, some of the men he associated with, or fought against: Stephen A. Douglas, for example, or Herndon, his old law partner; or even Edwin Stanton, whose innocence or complicity in Lincoln's death is still not firmly established, or John Wilkes Booth? All of these figures, and dozens of others, are relatively untapped resources for the enterprising and imaginative collector. Books about them, along with their own publications—and sometimes even their personal papers, memorabilia, letters, and so on, can still be gotten cheaply; but these—like rare-book prices generally—are rising, or are certainly about to rise, at a fast rate, and the collectors who buy in early will have an enormous advantage over all latecomers.

For the impecunious or simply adventurous collector who is interested in Lincoln there are many options other than focusing upon books by and/or about a historical character associated with Lincoln. One could very well focus upon twentieth-century books about the Great Emancipator; or collect fictional books with references to Lincoln; or stage plays about Lincoln; or film scripts; or references to Lincoln in the periodicals of his day; or books about the circumstances of his assassination; or books that have references to Lincoln's Indian policies (Harriet McConkey, in her *Dakota War Whoop,* speaks contemptuously of him as a bleeding heart, because his presidential edict allowed so many Sioux to escape the retribution of the Mankato hangings), or any of a score of fascinating subjects that relate to the man who—next to Jesus and Napoleon—probably has been the subject of more books than any other historical figure.

While there are many period collectors of Americana, as there are period collectors in literature and foreign histories, I have never known of a collector to fasten upon a specific decade and call it his own. No doubt the subject seems far too vast for anyone even to contemplate; and yet, what authority such a collection would have, no matter how incomplete!

Thomas Beer's *The Mauve Decade* is a vivid and informative book— the kind that might well invite someone to undertake collecting books from the 1890s; and yet, the supply of books still remaining from such a recent era is overwhelming. But why not a combination of principles—Chicago or Denver imprints from the 1890s, or books from the Scandinavian communities in Minnesota and the Dakotas from the 1890s, or books from those ten years dealing with social work? Of course, if one were to select an earlier decade—say 1810–1820—he might not have to compromise quite so much, although anything like the comprehensiveness available to a one-author collector is obviously beyond all hope of achievement.

The principle that obtains here, with regard to Americana collections, is a valid one, generally: a planned, unified collection is likely to possess a value above and beyond that of any mere accumulation of books. John H. Jenkins, the Texas dealer, writes:

> The key principle is seldom mentioned, but it is paramount: work towards building a collection which is more valuable than the sum of its parts. A thousand thirty dollar books on the Mexican War or South Carolina are worth more than thirty thousand dollars. Also essential is that the collection be useful. A gob of press books or poetry books or general Americana aren't, when assembled together, particularly useful as a unit. They may be worth more than what was paid for them, but they will bring these prices individually, whereas a useful collection will bring a much greater unit price. Also, I object to collecting at all if it is only for profit—building a unified, useful collection is its own reward. A good rule of thumb is, would an important institutional library like to own my collection if I spend twenty years building it?

Memoirs, diaries, and autobiographies of early preachers are among the richest and most fascinating Americana, and the beauty is that they remain a relatively untapped source. Such books need not be terribly old; after all, men who sit down to indite their memoirs are usually somewhat advanced in age, and many of those who participated in the settling of the far West did not write and publish their accounts until after World War I. (It is a little incongruous to think of Wyatt Earp being still alive when *The Great Gatsby* and *The Sun Also Rises* were published.)

In olden times, preachers were better educated than other folks, especially on the frontier; and their testimony is usually articulate, valuable, and often colorful. One such book is Bishop Talbot's *My People of the Plains,* published by Harper's in 1906. This is a common book, but it is delightful. Bishop Talbot (his first name was Ethelbert) was a missionary in Wyoming in the late nineteenth century, where he knew the great Shoshone chief, Washakie. Washakie, Talbot says, "was as autocratic as any Russian czar." He was also possessed of a tyrannical temper, and one day, in a fit of rage, slew his interfering mother-in-law—the dream of many a red-blooded white eyes, as well.

Rich in anecdotes, insights, and "social history," Talbot's book is only one of hundreds and hundreds published in this century, having to do with the settling of the old West, and containing priceless and entertaining material. Most of these books are still very low priced; but they are bound to shoot up before long, for there is no abatement in America's fascination with that great myth of Winning the West, nor with the darker side of that dialectic—the Indians, shadows that have inhabited the white man's dreams now for over four hundred years.

The earlier one goes back in American history, the more important and more interesting the preachers become. The roll call is impressive: Lorenzo Dow, Peter Cartwright, Jesse Lee, John Churchman, David Brainerd, Joshua Evans, John Wesley, George Whitefield, Ishbel Green, John Woolman, and on and on. Most of these were Quakers and Methodists; some were circuit riders—a tough and interesting breed, often ill-educated but powerful of spirit; many went forth to live among the Indians, and they brought back information about their languages and culture; all those listed above flourished in the eighteenth or early nineteenth century, and therefore recorded messages from a strange and distant world—that of ourselves two centuries ago.

Some of these accounts deserve to be called literature by any standard. In 1756, John Churchman was in Philadelphia, and witnessed the following events, not one word of which should be translated from his own speech:

> The Indians having burnt several houses on the frontiers of this Province, also at Gnadenhutten in Northampton County, and murdered and scalped some of the inhabitants; at the time of this meeting two or three of the dead bodies were brought to Philadelphia in a waggon, with an intent as was supposed to animate the people to unite in preparations of war to take vengeance on the Indians, and destroy them: They were carried

along several of the streets, many people following cursing the Indians, also the Quakers because they would not join in war for destruction of the Indians. The sight of the dead bodies and the outcry of the people, were very afflicting and shocking to me: Standing at the door of a friend's house as they passed alone, my mind was humbled and turned much inward when I was made secretly to cry: *What will become of Pennsylvania?* for it felt to me that many did not consider, that the sins of the inhabitants, pride, profane swearing, drunkenness with other wickedness were the cause, that the Lord had suffered this calamity and scourge to come upon them; the weight of my exercise increasing as I walked along the street; at length it was said in my soul, *This Land is polluted with blood, and in the day of inquisition for blood, it will not only be required at the frontiers and borders, but even in this place where bodies are now seen.*

Three years ago I came upon a copy of the first edition (Philadelphia, 1779) of this book in an antique shop and paid twenty dollars for it. I consider it priceless. While it is not listed in Wright Howes's indispensable second edition of *U.S.-iana,* I have seen modest auction records of £5 and £5½ for a later (1780) London edition. Churchman is an obscure figure in our literature. The title page of the above book reads, *An Account of the Gospel Labours and Christian Experiences of a Faithful Minister of Christ, John Churchman.* Which all sounds very dull and pietistic (and God knows that those early Quakers knew how to be dull when they put their minds to it). I wonder how many people have passed over this neglected masterpiece simply because of the title page and what it suggests.

Not all early American preachers have been neglected. John Woolman (a friend of Churchman) was also a scribbling Quaker, but his *Journal,* published in 1774, is something of a classic. Woolman (as if responding to some deep chord in his name) gave up wearing colored clothing when he learned that the dyes used were harmful to the workers who made the cloth; and he gave up sugar in silent, private protest against the slave labour required to harvest the cane. The writing in his *Journal* is celebrated for its clarity and simplicity; and this work has been praised by Whittier, Channing, and Lamb. Howes refers to it as "an autobiographical masterpiece, rivalled in 18th-century America only by that of Franklin." Reprinted often, Woolman's book is widely available, relatively speaking, and obviously collectable in just about any early edition. A good copy of the first edition, graded "aa" by Howes (i.e., from $25 to $100) might well bring close to $200 today. Possibly more, for who can tell with such rarities?

If one is severely limited in funds, there could be no better advice for collecting-investing than to "buy the preachers," at least those you can find at two, three, and four dollars each, and let them accumulate (as you read them, of course) while their values rise. You may be sure that their plentiful supply today is only temporary; and when the time comes that the last two-dollar copy is sold, and the next collector in line has heard about that particular book and wants a copy, then its economic fate has instantly changed: it has become a rare book.

By the mid 1800s there were many laymen who were sufficiently educated to keep diaries and write about their experiences, so in collecting western Americana one is not forced, even subtly, to buy the preachers, especially if he has a little more money to invest. There are thousands of books by soldiers, drummers, scouts, cowboys, schoolteachers, surveyors, buffalo hunters, railroad builders, trappers—just about any-

THE

CALIFORNIA AND OREGON

T R A I L :

BEING

SKETCHES OF PRAIRIE AND ROCKY MOUNTAIN
LIFE.

" Let him who crawls enamor'd of decay,
Cling to his couch, and sicken years away ;
Heave his thick breath, and shake his palsied head ;
Ours—the fresh turf, and not the feverish bed."
BYRON.

BY FRANCIS PARKMAN, JR.

NEW-YORK:
GEORGE P. PUTNAM, 155 BROADWAY.
LONDON : PUTNAM'S AMERICAN AGENCY,
Removed from Paternoster Row to
J. CHAPMAN, 142 STRAND.
1849.

body who had the fire and opportunity to venture beyond the wide Missouri, and who had learned his ABC's, was a likely author. And if he had experiences that were interesting (a prodigious likelihood), the book might be worth reading whether he was "any good at writing" or not.

It is no wonder that the prices of the best and earliest western Americana rise so swiftly and steadily, for they not only breathe forth the spirit of open-air adventure, but exude a joyous expansiveness that is unique to that time and place, and can be seen as both occasion and metaphor for some of the happiest and bravest, as well as some of the grubbiest, human qualities. Their appeal is everywhere manifest in dealers' catalogues and at auction.

The flux and variety of the western Americana market are an index to its general vitality. Purchases made from fairly recent catalogues have proved to be stunning bargains within a few years. In December 1971, Robert Hayman published his Catalogue Number 46, listing Charles D. Ferguson's *The Experiences of a Forty-Niner During Thirty-Four Years' Residence in California and Australia* (Cleveland, 1888), for only $22.50. On the previous page, there is a title by William Ellis (not what we usually think of as *western* Americana, to be sure), whose full listing is *An Authentic Narrative of a Voyage Performed by Captain Cook and Captain Clerke, in His Majesty's Ships Resolution and Discovery, During the Years 1776, 1777, 1779 and 1780; in Search of a North-East Passage Between the Continent of Asia and America.* Third Edition, 2 vols. in one, as issued. London, 1784. Hayman notes: "Two of the plates called for in the list of illustrations are not present in this copy, although there is no indication that they were ever bound in." The price for this early rarity? $15.

Today, these titles would sell at anywhere from three to five times Hayman's 1971 prices. As would another book about pioneer days in California: Hinton R. Helper's *The Land of Gold* (Baltimore, 1855) which Hayman offered for $27.50 in his next catalogue, that came out in the winter of 1972. In the Second Edition of Van Allen Bradley's *Handbook of Values,* the value of this book is listed at $125—probably a conservative figure for a copy in excellent condition.

While there is a robust glamour to western Americana that distinguishes it from every other kind of bibliophilic specialty, the mind-boggling prices are still pretty much monopolized by the very earliest Americana—much of it, of historical necessity, written in Spanish,

French, German, or even Latin. There are dramatic exceptions, of course: Josiah Gregg's *Commerce of the Prairies* (New York, 1844) sells for several hundred dollars in the first edition in good shape; the next first edition of Parkman's *The California and Oregon Trail* (New York, 1849), in the two-volume printed wrappers, may bring up to $2,000 when it appears at auction; and Zenas Leonard's fabulously rare *Narrative,* having brought $6,250 at auction in 1968, may come close to tripling that price whenever the next copy comes up for sale.

But most of the superlatively rare Americana were printed a century or more earlier, like John Ogilby's and Arnoldus Montanus' *America,* printed in London in 1671, which Dawson's offered at £2,850 ($6,840) in 1970. A first edition of John Smith's beautifully titled *The Generall Historie of Virginia, New England, and the Summer Isles* (1627) sold for £4,850 ($11,640) out of the same catalogue. Today, a good copy will bring twice that amount. Still another splendid rarity is the first edition of *A Journal of the Late Actions of the French at Canada,* by Nicholas Bayard (also spelled "Beyard" and even "Reyard") and Charles Lodowick. Printed in London in 1693, this gives an account of a French expedi-

V O Y A G E S

FROM

M O N T R E A L,

ON THE RIVER ST. LAURENCE,

THROUGH THE

CONTINENT OF NORTH AMERICA,

TO THE

FROZEN AND PACIFIC OCEANS:

In the Years 1789 *and* 1793.

WITH A PRELIMINARY ACCOUNT

OF THE RISE, PROGRESS, AND PRESENT STATE OF

THE FUR TRADE

OF THAT COUNTRY.

ILLUSTRATED WITH MAPS.

BY ALEXANDER MACKENZIE, ESQ.

LONDON:

PRINTED FOR T CADELL, JUN. AND W. DAVIES, STRAND; COBBETT AND MORGAN. PALL-MALL; AND W. CREECH, AT EDINBURGH.
BY R. NOBLE, OLD-BAILEY.

M.DCCC.L.

tion against the Mohawks—one of those chronic border actions that eventually erupted in the French and Indian War three quarters of a century later. Only three copies of this rarity have appeared at auction in the last fifty-seven years; the third and last brought $17,000, which even at that price was considered something of a bargain.

Not all of the earliest Americana is that expensive, of course. A first edition of Jonathan Carver's *Travels Through the Interior Parts of North America in the Years 1766, 1767 and 1768* (London, 1778) was offered by the Canadian firm of Laurie Hill for only $95 in their catalogue Number 34, in 1965. That had to be a bargain, as was the purchase at auction two years previous of a similar copy for $110. In 1974, a copy of the *second* edition sold at auction for $320. Whenever the next copy of the first edition is offered, its price will represent a most handsome appreciation over those mid-1960s prices. The same 1965 Laurie Hill catalogue also offered the third edition of Henry B. Fearon's *Sketches of America* (London, 1819) for $20. I only wish I had seen it then, for the price nearly tripled within eight years, when a copy brought £24 ($58) at auction.

A greater rarity is *A Voyage of Discovery to the North Pacific Ocean and Round the World,* a book in three volumes, with folio atlas, by George Vancouver, eponym of both city and island. In 1963, a copy was offered by Dawson's of Pall Mall for the bargain price of £ 60, or $168. Some eleven years later, a similar copy sold at auction for $1,150.

In his explorations, Vancouver was assisted by two Spanish ships, one of which was commanded by Dionisio Alcala Galiano, who probably (according to Wright Howes' *U.S.-iana,*) wrote his own account of these early west-coast explorations, sonorously titled *Relacion del Viage Hecho por las Goletas Sutil y Mexicana en el Ano de 1792 para Reconocer el Estrecho de Fuca* (Madrid, 1802). This title is rated "dd" by the scholarly and conservative Howes, which in 1962 signified his estimated value of "$1,000 and upwards"; given the natural appreciation of Americana since that date—particularly the crème de la crème—along with Howes' understandable vagueness concerning what such seldom-encountered books might bring upon their next availability, it is probable that a first edition of Galiano's "Relation" will bring something like the price of a new Lincoln Continental, with all the extras, when it next comes up for sale.

But as I said, not all of the real early Americana is that expensive; a lot of it is within the reach of many collectors' purses, if they want a particular title badly enough. And some of these books are genuine classics, hence genuine bargains at the going prices. If you had attended Parke-Bernet's 1963 auction of the library of Robert P. Esty, you would have seen a copy of the first edition of Crèvecoeur's famous *Letters from an American Farmer* (London, 1782) sell for only $80. At Sotheby's July 29, 1975, sale, however, the same title went for £260, or $624. This is a lot of money, no doubt; but $80 spent for such a book twelve years before would have proved a marvelous investment financially, as well as the satisfaction of years of possessing these delightful and perceptive "letters" of a man of sensibility, who claimed, among other honors, those of having introduced alfalfa, sainfoin, and vetches to American soil.

The absorption of the present into the past is perpetually adding to the store of collectable Americana, as well as to other books; but there is another kind of increment. New things are constantly being discovered about the past: facts, insights, connections, errors in older reports, lacunae, inconsistencies, problems, and so on. The past is never completed; it is always (like certain gaudy, promissory real estate projects) under development, being created anew, thereby always approaching its fulfillment, without ever quite reaching it.

From the sowing of new scholarship comes a harvest of new books, always. Some of these are already collectable, even though they were published long after the closing of the old West, by people whose connections with their epic material are indirect, even remote; but with scholarly zeal they have brought it to life again.

A few of these books are not only collectable, but acknowledged classics of their kind: Bernard DeVoto's *Across the Wide Missouri* (Boston, 1947); Walter Prescott Webb's *The Texas Rangers* (Boston, 1935); Mari Sandoz's *Crazy Horse* (New York, 1942); and J. Frank Dobie's *Apache Gold and Yaqui Silver* (Boston, 1939) are a few of these. The books listed above, in good condition and with the dust jacket intact, will sell from $25 to, well, some of them perhaps as high as $100—if not today, then you may be sure, tomorrow. And these authors have written several score other highly collectable books, as well; which are of course becoming more scarce with each revolution of the seasons.

There are still hundreds of books by other twentieth-century writers that move very much in the mainstream of Americana. They are for the most part handsomely done books, valuable in content, and most readable; in short, they belong on the shelves of those collections whose scope at one time might have been austerely limited to first editions of works within a precisely circumscribed area. This means that a collector of early books about cattle drives, who might have been content twenty years ago to specialize in titles appearing before 1900, will today have to buy a number of commercial and university press publications that contain not only facsimile editions of titles virtually unobtainable in their original editions, but recently published books containing new information, new ideas, recent discoveries, and other valuable contributions from the harvest of continued research—and not just buy them, but keep on buying them to build and maintain his collection. Their general historical importance, not to mention their indispensability for some collections, is enough to ensure a vigorous increase in both scholarly and monetary value in many of these books.

The fact that the supply of rarities is being augmented constantly by both the expansion of the market and duplication of titles is of great comfort and profit to book people. But reliance upon the growing market is not in any way an admission that the old, classic Americana rarities are no longer available. Now and then one will hear some dealer or collector say that good books simply are not available any longer. It is a familiar lament, in fact, but it simply is not true. There is too much public ignorance and neglect for rare books to hide in—they will never all be flushed out.

Within one recent week, I encountered two early Americana treasures offered for sale—one in a likely, the other in an unlikely, place. Both are rated "b" by Howes ($300 to $600). The unlikely place was a country auction nearby, where a copy of the first edition of Patrick Gass' *Journal* (Pittsburgh, 1807) had been put aside for special bidding. This book contains the first account of the Lewis and Clark expedition. Van Allen Bradley lists its value as $300 to $400, which seems to me lower than Howes' judgment of its worth, when you consider the general appreciation of books since 1962. Nevertheless, a copy sold at auction for $250 in 1972; and another (with the spine repaired) brought $300 in 1975, so it appears that Bradley's evaluation is realistic. For some reason, however, I have always considered this an underpriced book—which fact makes me all the happier in having been the successful bidder for that copy at $130.

The other Americana rarity I came upon was a copy of William Bartram's *Travels*, which Frank Klein (proprietor of The Bookseller in Akron) had just gotten when I walked into his shop the other day. This copy is the first edition (Philadelphia, 1791), in very good shape, of a book that is in Howes' judgment, "A work of high character well meriting its wide esteem." A naturalist, Bartram lived among the Creek, Cherokee, and Choctaw Indians in the late eighteenth century, and his first-hand accounts of that vanished world make wonderful reading. Klein has priced this gem at $800, which—in view of the fact that copies have already sold for over $1,000—will prove a solid purchase for some collector.

Americana prices have remained high since Americana emerged as a popularly collectable specialty at the turn of the century. Its appeal should be obvious for all Americans, for this is the stuff upon which our past is imprinted; these are our traces, and they show us what we were about and what we have been, and—by implication—something of what we are, and might be. As Robert G. Hayman, a dealer whose catalogues are informative, insightful, and often witty, says: "I specialize in historical Americana with special emphasis upon midwestern Americana. Probably the subject matter of the books is the primary appeal. It is a very broad field and filled with many fascinating topics—who can fail to be excited by the thought of wild Indians, outlaws, gunmen of the old west, cowboys and cattle drives, fur trappers and mountain men?"

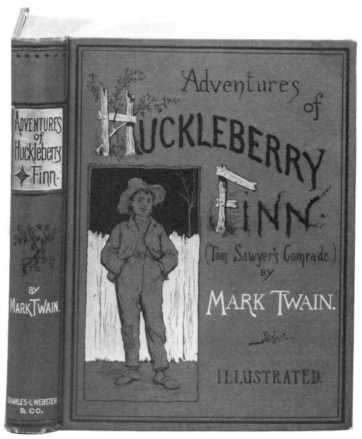

Courtesy of Sotheby Parke Bernet, Inc., New York

VII.

MODERN FIRST EDITIONS

ike the historian, the bibliophile learns to think as conveniently in terms of period and centuries as in years; therefore it is not surprising that the works of Mark Twain and Henry James, for example, should be included in the category of "modern first editions." The era of modern firsts in America begins conveniently with the end of the Civil War, and the fact that Twain and James first published books in the late 1860s is an auspicious start for just about any conceivable era.

There are always those who try to divide mankind into cat lovers and dog lovers, or into those who like Tolstoi or Dostoevski; but it is a shame that people have to crave such tidy divisions. Still there is something both strange and marvelous in the fact that Henry James and Mark Twain were contemporary Americans. (It's true that James was an exile; Twain spent a good deal of time abroad, too, and was not as uncouth as his lecture-circuit facade pretends), and yet the two men seemed barely to know of one another's existence. Maybe there is no such thing as a kind of person who *must* choose one author against the incompatible other, but certainly there is an isolatable sensibility that we can identify in ourselves that will at one time, and in one way, respond to the intelligence of one, and at another time, and in another way, to that of the other.

The breadth, insight, vitality, inventiveness, subtlety, and vision represented by both Mark Twain and Henry James would seem to be enough to encompass an era, rather than simply launch it. And yet, by the 1920s, when both men were just comfortably dead and out of the way, it was evident that there was a whole lot that they—in spite of their complementary geniuses—simply had no idea of. By this time, the two traditions that James and Twain had helped inaugurate were vitally alive and inextricably merged in the fiction and poetry of more than a score of what are now conceded to be "major figures."

It is only natural, then, that collecting these later people has almost seemed to eclipse the two founding fathers of the period. This is not just a literary judgment; Twain and James are both, and for different reasons, marvelously collectable authors. But with a few exceptions (and most of these, Twain's), their first editions simply do not bring prices commensurate with their stature. After his *Innocents Abroad,* Twain was simply too popular a writer for his books to achieve a rare status; first printings of his works were so huge that scarcity was out of the question, except for *Tom Sawyer* and *Huckleberry Finn* (both thought of as "boy's books," hence generally read to death). *Pudd'nhead Wilson,* which is in some respects a better novel than either of the above, has never achieved that popularity necessary for being labeled a "classic"; therefore, its price is a relatively modest one.

In spite of the large printings, Twain's first editions are still solid purchases, for interest in his fiction has never diminished. There are signs that the run-of-the-mill titles have leveled off somewhat. One collector complains that his first edition of *Life on the Mississippi* is worth no more today than what he paid for it several decades ago. I don't know what he paid for it, nor do I know what condition it is in, or what "price range" he is referring to; but I am happy to know that this man is genial in his complaint, happy to own this classic of Americana and plain good writing.

One of Twain's scarcer titles is *The Celebrated Jumping Frog of Calaveras County,* his first book and a classic. The first edition (New York, 1867) sold for $500 and $550 at auction in 1969; next year, its price plummeted to $160. (One must constantly keep in mind, here and elsewhere, that there are many "impure" factors that help determine price—thus, the $160 copy may have been slightly damaged, or in slightly faded cloth—neither fault grave enough for mention; or, there may have been only one bidder in the audience who really *wanted* that copy.) In 1974, however, another copy of the same first issue brought a lusty $1,200.

116

Henry James was never to achieve anything like Twain's popularity as an author, and while the first printings of his books remained small, they have never inspired collectors to manic heights. James' audience has always been a rather special one. Like those classic composers who were said to be "better than they sound," James' novels, short stories, and—especially—novellas (a form he virtually made his own) are better than they read. And they really are.

This is not to say that James is not collectable; his following today is as ardent, brilliant, and bull headed as ever, so naturally all this heat will affect the prices of his first editions. Especially coveted are his letters and inscribed copies; so much of his fiction reads like a splendid talking-to-oneself that the manner naturally spilled over into those occasions when he was explicitly talking to others, as in a letter, or on the flyleaf of a book. Such inscribed copies soar into the upper hundreds of dollars. And even some of his uninscribed first editions can bring several hundred dollars: the three-volume English edition (the true first, in this instance) of his *Portrait of a Lady* (London, 1882) is worth $500 or more; *The Princess Casamassima*—also three volumes and printed in London in 1886—brings almost that much.*

Most first-edition copies of the books from James' long and prolific career, however, are still to be had, in excellent condition (and many are very handsomely designed), modestly priced in the $25 to $100 range. His mastery of the art of prose is signalized by the famous twenty-six volume New York edition, published by Scribner's (1907 to 1917) in a format that is distinguished for its simplicity and elegance. This classic of bookmaking can still be purchased for anywhere from five hundred to a thousand dollars; and it will crown any James collection.

Henry James still bears something of the stigma of being an insubstantial, fussy, and effete "novelist of manners." No doubt this is a vestige remaining from random strands of naturalistic gutsiness and the cult of conspicuous proletarian suffering that has been the source of so much pleasure in modern literature. Furthermore, his novels tend to represent acts of seeing, rather than doing ("awareness" is ever the key word), and thus his characters can be thought of as impotent, which

*One interesting and occasionally bothersome problem encountered in collecting James' first editions is that of establishing the priority of English and American first printings. "Following the flag" is of little help with this writer, who bestrode the Atlantic in a textual as well as artistic sense.

means that they and he both are vulnerable to whole invasions of Freudians.

But his "mysterious wound" notwithstanding, James is a writer of great power, as well as subtlety. He has probed the twilight regions in ways and places no one else has reached, and some of his shorter works, especially, lift the art of prose to its limits, condign with, but different from, poetry. Read such short stories as " 'Europe' " (almost inevitably indexed incorrectly, without those quotation marks which are integral to the title) or "The Jolly Corner," and you will become a Jamesian, maybe even a collector of his first editions.

I have merely touched the surface of the collecting appeal of two writers who stand at the beginning of the era of modern first editions in America. Before the end of the century there were literally hundreds of writers whose works—carefully read and honestly experienced— might inspire collectors. Stephen Crane, in spite of his great stature as a writer, can be collected at modest expense, until one is forced to spend five or six hundred dollars for a first of *The Red Badge of Courage* and five to ten times that amount for a first of *Maggie* in the famous yellow wrappers.

On the other side of the Atlantic, there is Anthony Trollope, a writer who particularly irritated James. This was partly because of his mannerism of interrupting a narrative to call attention to the fact that it was, after all, something invented, and that as a writer, he, Trollope, had a serious obligation to entertain his readers, and what ought he to do with his characters in order to . . . and so on. James felt that such playful confidences were a betrayal of the high art—and in a sense they are, but they are replaced by another high art, that of self-irony. It is in fact as an ironist that I first read Trollope, for I was introduced to his work through his *Autobiography*, which impressed me as a sustained exercise in whimsical, Socratic self-abasement. It seemed to me that a man must have a marvelously sturdy ego to play with the reader as Trollope did in this book; and it still seems so to me, long after being introduced to the delightful world of his novels.

Trollope's virtues are many, and a few are not at all obvious in their effects. It is said that British soldiers in World War I often carried a Trollope novel into the trenches with them, sometimes even at the cost of food rations or some other more exigent supply. It is not only that Trollope can tell a good and robust story (although he can do that excellently well); it is not only that he is, in his way, as perceptive regard-

118

ing human character and motivation as his disapproving competitor, Henry James (although he is); it is not only his use of a kind of humor in giving his characters grotesque names, sometimes with an epic or childish significance, sometimes merely playfully (this was also a habit he shared with his austere rival). It is all of these things, of course; but in addition, Trollope had a very strange and extremely rare gift for a novelist: he was able to create a character that was perfectly credible, immensely subtle, of strong vitality, and *morally decent.* Furthermore, such characters were, through Trollope's conception of them, interesting. Doctor Thorne, eponym of that novel, is one of the mightiest in this regard. He is a sort of Squire Allworthy, but subtler, less stereotyped, and devoid of Fielding's genial irony.

It is only fair that the decent, hard-working Trollope—who weighed 235 pounds and was built like a linebacker with muttonchop whiskers (very much as linebackers wear them today) and loved to fox hunt—should have left a heritage of novels that produce big, solid prices whenever they are offered at sales or in catalogues. Most of them are three-deckers, exemplars of the Victorian novel at its best and most popular. One of them (part of the lesser canon, indeed) is titled *Ralph the Heir,* and at auction in 1970, a first edition copy "in parts" brought $3,000! Other Trollope first editions that have sold recently at auction are *Castle Richmond* ($575), *He Knew He Was Right* ($450), *The Struggles of Brown, Jones, and Robinson* ($550—this like *The Eustace Diamonds,* was first printed in New York; therefore, the American is the true first edition); *The Three Clerks* ($800); *On English Prose Fiction as a Rational Amusement* (a marvelous title, which stands as an essay in itself—$400); and so on.

Not all of Trollope's first editions are that high, however. There are a number of variables, the most important of which (aside from condition) is whether the copy is "in parts," as those listed above, or in the first book edition, as bound by the publisher. In most contexts, periodical publications do not approach book publications of the same title in value; but the Victorian tradition of issuing a novel periodically in thin paper-wrapped pamphlets much like the modern magazine (thus, "in parts") has given rise to a terrible snobbery (i.e., I don't have any) of insisting upon owning all of the parts, as issued, with the covers intact and unsoiled—a much less likely event than the same novel's having been preserved in book form.

In publisher's book form, Trollope's first editions can sometimes be gotten at astonishingly low prices. In a 1963 catalogue, Goodspeed's of Boston offered the two-volume first edition (in book form) of *He Knew He Was Right* (London, 1869) for only $10. This had to be a steal, even then, before Trollope's first edition prices soared to their present heights. The book has since that time sold for $100 and more—still a reasonable amount to pay for a copy of the first edition of such a fine novel. By dramatic contrast, a copy of this book in wrappers sold for $450 in 1974.

It would be impossible simply to refer to all the British writers who belong in the "modern first edition" pages of catalogues. Lewis Carroll, of course; George Meredith, Thomas Hardy, Oscar Wilde, Frank Harris, George Bernard Shaw, Joseph Conrad, Rudyard Kipling, and R. L. Stevenson are just a few of the obvious. First editions of most of these tend to be quite inexpensive today; although many—in spite of some leveling off among some (e.g., Stevenson and Meredith)—are still eminently worthy of investment, providing you are patient, prudent, and sufficiently interested in their books that you really do want them for reading, and to rest on your shelves while they either appreciate or at least hold their own in value.

It is impossible to ignore the Irish for long in any discussion of modern first editions. Shaw and Wilde were Anglo-Irish (and are incidentally relatively easy to collect, with fairly low-priced first editions of many titles). Yeats is good to collect: most of his first editions are physically handsome books, and—while they are sought after to a degree consistent with his being one of the handful of major poets of this century—some were produced in liberal printings, so that the Yeats collector can reasonably expect to gather most of the first editions around him at no great expense.

Sean O'Casey, Lord Dunsany, Frank O'Connor, Lady Gregory, Brendan Behan, Mary Lavin, James Stephens, A. E., and Sean O'Faolain are a few of the twentieth-century Irish writers who have exercised a brave influence on the language; and they are all collected to some extent. But the greatest challenge to the collector of modern literature is James Joyce, who when he lived was bothered by such things as drink and the problem of getting enough money to buy a new pair of trousers; but now these many decades after he has joined the obstreperous dead he presides like a confabulating God over the disposal of his first editions at almost incredible prices.

A copy of the first edition of *Ulysses* (Paris, 1922) in the rare printed blue wrappers, and signed by Joyce, brought $8,000 at auction in 1975. This was one of a limited edition of 100 on Dutch handmade paper; another (one of 150 on Verge d'Arches paper) has sold for $1,300, but that was almost ten years ago. In 1935, the Limited Editions Club brought out an edition illustrated by Matisse, who signed it along with Joyce. A single copy of this 250-copy edition will bring a price somewhere in the neighborhood of $2,000, which most people would agree is a pretty expensive neighborhood, in the context of modern books.

Joyce suffered the fate and good fortune of being labeled collectable during his lifetime, so there are "fragments from work in progress"—which is, in singular form, the subtitle of *Haveth Childers Everywhere* (Paris, 1930)—a selection in stiff printed wrappers that in its boxed Japan vellum edition of 100, signed by Joyce, brings over $500, enough money to keep Joyce in trousers and white wine for a whole year, if he were only around to collect. A signed first edition of *Finnegans Wake* brings $1,000 or more; and firsts of his earlier *Dubliners* and *A Portrait of the Artist as a Young Man* will each bring approximately half that amount. The collector need not haveth dollars everywhere to collect Joyce's first editions, but he will have to be able and willing to write a few heavy checks to build his collection; however, if one possesses the fervor of the true Joycean, he or she will make the family car do for another year, and apply the money saved for a signed *Finnegans Wake* or a holograph letter. By almost any standard, a finne joice.

In the progress of this survey of collectable modern authors, it will no longer prove useful to observe national boundaries in discussion, although it will almost always be necessary to observe them in following the flag in pursuit of the first edition.

D. H. Lawrence is an excellent author to collect, because of his literary importance, the notoriety of his work, his image as a crusader, and the wide availability of many of his titles, along with the steadily rising prices they bring. Signed copies of his *Bay: A Book of Poems* (1919) have brought over $600 each in recent years, and will go higher. Signed copies of *Lady Chatterley's Lover* (Florence, 1928) bring almost as much as do signed copies of *Women in Love* (New York, 1920). Lawrence's first book, *The White Peacock* (New York, 1911) is an extraordinary rarity: a slightly worn copy without dust jacket brought $4,350 at auction in 1972. The first English edition, published by Heinemann's one day after the American, was offered by John Howell for only $75 in 1971; two years later, a copy sold for £50, or $120—a very good appreciation.

121

Because of the controversial nature of his work, Lawrence's first editions are widely scattered, with several of the true firsts published in Florence or even New York, while most should have "London" on the title page. An expatriate like Joyce, he found publication where he could, and anyone who wants to collect his first editions should know his bibliography in every detail, which will require a little more care than with most authors. Not all Lawrence first editions are expensive. In his Catalogue Number 24, issued two or three years ago, Douglas M. Jacobs offered a first edition copy of *The Virgin and the Gypsy* (Florence, 1930) for only $85, a price that echoed an auction sale of £20 (about $48) shortly before. The general appreciation of Lawrence's titles, as well as of modern first editions generally, is represented by the fact that several years before, in 1969, Alan Hancox offered a first-edition copy of *The Plumed Serpent* (London, 1926) for only £3/10, or approximately $8. This would have been a good investment in anyone's market, in view of the fact that another copy sold at auction in 1974 at £16, or $38. A fine rise in value, but still at that later price a bargain for the first edition of a major novel by a major twentieth-century writer.

After the First World War, the literary scene becomes gloriously crowded with figures that are so active and so various that no survey can do them justice. And in addition to their miscellany of virtues as writers, most of them are excellently collectable as investments. Possibly the oldest, most powerful figure in terms of influence is Ezra Pound, whose first editions sell higher and higher each year. In 1970, two copies of his translation from the notes of Ernest Fenollosa, *Cathay,* sold at auction for $65 and £28. Four years later, another copy appeared at auction—this one with soiled wrappers—and sold for $140.

T. S. Eliot, whose achievements are interestingly implicated with the ideas, doctrines, and prejudices of Pound, is of course a classic author of the modern era; and a copy of the first edition of *The Waste Land* brings nearly a thousand dollars—a price which the Hogarth Press first edition of his *Poems* (Richmond, England, 1919) will likely reach first. As with most writers of established reputation, fully canonized by the literary-academic establishment, Eliot's first editions seem to be firm investments, with suitable appreciation rates. As simply one more indication that a shrewd collector may actually buy from a dealer and realize investment profits from the purchase, I will cite Alan Hancox's listing—in his Catalogue Number 113, Autumn, 1969—of the first edition of Eliot's *Anabasis* (London, 1930) for only £4/10, or about $10. Five

THREE STORIES

Up in Michigan

Out of Season

My Old Man

& TEN POEMS

Mitraigliatrice

Oklahoma

Oily Weather

Roosevelt

Captives

Champs d'Honneur

Riparto d'Assalto

Montparnasse

Along With Youth

Chapter Heading

ERNEST HEMINGWAY

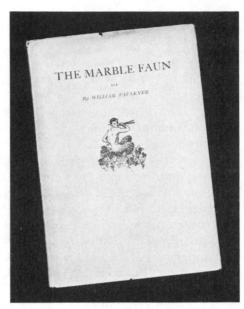

Courtesy of House of El Dieff

Courtesy of House of El Dieff

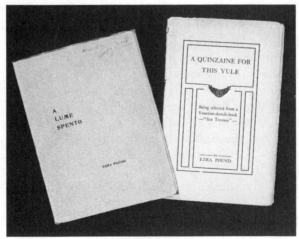

years later at auction, two copies of the same title, same edition brought $130 and $140. What a pleasant contemplation the thought of this appreciation must be to the owner of that copy purchased at £4/10; I hope the owner knows about these recent sales, and hope his satisfaction is not marred in any way by a desire to cash in on the book's present value.

The roll call of investable twentieth-century American writers is a long one, and begins to sound like the catalogue of ships that sailed for Troy: William Faulkner, Ernest Hemingway, e.e. cummings, F. Scott Fitzgerald, John Dos Passos, John Steinbeck, Thomas Wolfe, Edmund Wilson, Vachel Lindsay, Marianne Moore, Robert Penn Warren (and virtually all the Southern Fugitives—Allen Tate, John Crowe Ransome, Andrew Lytle, et al), Theodore Roethke, Robinson Jeffers, Yvor Winters, Janet Lewis, Wright Morris, Edward Dahlberg, Hart Crane, Robert Frost, Katherine Anne Porter, Sherwood Anderson, Djuna Barnes, Conrad Aiken, James M. Cain, Ring Lardner, William Carlos Williams, James Thurber, John O'Hara, Nathanael West, Wallace Stegner, Eudora Welty, Walter Van Tilburg Clark, Theodore Dreiser, Gertrude Stein, H. L. Mencken, Eugene O'Neill, and of course T. S. Eliot and Ezra Pound, and indeed, on and on. First-edition titles of all those listed, plus many others, already demand a special premium in catalogue listings in recognition of the fact that they have achieved status as "important" writers.

Most of those listed are from the generation that came to maturity during and immediately after the First World War. Many of the men fought in that war and celebrated it in one way or another in their writings. Some on that list are still very much alive, very much with us, and very much continuing to expand their bibliography.

The first editions of the most famous of these writers seem to be rising swiftly and effortlessly with each auction season. A first of Eliot's *Prufrock and Other Observations* (London, 1917)—signed by Eliot—brought $1,100 early in 1976 at Parke Bernet. At the same (February 25) sale, a copy of the signed, limited edition of Faulkner's *Go Down, Moses* (New York, 1942) brought $2,000! First-edition copies of *Sartoris* (New York, 1929) and *Mosquitoes* (New York, 1926)—lacking the dust jacket, and with the spine slightly wrinkled—brought $150 at the January 15, 1976, sale at Swann Galleries. A copy of the first of *Sanctuary*, with dust jacket, brought $130 at the same sale. Faulkner prices have risen steadily over the past two decades, not even wavering significantly in the aftermath of Faulkner's death.

Generally Hemingway's first-edition prices have risen coordinately. A copy of the first issue of *A Farewell to Arms* sold at a 1971 auction for only $36; in 1974, a copy sold for $150. This is a fairly common book, but the demand for it is always just a little ahead of the supply. This combination of factors results in a price variation much greater than that of most rarities; next year, good, dust-jacketed copies of the first may sell anywhere from $75 to $300. (*A Farewell to Arms* contains the well-known first-issue point of *not* having an editorial disclaimer before the text; second issues do have such a disclaimer, thus destroying most of the copy's bibliophilic value.) Other Hemingway first editions share this market instability, probably for very much the same reason: like Fitzgerald, he was sufficiently popular during his lifetime to command large first printings, and while there are enough collectors to absorb this plenty, the abundance of both supply and demand make for a shaggy market, lacking in discipline and definition. A first edition of *Death in the Afternoon* (New York, 1932) sold at auction for $225 in 1974, and was listed in a catalogue shortly thereafter for only $35. Such a wild fluctuation can be partly explained by differences in condition— the one listed in a dealer's catalogue had a torn, but complete, dust jacket but this defect was not great enough to make *that* much difference.

It is difficult to know how much influence the growth of women's liberation movements has had on the first-edition prices of female authors, but obviously it is a factor in their appreciation. A modern author whose importance was acknowledged long before the women's movement became articulate is Virginia Woolf. One of her most elusive first editions is that of *The Waves,* published by the Hogarth Press in 1931. A copy in dust jacket was offered in a 1966 dealer's catalogue for £12/12; eight years later, the same title brought £45. One of her subtlest and most perceptive books is *A Room of One's Own,* a copy of which—first edition in dust jacket—sold for only £3 ($7.50) in a 1969 catalogue. At auctions in 1975, similar copies sold for £18 ($43) and $40.

Years ago, a bookseller in Hingham, Massachusetts, told me that it was possible to argue that America's three greatest modern writers were all women: Willa Cather, Edith Wharton, and Ellen Glasgow. Although this idea was suggested somewhat playfully, it may have the merit possessed by any controversial or unexpected idea in stirring up honest thought. And while it isn't the sort of thing reasonable folks will argue about (the word "greatest" assumes a protean nebulousness when heated by a discussion like this), those authors have, in truth, produced some powerful and original work; and this fact is reflected by the fact that their first editions regularly bring good prices.

Willa Cather's first editions, especially, attract high prices. Her beautiful and lyric novel, *My Antonia* (Boston, 1918), sells for near $200 in fine condition in the dust jacket; *O Pioneers!* and *Death Comes for the Archbishop* for somewhat less. Her favorite novel (and one of mine, of hers I've read), *The Professor's House* (New York, 1925) sells for anywhere from $15 to $30; and that's the first edition, in dust jacket—surprisingly low for so excellent a book.

The salvation of the collector-investor lies in the ever-expanding rare-book market; and there is no more exciting or more challenging quarter in this advancing frontier than that of the modern first edition. New books are constantly being made, and they flow into circulation with the power of an Amazon. However, most are windup toys of the moment, fabricated to entertain or ostensibly instruct, or they may be thought of as servants of fashion and relevance destined soon to pass away.

Nevertheless, in this massive production there will have to be some few books that speak to the mind and heart; a few must surely, as in the past, have a vitality that will enable them to survive the fashion of their time. Nothing is more natural for a lover of books and the written word than to try to identify these *as his own,* and gather them in for himself.

What the collector-investor desires, of course, is to rise above the ephemeral little fashions of his time into those larger, more enduring ones, whose configurations more and more nearly approximate the truth, or at least, established Literary Reputations. But how can you separate the good from the bad in the midst of such an incredible profusion of new books? In slightly cruder terms, how can you know what will last and what won't? Well, the truth is, you can't; not really. But you can exercise ingenuity and judgment and even—if you're very lucky—honesty. You can learn somewhat to read the signs, the clues. But these signs and clues should lead you only to the occasion for judgment; for in the last analysis, it just doesn't make sense to add a book you don't respect or even love to your own collection. If it's a smashing bargain, buy it; then sell it for a profit, or trade it to another collector, or a dealer for a book you will cherish.

How do you know how to go exploring? How can you hear anything sweet and clear in this babble of noise? Consider the contemporary situation in poetry. Everybody's writing poems, and a lot of it seems to be vital, powerful, excellent. Someday, we really *might* be judged to have been living in the midst of a poetic renaissance; but now the profusion is so great that it is hard to see how literary scholars will ever be able to tell what's happening, let alone separate the good from the bad, not to mention that huge bulk which doesn't manage to be either, but only second-rate.

Furthermore, the worst sometimes looks dangerously like the best; and of course, vice versa. And not only is there this staggering volume of books, chapbooks, poetry pamphlets, and periodicals being produced by a large number of compulsively articulate people, but there is such a rapidity of change in fashion that by the time the ink on your check dries, you may find you have invested in a moonbeam or, even worse, a garbage-school period piece.

Late in the 1960s I had some of my own poems rejected by an editor, who wrote, "God, I didn't think anybody had been writing poems like this since the 1950s!" At first, I didn't know whether to take that as a negative criticism or not; but upon reflection, I decided it probably was. And you can see that if a *poet* has to dig what's happening, the collector-investor *really* has to be in on the know.

The situation is difficult, but not impossible. Every metaphorical jug has two handles; in almost every difficulty, there is an implicit advantage. Consider those I have enumerated: the sheer mind-boggling volume of poets and titles, representing what might at first seem to be an equally staggering variety of insight, taste, and value, but proves, upon closer scrutiny, to be somewhat less. This very amplitude of production, however, presents marvelous opportunities for the serious collector. If books of poetry are published by the thousands, then they are available by the thousands, in spite of the shamelessly narrow channels of distribution that prevail in supplying bookstores. The fact is, such an exuberant proliferation cannot be inhibited, and almost any conceivable book, or type of book, can appear in almost any conceivable place.

127

Not even the glossiest and most conservative bookstores—committed to the sale of paperbacks and new books in shiny dust jackets—are invulnerable to the rich confusions that are meant to serve the collector.

A personal anecdote will show what I mean. Several years ago, I visited another university and, of course, went to the campus bookstore in search of collectable books that might have found their way into the stacks of new trade books, or even on to the shelves of assigned texts. It was on the latter that I came across three high stacks of new, hardbound, dust-jacketed copies of Saul Bellow's *Mr. Sammler's Planet* that some enterprising instructor had assigned for his course. This book had been published less than a year before, and following a hunch, I looked through the copies, one by one, checking the fly leaves. Sure enough, I soon came upon one signed "S. Bellow"; and in going through the others I found still two more signed copies. Of course, I bought all three at the standard retail price, and eventually traded two of them ("duplicates" to me) to dealers for some books of similar value I did not already own.

What had happened? Apparently, this: Saul Bellow had been invited to an autograph party at some large book or department store, where he had been given a seat and asked to sign a hundred or possibly five hundred copies of his recently published novel. Eventually, when sales subsided (the commercial life of most books is less than three months), a few of those that still remained were removed to a back table, somewhere, and still later (when the sales arc was virtually completed), some unknowing clerk was assigned to the task of reducing stock, and returning to their publishers unsold copies of all books stored or shelved in a particular area; whereupon he crated up the signed copies of Bellow's novels along with others, and returned them. When the instructor of the course I referred to assigned the novel for his class, and the campus bookstore ordered them, these signed copies were waiting in the warehouse to be shipped out.

This is of course similar to the episode with John Berryman's *Love & Fame,* which I described earlier. And, as a matter of fact, I have found many other collectable volumes mixed in with, and shoved behind, the hyper-promoted inanities of the moment, only waiting for someone who was not simply "buying a book to read," but buying it with the hope of reading it and liking it and wanting to add it to his collection.

Opportunities of this sort spring up everywhere, constantly, and it is ridiculous for a collector not to take advantage of them. In a bookstore in Toronto, William Heyen came upon thirty-five paperbound first editions of Dick Hugo's *Good Luck in Cracked Italian* offered for twenty-nine cents apiece, and bought all of them. (He'd gotten the hardbound first edition for $6.50 a year before.) He gave part of this new windfall to Hugo, had others signed, gave some to friends, and still had plenty remaining for "trading stock."

Another collector says, "I love rare books, and buy a lot; however, I'm just a trifle dubious about buying them as an investment; but there is no doubt whatsoever that the occasional find can be a *marvelous* investment." And of course he's right about the "find." What you have to do, if you are committed to this kind of collecting adventure, is to work harder at finding the find. Serendipity is as much a gift from within as from without. Which means, you have to know a good or promising book when you see one.

Ask any two book people who the most collectable of today's writers are, and you'll get two different lists. A practical way to arrive at a list would be to cull one from a study of current dealer's catalogues. Presumably writers are listed only if they are 'collectable' in the opinion of a dealer. No doubt, a book is occasionally included because a dealer personally likes it and thinks it deserves to have some premium as "rare," or possibly he has a hunch, maybe even an educated one, extrapolating from evidence of cash sales.

But there are a lot of godawful writers who are considered collectable today; and there is no point (to reiterate this cardinal truth) in collecting books that you don't honestly and deeply respect. Many of these authors listed are collected for adventitious reasons—not because they have a unique vision or powerful voice; in short, they are "relevant," and their value will evaporate with whatever cliché-clotted fashion they exemplify. You might just as well invest in the stock of a corporation to whose activities you are utterly indifferent—you can secretly despise these, too, deprived only of the comfort of knowing that you have surrounded yourself with, if not unread, at least unreadable, books.

There is a problem in studying the market intelligently, not because of a lack of clues, but because of too great an abundance. Here, the axiom that one should always buy what he likes is tempered somewhat by the truth that the premium required for puchasing a first edition is not an essential part of simply reading that author; you pay that premium for the pleasure of possessing the true first, and for the pleasurable anticipation of having the price spent on the book validated by a rise in the market. And for all that is implicit in this second value, you have to be informed.

Any enlightenment you get on investing in contemporary writers will prove to be composed of part shrewdness, part luck, and part prophecy. Just like any other kind of investment advice. No one can assure you that the writers whose first editions are riding so high today will continue to ride high. Maybe they'll even fall. There are no safeguards. But of course, there are all those multifarious clues: critical reputation, popular reputation, auction records, dealer's listings, size of printings, physical quality of the books, and so on. These clues are not always easy to interpret. Popular reputation is ambiguous, insofar as it entails large printings, thus tending to deflate the price value of a particular title, and yet betokens a solid—and possibly enduring—general interest in that author's work. In a situation like this, we need all the help we can get. Which means we go to the experts, the more the better. In 1975, *Antaeus,* a literary quarterly, began a series called "Neglected Books of the 20th Century," which lists titles submitted by a number of successful and well-known writers, critics, and public figures. While many of these "neglected" books were written by writers now dead, many others are by writers who are living and still producing. Being "neglected," these books may be considered potential high spots—which also means they will probably be easier to find, and a lot cheaper than after the prophecy they figure in is fulfilled. Another source is *Rediscoveries,* edited by David Madden (New York, 1971); this is a book of essays by writers on neglected books, and many of these books, too, are by living writers. There is, in fact, something of a movement toward critical reappraisal and the rediscovery of forgotten or neglected books and authors. All essays and volumes devoted to this idea are likely to prove rich sources of knowledge and profit for the collector-investor.

William Targ in his lively book of memoirs, *Indecent Pleasures* (New York, 1975), has a section with a title that is something of an essay in itself: "Book Collecting for the Smart Money; or, What the Disillusioned and Bewildered Stock Market Speculator Can Turn to for Solace, Culture, and Some Profit." Here Targ lists his own favorite modern authors, in terms of his estimate of their investment potential. This list is part of the distillation of a lifelong study of, and a passionate commitment to, rare books. His list includes many of the inevitable dead (Joyce, Faulkner, Yeats); but it also includes a number of living writers. Samuel Beckett and Tennessee Williams are in the top ten; Edward Albee, Stephen Spender, Gwendolyn Brooks, Henry Miller, Edward Gorey, James Baldwin, and Vladimir Nabokov, are in the second twenty; and John Ashbery, Saul Bellow, Elizabeth Bishop, Ray Bradbury, Truman Capote, Edward Dahlberg, John Hawkes, Carolyn Kizer, Anaïs Nin, Laura Riding, Adrienne Rich, Gary Snyder, William Styron, and Allen Tate are only some of those listed in the remainder.

A list like this, or like that in *Antaeus,* is a good place to start. The second move is, of course, to read and read, and think and think. Then when you have learned to like and respect an author, move in and gather up all the first editions you can, with the conviction that you have gotten there early, when the supply is plentiful and the prices are low.

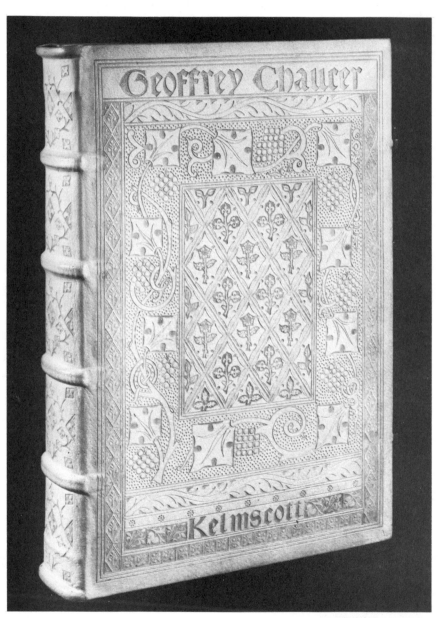

Courtesy of House of El Dieff

VIII.

ILLUSTRATED AND

PRIVATE PRESS BOOKS

Books have always exercised a particular torque upon the imagination, and have inspired an extraordinary variety of effects in artistry and design. Given the basic, powerful fact of *bookness,* the ingenuity, inventiveness, and—yes— kookinesss of mankind have been liberated in exotic ways. Books have been made of all kinds of materials—wood, velvet, linen, silk, leather (including the skins of calves, steers, horses, goats, pigs, dogs, deer, and foxes, as well as the skin of human beings and animal embryos), plastic, paper, cloth, cardboard, and, for all I know, of cobwebs, button hooks, and chewing gum. They have been equipped with brass hinges and leather loops; tied with cloth bands, decorated with marbled boards, gilt-stamped, blind-stamped, done in art nouveau morocco, vellum, large heavy paper bindings, boxed, slip-cased, and on and on to the very limits of the imagination.

Books have been made in all sizes, convenient to palm in church, while the alabaster-nosed deacons of yesteryear scanned the congregation with a bilious eye; or large enough to fill both arms, as cumbersome as an infant's cradle, and as heavy. Varieties in style and size of type are also striking (in a manner of speaking); and there is a thriving species of bookworm—the typophile—whose existence in one form or another is a prerequisite for the modern fine press movement.

One oddity of bookmaking that may serve to represent a number of these design peculiarities is the fore-edge painting. In one sense, this is an old art, for decorations were painted on the fore-edges of incunabula, even—a sign and token of Renaissance exuberance. But as we think of them, fore-edge paintings are a sort of pictorial message concealed in a design code, hidden from all but the knowing eye. This technique was perfected and popularized in the late eighteenth century by William Edwards, one of a famous family of binders in Halifax. It consisted, basically, of placing a volume in a frame so that the pages were tightly fanned out, and then painting a scene (usually, but not always, relevant to the text) on these fanned edges. When the book was closed, the painting disappeared. After the painting dried, the edges were gilt in the customary manner, thus compounding the deceitful appearance under which a secret, "inner" truth was hidden.

It is perhaps a little more difficult to explain the charm of fore-edge paintings than it is to explain other aspects of the bibliophile's passion. And yet, for all the sheer pointlessness of expending so much labor and craft on so trivial and peculiar a canvas, the charm is unquestionably there. As a curiosity, in fact, it may communicate with people who are otherwise impervious to the delights of book collecting. The fore-edge painting of Boston Harbor on my copy of James Fenimore Cooper's *Lionel Lincoln* will, at the climactic moment when I fan the pages before the eyes of guests, evoke an exclamation from those who have managed to remain heroically unmoved up to that instant. It is a little like an act of prestidigitation and perhaps as transitory in effect; although it does exist, and does sing to the mind—if ever so briefly and quietly—of the pleasures of insight.

As a matter of fact, during the 1930s the charm of fore-edge paintings proved so great that it gave rise to a flourishing business, in which several upper rooms in prominent London establishments were converted into studios where artists assiduously created genuine eighteenth- and nineteenth-century fore-edge paintings in order to satisfy the lusty popular demand for these embellishments. This was done, John Carter says, "sometimes as an avowed modern craft, on modern books, but more often applied to suitable earlier books with intent to deceive." Usually, the book with a genuine fore-edge painting will have the binder's name or imprint stamped on the extreme outer edge of the front board. This is not always the case, however—which gives me some comfort in view of the fact that my copy of *Lionel Lincoln* does not bear such evidence.

134

Fore-edge paintings were so furiously the vogue a few decades back, that some collectors are surprised to see them still around—still listed in catalogues, still bought and sold. That they remain very collectable is evident in the fact that a section of 39 books with fore-edge paintings was offered at a recent Park-Bernet sale, bringing a total of $11,585, or an average of just under $300 per title in spite of the fact that two of the books offered were not in good condition (bringing $50 and $60), and another was one volume of a two volume set ($150). That people were buying fore-edges and not "content" is indicated by the fact that books with a reasonable claim to literary merit (a two-volume Milton, London, 1796—$275, or Scott's *Marmion,* with an angling scene on the fore-edge—$175) brought considerably less than other titles of less famous authors. Beyond doubt, these purchasers were intent upon the edges of the pages, not upon those flat surfaces, where the print lies.

Fore-edge paintings, however, comprise a mere curiosity in the history of fine books; and my reference to them is deservedly brief. Books collected and admired primarily for their physical beauty fall into four general categories: illustrated books, those noted for the excellence of their typography, books with fine bindings, and private press books. These categories are necessarily crude, and they are neither exclusive nor coordinate. No book will emphasize one quality to the total exclusion of the others, and this variety of emphasis, combined with other factors of skill, expense, and intention will occasionally wreck any system of classification. For example, a book whose chief pride is its binding may nevertheless have finer typography than another, cheaper volume whose emphasis *is* typographical. Furthermore, there are complications within these categories: for example, typographical excellence will be lost on inferior paper, which fact suggests that papermaking (an old and venerable art) might well claim a condign place with typography and fine binding. But for the sake of convenience and clarity, we may combine papermaking and typography, since neither can be appreciated without the other.

The private press book is unique among these categories in that it deliberately exploits most of the values implicit in the other three: illustrations, typography, and fine bindings. Some private presses, it is true, have among their most opulent offerings books that are issued in wrappers—thus, lacking bindings of any sort, either fine or gross. But these wrappers are usually of rich and heavy paper—sometimes in themselves handsomely designed; or, as is the custom in France, they are in-

135

tended as only a temporary stay against usage and elements until the volume is custom-bound for the owner.

Illustrated books are difficult to classify, for they comprise a great variety of books, extending from those which exist primarily for the purpose of displaying the illustrations to those in which only a handful of undistinguished illustrations appear, constituting little of the bibliophilic value of the book, except as points. In between these two extremes, lie most of those books we designate as "illustrated"—the illustrations forming a sort of pictorial counterpoint or commentary upon the basic narrative or argument of the book.

As a visible presence, illustrations have been an important factor in the value of many of the rarest books already discussed, including such illustrated incunabula as *Hortus Sanitatis* and the *Nuremberg Chronicles.* How much of the value of these books can be attributed to the illustrations, how much to text, and how much to their simple existence as antiquarian objects is impossible to say. But fine or old illustrations have an enormous appeal to booklovers of almost every description; and whether they are ancient or modern, books which feature illustrations are high in investment potential.

In the early days of printing, pictures of such famous artists as Holbein and Dürer (Dürer was himself an engraver) were translated into woodcuts for book illustrations. But it was relatively late before collectors began to concentrate upon collecting the illustrators, rather than the authors, of books. Hogarth is the first English illustrator to become collectable as a name. Books with Hogarth prints may or may not have bibliophilic interest in the text, but the presence of his prints alone in an eighteenth-century book make that book valuable. Two copies of Hogarth's *Works,* "from the original plates restored by John Heath, edited by John Nichols," including 150 engravings on 114 plates, were sold on July 28, 1975, by Sotheby's. One copy, slightly damaged and lacking two suppressed plates, brought £220 ($528).

In the latter part of the eighteenth-century, two brothers—Thomas and John Bewick—were prominent wood engravers, whose illustrations in contemporary books render them valuable above and beyond the text. Thomas was the older and more famous of the two, and is honored for developing the "white line" engraving, by means of cutting his woodblocks on the end of the grain. He also had a sense of humor that did not depend upon satiric effects or caricature, thus making him something of an exception in his day. One of the blocks he cut to illustrate Newberry's *The Life and Adventures of a Fly* shows a small boy rescuing a fly from his soup, while his entranced father looks on. A five-volume set of Thomas and John Bewick's illustrated works, consisting of the *History of British Birds* (2 vols., 1804), *Select Fables* (1820), *Fables of Aesop* (1823), and *Quadrupeds* (1824)—the first two titles first editions—sold at the Josiah M. Erickson sale in 1967 for a total of only $85. At the Swann Galleries sale of July 31, 1975, a first edition copy of the *History of British Birds,* along with the eighth edition of *Quadrupeds,* brought $200—which is the exact price that *Select Fables* has also brought at a recent auction, and was as good a bargain for 1975 as the Erickson price was for that larger lot only eight years before.

The remaining eighteenth-century illustrator to be considered is so much more than what we normally mean by the word "illustrator" that the only alternative to devoting a whole chapter, or book, to his work alone is simple acknowledgment of his unique presence in the history of literature as well as illustration. This is of course William Blake, whose first editions are so superlatively rare, and so passionately sought-after, that it would almost seem possible for whole industries to exist simply in reprinting newly designed and facsimile editions of his work. One of the latest appearances of a first-edition copy from the Blake canon at auction was on May 29, 1971, when *The First Book of Urizen* (Lambeth, 1794) sold for £24,000. A first edition of this title had sold in 1924 for £580, indicating that Blake's position among collectors is hardly new. The sale prices of other Blake first editions—on those few occasions when they are offered—are comparable.

As for the facsimile editions, they have also appreciated exuberantly, since to most Blake collectors they represent the nearest and best substitute for the original. A London 1958 facsimile edition of the *Urizen* mentioned above, bound in half morocco and limited to 480 copies sells in the $200 range; the full morocco issue, consisting of only twenty copies, sells for over twice that amount.

The Nonesuch Press printings of several Blake titles, edited by Geoffrey Keynes, all sell in the hundreds of dollars. The Trianon Press facsimile edition of *Songs of Innocence* appeared in 1955 in a limited edition of 526 copies. By 1970, these copies were selling in the $400 range (£170 at auction in October of that year); and in 1974, a copy sold for £220, or about $525. The Grabhorn Press edition of this title came out in San Francisco in 1924, with a printing of 100.

In spite of the interest and fascination of eighteenth-century engravings, the day of the illustrator did not arrive until the nineteenth century, issued in with the rich and earthy satiric drawings of Thomas Rowlandson. These caricatures of Rowlandson have eclipsed the happy doggerel of William Combe, who wrote the once-famous "tours" of a quixotic schoolmaster named "Dr. Syntax." Syntax is an impoverished and scholarly eccentric who decides to go forth and seek adventures for "material," so that he can write a book and make money. "I'll make a tour—and then I'll write it," he tells his shrewish wife, and then continues:

> You well know what my pen can do,
> And I'll employ my pencil too:—
> I'll ride and *write,* and *sketch* and *print,*
> And thus create a real mint;
> I'll *prose* it here, I'll *verse* it there,
> And *picturesque* it ev'ry where.
> I'll do what all have done before;
> I think I shall—and somewhat more.

Dr. Syntax may have fallen short of making a real mint, but he certainly made a real diphthong out of the vowel in the word "real" in line four. He also made a real classic in the history of the illustrated book, about which Combe tells an interesting story. The droll doctor's itinerary was planned in the following manner: an etching or drawing by Rowlandson was sent to Combe every month, upon which Combe composed a certain number of pages of verse—thus illustrating the illustration; the rest, Combe modestly wrote, "depended upon what my imagination could furnish."

The three volumes comprising the three tours of Dr. Syntax are solid standbys on the rare-book market. They are lusty and colorful, and it would be hard to think of anyone who could not respond to them. In 1972 the three volumes together brought $275 at auction; only two years later, the same set brought £550, about $1,420. In a 1975 auction a complete set sold at $800; another, rebound, at $650. Not all books illustrated by Rowlandson have appreciated so abruptly; but they have proved themselves solid and vigorous investments the past few years—a fact borne out by the auction records of Combe's *The English Dance of Death* (London, 2 vols., 1815–16), also illustrated by Rowlandson. In 1972, a first edition copy of this title sold for £85; in 1974, two sales showed prices of £170 and $625. Late in 1975, this title, along with the one-volume *The English Dance of Life,* sold for $1,100; also, a less fine copy of the first title sold for $500 at the same sale. Sotheby's January 26, 1976, sale had a copy of *Poetical Sketches of Scarborough* (1813), by Rowlandson and J. Green, sell for £70. In 1967, 1968, and 1970, three copies of the same title had sold at £9, $90, and £38—an average price of about $67.

Gustave Doré, J.J. Grandville (Jean Ignace Isidore Gerard), Harrison Ainsworth, H.K. Browne, George Cruikshank, and John Tenniel are just a few of the famous illustrators whose work graced nineteenth-century bookmaking. Any first edition of a book illustrated by these artists will have some value in that fact alone. Grandville's work somehow manages to achieve a quality both macabre and vigorous. His *Les Metamorphoses Du Jour* (Paris, 1869) was offered in a 1970 catalogue for £21; at auction on April 9, 1974, a similar copy sold for $100.

Browne, who was the illustrator of books by Robert Smith Surtees, Charles Lever, and Dickens, achieved his greatest fame as the pseudonymous "Phiz," whose lively conceptions of Dickens' characters have almost become a part of the novels themselves. But the great popularity of these novels brought about such large printings that not even with Phiz's genius grafted upon that of Dickens has the cost of first book editions of such treasures as *Little Dorrit* and *Our Mutual Friend* risen above $100—a nifty bargain, considering the fact that they keep making more years and more people, but they don't keep making more first editions of the novels of Charles Dickens.

Several years ago, my wife paid $37.50 for a first edition copy of Jane and Ann Taylor's *Little Ann and Other Poems* (London, no date, but probably 1883). These authors are best known for writing "Twinkle, Twinkle, Little Star," but their importance in this context is that their book of poems was illustrated by Kate Greenaway. Van Allen Bradley, in his indispensable *Handbook of Values* (second revised edition, New York, 1975) puts this book in the $80 to $90 range; however, at a recent auction, a copy sold for $120—one of several instances where Bradley's evaluation, which some have criticized for being too bullish, was actually a little too conservative.

Other Kate Greenaway books have proved good investments over the past decade. Her *Almanac for 1883* sold for only $4.90 in 1963; in 1974, a copy sold for £22, or $50, making a tenfold increase in that eleven-year period. Today, their value is much greater. *Almanacs* were issued from 1883 through 1897 (excepting 1896), and according to

Bradley, "Complete sets in fine condition are worth $1,250, possibly more at retail."

In a 1971 catalogue, John Howell listed a copy of *Mother Goose or the Old Nursery Rhymes* (London, 1881) illustrated by Kate Greenaway, and the first edition, as such. Howell's price for this copy, which was slightly imperfect, was only $45—an excellent bargain in view of the fact that a copy of the same book sold at auction in 1974 for $375.

Kate Greenaway is one of the first distinctly modern illustrators; and her work exists not only in a world of sweetness and light, but in a world fresh and alive with colors that were not possible in the reproduced plates of earlier books. The plates of earlier artists had to be colored by hand, individually; but with the invention of more sophisticated techniques for printing color plates late in the nineteenth century, the emphasis in illustrating naturally shifted toward the exploitation and realization of these techniques.

No one has to believe that the medium *is* the message to understand the enormous influence technology has upon the arts; and nowhere is this influence more evident than in the development of modern color-reproduction techniques, and the responsive growth of a whole population of brilliant color illustrators. Some of these are not famous, and yet their work is solidly collectable. Edward Penfield's *Holland Sketches* (New York, 1907) is an unpretentious book, containing large print, wide margins, and color illustrations of a simplicity and clarity that freshen the eye. A copy recently sold at auction for $50. C. Coles Phillips' illustrations for Gertrude Atherton's *The Gorgeous Isle* (New York, 1908) possess a delicate and precise beauty, indicating that Phillips is a master illustrator whose work is deserving of attention. (*The Gorgeous Isle* is, incidentally, a completely beautiful book, with the Chinese red cloth handsomely stamped in gold and silver.)

Mary Russell Mitford's *Our Village* (London, 1824) sells for about $200 in the first edition. It has also been reprinted in a 1910 half-leather edition, illustrated by Hugh Thompson, which sells for as much as $50. I like my 1904 (London: J. M. Dent; New York: E. P. Dutton) edition, "with twenty-five coloured illustrations by C. E. Brock"—a lower-priced book, but an attractive one. Howard Chandler Christy's illustrations are actively collected. I have Brand Whitlock's nicely printed *Her Infinite Variety* (Indianapolis, 1904) illustrated by Christy, and inscribed by Whitlock to his brother Elias. Christy's style is strikingly like that of Charles Dana Gibson—the creator of "the Gibson Girl"; but Gibson's price is considerably higher than Christy's: his two-volume, oblong folio edition of *The Gibson Book* (New York, 1906) sells for $100 and more. Amelia M. Watson's cool and delicate marginal illustrations for Thoreau's *Cape Cod* (2 vols., Boston, 1904) contribute toward a delightfully designed book, whose value is $50 and more. At a recent auction, a copy described as "worn and shaken" brought $30.

Prominent among these color illustrators are Howard Pyle and N. C. Wyeth—leaders of what has been called "The Brandywine Tradition." The washes, colored drawings, and line drawings of Pyle have gained a wide and loyal popularity among collectors. He wrote books as well as illustrated them, and the freshness and vitality of his works soon created so great a popular demand that they were liberally printed, with the result that most titles are available today in the first edition at modest prices, ranging from $20 to $100. There are a few exceptions: his first book, *The Merry Adventures of Robin Hood* (New York, 1883), in full leather, goes for $150 to $200. A number of reprint editions are sufficiently handsome to sell for $50 to $150. One of his titles, *Howard Pyle's Book of Pirates*, edited by the excellent bookman Merle Johnson ten years after Pyle's death, came out simultaneously in a trade edition ($50 to $75 when perfect, in dust jacket) and a limited edition of fifty on vellum, signed by Johnson. The price for this boxed pirate treasure is about $150.

N. C. Wyeth's gifts as an illustrator are somewhat underrated. Like Pyle, Wyeth had something of a young boy's love for what might be called "wholesome violence." No doubt, the strangely romantic image of the pirate derives largely from the paintings of these two artists. Wyeth's illustrations for *Treasure Island* are marvelous—with heavy, sculptural shadows lying in tension against a cool delicacy of color; and the brutality of gesture and expression lying in tension against an inventory of lovingly wrought details. For all their excellence, books illustrated by N. C. Wyeth are greatly underpriced—many available at the price of a bottle of whiskey or a new fishing reel—therefore a good bet for the collector-investor.

Wyeth's situation is proof that artistic ability in itself is not enough to ensure a high premium among collectors. Some highly collectable illustrators are famous for reasons that are not always clear; others for perfectly valid but nonartistic reasons. Sentiment and association are factors in every branch of collecting, and sometimes they exercise rights of priority over the more sophisticated virtues of technique and skill.

Books illustrated by Charles M. Russell, the "cowboy artist," have been appreciating mightily over the past decade. His colorful and energetic pictures have been collected into handsome books, some selling in the $300 to $500 range, and others—limited, signed, and a few with original drawings—sell for much more. In 1973, Fred A. Rosenstock, of Denver, gathered a collection of Russelliana for auction. According to *American Book Prices Current* for that year, "Parkman's *Oregon Trail,* with a presentation inscription, and eleven original watercolour drawings by Russell fetched $13,000."

Born three years before Russell, Frederic Remington illustrated books that have also continued to do well on dealers' shelves and at auction. Like Russell, Remington's collectability has as much to do with his subject matter, and his own intimate connection with it, as with his considerable ability as an artist. Remington traveled widely in the "late Old West," and like Russell—who actually was a cowboy in the 1880s—identified with it and left his impressions as invaluable documentary evidence concerning a world that is gone forever. Remington's *Done in the Open* (New York, 1902)—a folio of classic drawings, accompanied by the simple rhymes of Owen Wister—sells for $150 and up, *if* Remington's first name is misspelled "Frederick" on the front cover, thus designating a first issue. Remington was also a lively and interesting writer, as evidenced by the fact that his *Men With the Bark On* (New York, 1900) sells for as much as $100, providing the book is only ⅞ inch thick, instead of 1⅛, as in later issues.

Remington was neither the draftsman nor the colorist that Pyle and Wyeth were; his merit lies elsewhere. The merit in Aubrey Beardsley's work is even more elusive, in spite of the fact that his illustrations are very much coveted by collectors—at least enough of them to keep the prices of Beardsley's books in the $50 to $150 range.

Perhaps the most avidly collected modern illustrator is Arthur Rackham, whose superb inventiveness and skill enabled him, throughout a long career, to contribute a score of illustrative masterpieces to the world of books. Deluxe limited editions (often bound in white vellum), signed by Rackham, are priced high in the hundreds of dollars, and will likely soon reach a thousand if they haven't already. Even the trade editions of such masterfully illustrated books as the *Vicar of Wakefield,* Grimm's *Fairy Tales, Ingoldsby Legends,* and *Gulliver's Travels* are priced in the $50 to $100 range, and well worth these prices, for they keep going up. One example of his popularity among collectors is his *The Allies*

Fairy Book, which Bertram Rota offered for only £5, or $12, in 1970; in 1974, the same title brought £35, or $84, at auction.

Rackham's style is unique and unforgettable. It is well described in the following conclusion to the entry on Rackham, from *Contemporary Illustrators of Children's Books,* compiled by Bertha E. Mahony and Elinor Whitney, Boston, 1930:

> Color, or rather brilliant color, does not interest him. He frequently seems more interested in true relation than variety of hue. The subtle blues, the gray greens, golden browns, and that quality of warm old ivory with which he envelops his drawings are more potent than mere brilliance. [p. 62]

Contemporary illustrators are wondrously prolific, talented, and diversified in talent, style, and media. Often they are of a stature to determine the price of a book, or to justify its being issued in a limited edition. Leonard Baskin, Ben Shahn, Edward Gorey, Percy MacMahon, Joseph Low, Lionel Kalish, Larry Ross, Edward Ardizzone, Helen Oxenbury, Ramond Briggs, Mercer Mayer, Anne Rockwell, John Burningham, and a hundred others are eminently worth collecting. Some of those listed are thought of as illustrators of "children's books," which of course means even less as a grading category to the art lover than it does to the lover of stories. Burningham's color illustrations for the book *Cannonball Simp* are simply magnificent. MacMahon's dust jacket design for Edward Maze's *Kirie, Pirie, and Kalikoolin's Pipe* (New York, 1964) is breathtakingly beautiful. (MacMahon and Maze, pseudonyms of two Americans living in Sweden, first published this book there in English and then in Germany before the titular "first edition" was published in the United States.)

There are too many good and interesting illustrators doing too many different things for me to attempt anything like a lucid summary. Some will be referred to in the section on private press books. As for the great majority, they are still thriving and working. The opportunities they present are glorious. Most of their reputations have not yet congealed into that state whereby the books they have embellished may be said to have a predictable value. They are still working, still changing, still growing; and their manifold audiences are still learning to see what their illustrations are trying to create and reveal. The thousands of illustrated books that pour out of the presses each year—particularly the juveniles—have among them some that will prove an abiding joy to possess, as well as a handsome investment in coming years. They are, of course, "limited and reserved"—for those who have eyes to see their beauty and the desire to acquire them as their own.

Before leaving the subject of book illustrations, it would be wise to refer to the growing interest in collecting books with photographic illustrations. Primarily, photographs are used to convey lifelike images of people and places for informational, nonfictional purposes; therefore, in some ways, and in the hands of a careful and talented photographer, photographs can afford the best possible "illustrations" for a text. Early photographs of people and places are especially desirable in a book and their prices have been rising steadily. When this documentary power of the camera is focused upon Americana, as in Edward Curtis' *The North American Indian (1907-1930)*—a prodigious twenty quarto-volume set, containing over 1,500 photographic plates—the cost will be princely. Planned as a limited edition of 500, only about half this number were issued, signed by Curtis (with some signed by Theodore Roosevelt, who wrote the preface). This book was sold for $3,850 when it was published. In 1972 a set went for $26,000 at auction; two years later, another brought $31,000.

Books of photographs, as well as books with photographic illustrations, are commanding ever-higher prices on the market. Lavish coffee-table productions, however, tend to be overpriced at publication date, inviting many collectors to bide their time until they are remaindered, *if* they are remaindered, or remaindered in a reasonable time, which is a gamble one has to consider in deciding upon such tactics.

There have been experiments in using photographs to illustrate fiction. I have one such curiosity—the Dodd, Mead 1901 reprint of J. M. Barrie's *A Window in Thrums,* with photographic illustrations by Clifton Johnson. This copy has a colorfully decorated binding in the turn-of-the-century style, and the photographs are of some interest, simply because of their age. But the whole thing seems to me to be the issue of such a monstrously incompatible marriage that I cannot gather the interest to read it. Maybe I'm missing something worthwhile; but my instincts tell me I'm not.

The price stability of illustrated books seems about as sure as anything in an unstable world. Dealers who once circumscribed their activities with spartan discipline, now include illustrated books in their want lists, regardless of where their primary interest lies. The whole matter was summarized very well, over a century ago, when the illustrated book as we know it had hardly begun: "A passion for books illustrated, or adorned with numerous prints . . . is a very general and violent symptom of the Bibliomania." The author of this was that great bibliophile Thomas Frognall Dibdin—a man who should know, as all will agree.

Today, within the expanding market, there are many noticeable trends in book collecting, but perhaps the most active, the most vital, and often one of the most expensive, is the collecting of modern private-press editions. The majority of these productions are very attractive; some "possess the splendour of a small sunset." Most represent, in one way or other (and no matter how profitable they might be), a labor of love. The field seems infinitely rich: there are constant announcements of the forming of a new press. Perhaps a husband and wife in a farmhouse in Vermont are bringing out a book of poems by a friend; do not be prejudiced or contemptuous—the result may be surprisingly good, in every way. This may seem to be vastly different from the noble Kelmscott, Ashendene, Grabhorn, Doves, or Golden Cockerel productions; but essentially it is not, for all exist in the service of the venerable handicraft and guild ideals that were so ardently celebrated and promoted by William Morris at Kelmscott.

In 1974, the British firm of Bertram Rota issued from their Savile Row address their Catalogue No. 192, titled *The Printer and the Artist.* Like many special productions of what is ostensibly a price list, this catalogue is actually a work of art—bound in heavy cream paper, bearing on the front cover geometrically constructed monograms (*B* and *R*) taken from the Grolier Club facsimile of Pacioli's alphabet, and printed handsomely on fine paper within. The catalogue was priced at two pounds—a bargain if you can by some chance still find one. Like all the best catalogues, it is far more than a price list: it is a reference work, a learned treatise on the subject therein, which is, in the wording of its subtitle on the cover, "A Catalogue of Private Press Books & Illustrated Books from the United Kingdom, Europe, & America." There are 1,320 books listed, representing 174 private presses, along with varous designers, typographers, and illustrators listed separately. All but a handful of these books were published in the twentieth century. Their prices range from five pounds, about $12, to £3,200, which then translated into something like $7,680.

145

This top price belongs to a copy of the famous Kelmscott Chaucer, specially rebound in vellum with white morocco lettering, and signed by William Morris, the founder of the Kelmscott Press, the inspiration and prototype of the modern private-press tradition, especially in England and America. It so happens that this book is one of the oldest listed in the catalogue (1896); but this is not at all old for a book, and it is valued for reasons that have little to do with age. It just also happened to be a smashing bargain for someone, in view of the fact that in 1973 two copies of the Kelmscott Chaucer were sold—one (bound by Sangorski and Sutcliffe) for $36,000; the other (bound in pigskin by the Doves bindery) for $11,500. And in 1976, a dealer offered a copy for $15,000. Another expensive book listed, featuring thirteen poems by W. H. Auden, along with twenty-one lithographs by Henry Moore, was actually a new book, just published and offered at its "retail" price: £1,400, or $3,360. (This edition is one of 150 numbered copies, signed by Moore.)

Bertram Rota's catalogue bears testimony to the fact that today, limited edition, private press, and fine illustrated books are flourishing as never before. For years there have been collectors—some of the wealthiest and most active, in fact—who have sought out the physical book, not necessarily independently of content (although in extreme cases, this was, and remains, true), but giving the body priority over mind or soul. Many of these bibliophilic specialists were typophiles, striving for comprehensiveness in their collection by possessing Baskerville's and Aldine italics, Bodoni's and Caxton's, and on and on through the canon of early printers, and continuing to the typographers, designers, and printers of today. Typography can be an exalted art and is capable of extending its fascination to a great variety of mind and temperament. In his *In Quest of the Perfect Book* (Boston, 1926), William Dana Orcutt makes the curious claim that if William James "had not taken up science as his profession and thus become a philosopher, he would have been a printer." This is curious because of the old-fashioned commingling of science and philosophy, not because of a too-honorific notion of the art of printing. James himself would have agreed: in a letter to his mother in 1862, he made reference to "the honorable, honored, and productive business of printing."

There are times and places in history that seem to pulse suddenly and brightly with a vision, and thereby illuminate the years that follow. Nobody knows exactly why this is so; it is more than what we usually

146

mean by *Zeitgeist*. There seems to be a convergence not only of thought, but of ideal and feeling; and this convergence is so powerful that the results are vivid and lasting. One such time and place was England at the end of the nineteenth century, when several remarkable printers and book designers began their careers.

William Morris was the first, with the founding of the Kelmscott Press in 1891; soon afterwards, C. H. St. John Hornby and James Cobden-Sanderson (with Emery Walker)—founded, respectively, the Ashendene Press and the Doves Press. Morris, St. John Hornby, and Cobden-Sanderson have been called the triumvirate of great English printers. Since Morris was the first, and in view of the fact that his Kelmscott Chaucer is probably the most expensive book of its kind in the world, it is not surprising that he could be considered "the greatest and most inspiring of all these venturers in ink."* And yet, referring to the Kelmscott, Doves, and Ashendene Presses, Will Ransom asks rhetorically in his *Private Presses and Their Books*, "What need is there of opinion or discrimination amongst the noble three . . . ?"

Titles from these three classic modern presses have long been prime acquisitions for the collector-investor. In fact, this premium is of such a long duration that there are those who believe they have peaked and leveled off, more or less permanently. There are, of course, signs to support such a view: the Kelmscott edition of Ruskin's *The Nature of Gothic* (1892), for example, was offered in a 1970 dealer's catalogue for $144; but at auction in 1974, three copies of the same book brought only $180, £35 ($84), and £95 ($228). Similarly, the Nonesuch edition of *The Notebooks of William Blake* did not rise appreciably in its sales prices over this period.

But of course, every market has aberrations, periodic flats and lows, downswings, and plodding, uninspiring, almost undetectable climbs. And there is no clear way to establish a peak for any market as complex as this. As long as inflation continues, prices of certain valued commodities will rise by that fact alone, so that maybe the time has come when the only sure losing investment will prove to be currency in the pocket and nonsilver coins in the piggy bank.

And the fact is, most books from the great presses of the nineties—along with their illustrious successors, Nonesuch, Golden Cockerel,

*C. J. Sawyer and F. J. H. Darton, *English Books 1475–1900*, Westminster vol. 2 (1927) p. 372.

and a hundred others—continue to do well as investments. Auction records of the Kelmscott printing of Caxton's *The History of Reynard the Fox* (1892) afford an example. In 1970, three auctions showed sales of $270, £20 (!), and £110. Four years later, three copies of the same book sold at £260, £140, and $475; and in a 1975 Parke Bernet auction, a copy brought $500. The Ashendene *Decameron* (1920) sold for £170 in 1970, but by 1974 its price had gone to £310. And the Doves Press edition of Tacitus' *De Vita et Moribus Julii Agricolae*, designed by Cobden-Sanderson sold for $40, $60, and $80 in 1969; while in 1974, one copy of the same title brought $450, while another was offered in a dealer's catalogue for $550. Here is as vigorous an appreciation as one could hope for.

A more detailed study of auction records of books from these three presses over approximately the same period reinforces the general conviction that they have proved themselves as investments. A copy of the Ashendene edition of the Jowett translation of Thucydides's *History of the Peloponnesian War* (1930) was offered in Bertram Rota's Catalogue Number 156 (Spring 1968) for $324. At auction in 1974, copies of the same title sold for £190 ($456), £140 ($336), £320 ($768), and $1,000. Next year, a copy sold for $650. The Ashendene *Ecclesiasticus* was listed in the same catalogue at $252; at auctions in 1974, copies sold at $744 and $576, and another was listed in a catalogue at $1,000.

The Doves Press *Shelley* (selected poems) sold at $200 in 1969 and at $500 in 1975. In 1974, Monk Bretton's catalogued a copy at $275—an excellent price. The Doves edition of Emerson's *Essays* (one of 300) sold for £65 ($156) in 1970 and at $200 three years later. This is okay, although hardly inspiring; but there is a principle in rare books which says that as titles rise in the scale of rarity, their values accelerate disproportionately. Therefore, a copy of the Doves Press Emerson limited to 300 copies is a desirable and valuable possession, no doubt; but Doves also issued a special 25-copy edition (sort of a *limited* limited edition), printed on vellum and exquisitely wrought. William Targ refers to his wife's buying him a copy of this edition as a gift one day for $225 at John Fleming's establishment. Nine years later, Paul Getty, Jr., bought a copy of the same title at auction for $2,600; and shortly after that, Fleming asked Targ if he would be willing to sell his copy for $3,000, since he thought he had a buyer at that price.

The Private Press tradition established by these gifted and dedicated men in England has continued both there and in this country. The

Nonesuch Press was created and built by Francis Meynell, who in his autobiography, *My Lives* (New York, 1971) wrote, "For me Nonesuch was a craft, a trade, a happy synthesis of my two fervours—poetry and print." (p. 155) The formats, the quality of materials, the typography of Nonesuch books are truly exceptional. One of its more famous productions is the 23-volume set of Dickens, which actually has 24 volumes—the extra one being a container for the metal plate used for an early Dickens illustration. This great enterprise was accomplished in two years—1937–38—and was issued in a "definitive" edition of 877 copies. Meynell's goal was to achieve printings larger than those thought compatible with fine-book production, and to do this with no compromise in quality. One set of the Nonesuch Dickens sold at a 1970 auction for £650; in 1971 there was a sale at £780; in 1972 another at £936. In 1973, three sets were sold at auction for £1,050, £800, and £840, showing an average annual appreciation rate of just under twenty percent. A 1974 catalogue offers it for $2,350—a good fair price.

Other Nonesuch books are less expensive. Montaigne's *Essays*, edited from Florio's 1632 (3rd) edition by J. I. M. Stewart* is one such Nonesuch. In good condition a copy will sell for $100 or more; although recently a rubbed copy, with somewhat faded spines, went at auction for only £20, or $48 at the then current exchange rate. And I recently purchased a copy at the bargain price of $65. *Selected Poems* by Alice Meynell, the mother of Francis, had an introduction by her husband, Wilfrid. This is an unlimited edition and sells modestly at $10 to $25. Meynell's inspired integrity has left its mark on contemporary book production. In his way, he seems to have overcome some of the difficulties in reconciling a relatively large production with an utter dedication to artistic principles. Part of this seems to be simple clear-mindedness. In addition to all his other affairs and accomplishments, Meynell spent years writing advertising copy. One of his "clients" was his own Pelican Press. In an early puff, he wrote: "The eye first will be pleased; and then the mind's eye." Which might stand as an ideal not only of the Private Press tradition, but of the book itself.

In 1931 the Golden Cockerel Press published its special 488-copy

---

*Stewart himself, under the nom de plume Michael Innes, has written detective novels that are scholarly, interesting, and no doubt solidly collectable in their own right.

edition of *The Four Gospels of the Lord Jesus Christ*, featuring the first book appearance of 18-point Golden Cockerel type designed by Eric Gill. Here is one of those types that hold sound and meaning as a "crystal goblet" (in Beatrice Warde's good phrase) holds wine or brandy. At auction in 1976, a copy of this edition sold at $850, a sensibly low price for this famous book. Two years before, however a copy was offered by a dealer for $1,250. Overpriced? Not really. The dealer's copy had been rebound—normally a disaster, or quasi-disaster, for a rare book; only this copy had been custom-rebound by Sangorski and Sutcliffe, which fact constitutes a defect of considerably ambiguity.

Golden Cockerel is one of the fine modern presses, but in spite of the high level of craftsmanship, its productions on the whole are low to reasonable in price. Some of its titles (e.g., Shenstone's *Men and Manners* [1927]) can be bought for as little as $25 to $50. Others (e.g., La Rochefoucauld's *Moral Maxims* [1924]) will cost about twice that amount—still very much a bargain. Robert Gibbings was the guiding genius of this long-lived establishment (it lasted forty years, which is near to being a record for private presses); and its existence would be justified by only a fraction of its long list of distinguished titles—including the celebration and perpetuation of the work of that artist of the short story, A. E. Coppard.

American private presses were flourishing simultaneously, in this Nonesuch era, and producing their share of great typographers and designers: Bruce Rogers, D. B. Updike, Thomas B. Mosher, and Dard Hunter, to name only a handful. Hunter, who spent an apprenticeship of a Biblical seven years at Elbert Hubbard's Roycroft Press, gained recognition as the world's foremost authority on papermaking. After travel and study abroad, Hunter returned to his home in Chillicothe, Ohio, where he went to work with a 300-year-old Wiltshire paper mill, an old hand press, and a motley of ancient typefounder's tools. He manufactured his own paper out of Irish linen and cut his own type. His subsequent accomplishments are unique: for he single-handedly created entire books—writing them, making the paper and cutting the type, printing and then hand-binding them. Copies of these genuinely limited editions are worth a thousand dollars and more—much more, in a few instances. Two copies of his *Papermaking by Hand in India* sold at 1968 auctions for $170 and $275. Late in 1975 a copy brought $1,600. Even more impressive is the price differential between a 1966 auction sale of *Papermaking Through Eighteen Centuries*—$17—and the same late-1975 auction sale price of $400. Also at this auction, Hunter's *A Papermaking Pilgrimage to Japan, Korea and China* (New York, 1936) went for $2,000; and his *Chinese Ceremonial Paper* (Chillicothe, 1937) brought $4,000.

In the 1920s, two brothers named Edwin and Robert Grabhorn founded a press in San Francisco, which has enjoyed a long and illustrious history. Three of Grabhorn's best-known books were printed for Random House and illustrated by Valenti Angelo: *The Red Badge of Courage* ($50 to $100), *The Scarlet Letter* ($35 to $75), and *Leaves of Grass.* The last is considered by many to be Grabhorn's finest production. Recently it has been listed in a catalogue, as well as sold at auction, for exactly $600—which must indicate its dollar value pretty accurately.

The Grabhorn edition of John W. Audubon's *Drawings Illustrating His Adventures Through Mexico to California, 1849–50* (San Francisco, 1957) is limited to 400 copies. The original edition is rated "dd" by Wright Howes, which "represents superlatively rare books, almost unobtainable, worth $1,000 and upwards." Howes also describes the book's four-color plates as being of "outstanding beauty." Like most press books, the Grabhorn edition isn't *contemptibly* accessible to an impoverished but enthusiastic collector. In 1970 a copy sold at auction for $60; exactly four years later, its price had doubled at auction.

One of the most important functions of such presses lies in their ability and willingness to reissue old, difficult-to-obtain classics of travel, science, philosophy, folklore, and literature; and bring out ever-new, freshly designed editions of the canonized classics, from *The Canterbury Tales* to *The Voyage of the Beagle.* The Gehenna Press, located in Northhampton, Massachusetts, issued a new edition of Melville's *The Enchanted Isles* early in the 1960s at a price of $1,000. The Allen Press, operated by Lewis and Dorothy Allen in Marin County, California, printed a 150-copy issue of Byron's *A Venetian Affair,* costing $40. Victor Hammer of Lexington, Kentucky, issued a volume of Holderlin's poetry in a 100-copy edition at $100 each. (Hammer's influence and inspiration were so great that the Lexington area became something of a center of fine printing.) Prices for all of these titles—along with those of scores of other private presses engaged primarily in reprinting older works—have continued to appreciate vigorously over the years.

The activities of the modern private-press movement, including some of those referred to above, are not limited to reprinting older works. Increasingly, private presses are operating as vehicles of the avant-garde, promoters and defenders of the newly creative, the experimental, and sometimes the revolutionary. Private presses are responsive in both directions—to writer and audience both—in ways that are virtually impossible to the large commercial publishers. An edition of 100 copies is qualitatively, as well as quantitatively, different from one of five or ten thousand. The smaller is conceived of as communicating with a different clientele—a more definable one, perhaps—and its emphasis in value is therefore different. For one thing, the visual dimension of the poem can be explored in interesting ways. An aesthetic interest in the appearance of the page merges into the poet's concern with spatial values in the organization of his poems. Francis Meynell's reference to his "two fervours—poetry and print" is not as eccentric as it may at first seem. Also it is no great surprise to learn that e. e. cummings was a painter as well as a poet, for he took a draftsman's interest in organizing his poems with a view toward their temporal-spatial effects on the page. And in fact most poets are acutely aware of typographical matters.

Regardless of its deriving from ancient oral traditions, poetry in the modern world is domesticated and lives in the rectangular rooms of the printed page. Who designs and "makes" these rooms? The typographer-as-architect. Beatrice Warde expresses the matter vividly:

> In the sense in which architecture is an art, typography is an art. That is, they both come under the head of "making or doing intentionally with skill." But they are not one-man arts like painting or oratory. The thing made, the finished work, is in every case the work of a team. Every work of Typography depends for its success upon the clear conveyance of intentions, in words and otherwise, from one human mind to others: from the man who is supposed to know how the finished thing should look and function, to a concert of specialists who are responsible, not only to the master-designer, but also to the public. Faulty masonry, or a misprint, is not simply a betrayal of the whole intention, it is also a matter of public concern. The defectively set coping-stone might kill a man, the misplaced comma might start a riot or a suit for libel. [*Specimens: A Stevens-Nelson Paper Catalogue,* from *The Crystal Goblet,* 1956]

Since this noble statement articulates one of the principles inherent to the domain of the printed page, it applies to much more than poetry.

And of course, the design of the page affects even the most unimaginative reader addressing himself to the most functionally informative page. But novelists and poets are not deceived; they know where their words will have to live. And some have an almost morbid concern about this future abode: George Moore thought title pages should be "as formal as gravestones"; and I have had fantasies of writing a novel by means of a whole symphonic orchestra of typewriters—each with a different typeface to represent a different voice, if not necessarily a different character. But such visual concerns are generally thought to be more important in the printing of poems than prose.

There is, in fact, a tradition of poetic "compositors"—part of which tradition can be clearly labeled as "concrete poetry"; and part of which is blurred, because there are many poets who utilize typographical means for their effects in greatly varying degrees, sometimes in the same poem. However, the effect itself is clear: whenever a poetic line is ended for nonmetrical or nonsyllabic reasons (any poem with ragged contours on the page), or for arbitrary metrical or syllabic reasons with a view to their placement on the page (e. g., the poems of Marianne Moore), then the poet has demonstrated a concern for visual design, since he has used typographical means to achieve his effects. It is no accident that a large percentage of the books published by today's private presses are volumes, or pamphlets, or broadsides, or chapbooks, or postcards, or even foldings of poetry. Their productions at best manifest a felicitous marriage, not only of form and content, but of form and form; and they are largely responsible for the flourishing and vitality of contemporary poetry.

These presses are often the work of one person, or a small group of people who share certain ideals of poetry and bookmaking. Old, seemingly atavistic craft values have been revived by these enthusiasts, and it is perhaps not surprising that their products are often characterized by the integrity and loving attentiveness that we associate with handcrafted things in a bewilderingly synthesized and mass-fabricated world. Though the individual operations are small, the movement is not. William Henderson, editor of The Pushcart Press, estimates that there are 2,500 small presses in the United States. From all this richness, he selects *The Pushcart Prize,* an anthology of pieces published each year in the small presses.

Given so much hard work and enthusiasm, it is no wonder that innovative techniques have been generated—not just in the making of chapbooks and poetry volumes, but even in "packaging" and "marketing" these products.

One of the most interesting of these new entrepreneurs is Ryan Petty, with his Cold Mountain Press in Austin, Texas. Cold Mountain was one of the first, if not the first press to make poetry postcards, selling a packet of five (one of which is signed by the poet) for only $1.50. Many of these poets (most are young) are unquestionably talented; and in a purely investment sense some of their autographs will no doubt be worth many times the cost of the packet in a few years.

Petty's distribution ideas are interesting, and best expressed in his own statement:

> My major premise is this: a small press desiring to publish poetry can do so using proceeds from the catalogue sales of modern first editions, autograph items, etc. It is based upon an observation: there are a substantial number of persons who earn their livelihoods in the rare-book business. Many of these people regularly sell items which were originally published by small presses . . . items which have subsequently become both well-known and scarce. At the same time I have observed that contemporary small press publishers *almost* never earn their livelihood through their publications (i. e., as a general rule, small press publishing is *not profitable*.) In the short run, it is almost a sure-fire loser. So my idea in broad scope has been to do the profitable (i. e., catalogue "rare" modern first editions and autographs) as a means to raise funds with which to do the unprofitable, the publication of modern literature. One subsidizing the other. The past literature recycled into the present. I sold my own rare-book collection to get started and now have none to my name. But I remain keenly interested in the market and occasionally buy and sell as I can.

"Innovative techniques" is hardly sufficient a term to describe Jonathan Williams' The Jargon Society. Williams has been referred to as "a poet, publisher, essayist, hiker and sorehead"—and listening to his prose, one wonders which function gives him the most pleasure. His Jargon Society is almost unlabelable—which sounds like echolalia, but tells the truth in this case. Williams lives his summers in England and his winters in North Carolina. He is also (in addition to all the offices celebrated above) an evangelist for poetry and art generally. His witnessing goes back to, in his words, " 'Bardstorming for Poetry' exploits of the 50s and 60s, when I was everywhere at once, selling books out of the back of ancient, oil-thirsty Pontiac station-wagons."

In one of Williams' brochures, a *New York Times Book Review* is quoted as saying, "Jargon had come to occupy a special place in our cultural life as patron of the American imagination . . . . But however attractive the books are to look at, and they are justly collector's items, the chief pleasure they afford is the intellectual shock of recognizing an original voice ignored by sanctioned critical opinion."

Williams is a born polemicist, a born advocate, and he stings the mind in unlikely places, waking it where it's been sleeping comfortably. Above all, he cares; and he cares about more than himself—his fury is not infantile; it is intended to be spent for others, for society, the world, us. If a writer is neglected, ignored, and gains Williams' respect, he is thereby fitted with a champion. One such victim is Alfred Starr Hamilton, a man now in his sixties, whom Williams sees as "an ignored caitiff; an 'original' poet, tuned in like Blake or Dickinson, vey occasionally, to a singular and moving world of words that he offers to one and all."

Another sturdy Jargonaut, sailing dangerously near to the Coast of Oblivion, is a novelist named Douglas Woolf, a copy of whose first book, *The Hypocritic Days* (no place of publication, The Divers Press, 1955), I recently got from Jim Lowell's Asphodel Book Shop for $12.50. (It was sold for $1.25 when first published.) Lowell recommended it to me when I asked, "Who are today's good but neglected writers?" It is a powerful short novel of some 35,000 words; and I consider myself fortunate to have this beautiful little handset, paperbound edition, printed in Mallorca over twenty years ago, typographical errors notwithstanding. (*These* will start no riots, Ms. Warde!) Woolf has continued writing, and I have already ordered another of his novels, and I intend to read and collect him further. How many other good, insightful, *needed* writers are toiling in that twilight of "silence, exile, and cunning"? The question is profoundly rhetorical, and the mere fact that it can be raised is something of an embarrassment to the mind and taste of our time.

Another writer Lowell recommended in response to my question was Haniel Long (I had never heard of him, either), a selection of whose work *If He Can Make Her So* (Pittsburgh, no date) is a beautifully made

155

book, containing a reproduction of a painting by John Kane that is splendid. For a hearing of Long's prose, I recommend the selection "Homestead" in this book—the work of a deep and honest writer.

What investment potential is there in books such as these? I don't believe a clear answer is at all possible now. Haniel Long, now deceased, lived a reasonably long and productive life, but he is hardly well known as a writer. Douglas Woolf, Alfred Starr Hamilton, and Lorine Niedecker—to use three writers promoted by Jargon as a sample—do not command high prices from dealers; and so far as I know, they have not reached that state where their works are listed at all in book auctions. Haniel Long's *Pittsburgh Memoranda* (Santa Fe, 1935) is offered for $10, and a copy of the signed limited edition of Lorine Niedecker's *North Central* (London, 1968) for $13.50, in The Phoenix Bookship's Catalogue No. 119. Elsewhere, the works of these writers are offered at a very low premium, if any at all—which suggests a good opportunity for these who like what they have to say, and how they say it.

The emphasis upon the Jargon Society publications is only a token acknowledgment of the tremendous proliferation and flourishing of small presses throughout the United States. It would be impossible simply to list them all, let alone do justice in describing their various qualities (and some are superbly worthy). Often a collector will cultivate them because of their promotion and advocacy of specific writers he collects: if you collect Henry Miller, you will want to know about the Capra Press in Santa Barbara; if you collect Gary Snyder, you will need to have a copy of *The Fudo Trilogy*, published in 1973 by the Shaman Drum in Berkeley; if your interest is Charles Bukowski or Diane Wakoski, you will need to be familiar with the Black Sparrow Press in Los Angeles. All of these presses like to print contemporary poetry, do handsome work, and happen to be located in California, but beyond those facts have little in common. Other states and regions have their share of presses that bring out fine editions of living writers. Sometimes these come from seemingly unlikely places, but most have some direct or indirect connection with colleges and universities. A few university presses, "Friends of the Library" groups, and even special collections are engaged significantly in publishing ventures such as these. The Kent (Ohio) University libraries, for example, brought out in 1971 *Six Poems/Seven Prints*, featuring poems by John Ashbery, Gwendolyn Brooks, Denise Levertov, Gary Snyder, and others, and prints by Alex Katz, Mary Ann Begland Sacco, Robert Smithson, and others. Referred to as a "special edition of *Occasional Papers*," this excellently designed little packet deceives no one—it is a collector's item, pure and simple; and a few years after its publication, found listings in various catalogues in the $25-to-$50 range.

Experiments in format, lush sheaves of heavy paper, bold and colorful type designs, a wild variety of illustrations—from photo montage to color adaptations of American Indian designs—all of these characterize the small-press movement today. But at their heart will be the ultimately undeniable fact of the language—the poem which is the cause and occasion that has called forth all this skillfulness and joy.

In response to the term "poet's poet," someone once asked rhetorically, "Is there any other kind?" We seek out our own mysteries and solutions in others as well as in ourselves. Thus it is natural that poets who in their own work show a concern for typography, visual design, format, and quality of materials (paper) should also be interested in such matters beyond the horizon of their own productions. One of the greatest (and of course, one of the most collectable) of modern poets is Wallace Stevens. The Spring 1974 issue of *The Book Collector* (Vol. 23, No.1), contains an essay by J. M. Edelstein, titled "The Poet as Reader: Wallace Stevens and His Books," in which Stevens' lifelong interest in fine printing is discussed. This interest, Edelstein claims, transcended the poet's natural concern over the appearance of his own books.

> . . . his [Stevens's] letters to J. Ronald Lane Latimer at the Alcestis Press, to Katharine Frazier and Harry Duncan at the Cummington Press, to Victor Hammer at the Anvil Press, to James Guthrie at the Pear Tree Press and to others show a man with great knowledge and a refined taste in all matters of book production and design. He liked press books and he bought them. The Nonesuch Press edition of *The Anatomy of Melancholy*, 1925, is one; the Nonesuch Press *Selected Poems of Coleridge*, 1935, is another; the Pear Tree Press *Life of Saint David*, Edited by Ernest Rhys, 1927, is another; and there are more.

Near the end of this interesting essay, Edelstein makes the astonishing assertion that "Wallace Stevens was not a bibliophile or book collector in the usual sense." His argument is that, while Stevens bought a great many books, he had the means to have a much grander library than he did in fact have; and then Edelstein says, "To Stevens books were useful instruments of knowledge before they were objects of aesthetic value." This is of course nonsense, if it is true (as Edelstein has previously asserted) that Stevens liked and bought press books: no one would ever buy the Nonesuch *Anatomy of Melancholy* for the "content" alone—there are too many cheap editions that are perfectly legible, and just as useful as the Nonesuch edition. Apparently for some people, the term "book collector" is as semantically charged as "invest" is for others.

I doubt very much if Wallace Stevens had any such problem however; and Edelstein quotes a delicious notation which the poet made in the margin of his Hogarth Press edition (he was a subscriber) of Charles Mauron's *Aesthetics and Psychology* (translated from the French by Roger Fry and Katharine John, and published in 1935):

> Originality is an accumulation through sensibility, or difference perceived . . . the sensibility of the artist makes an original being of him, an *amoureux perpétuel* of the world that he contemplates and thereby enriches. He adds to the pleasures of the world his own.

With a few adjustments, this could be scored as a poem. And in the present context, one cannot read it without thinking of Stevens himself, who knowingly and sensitively collected fine books so that they could accumulate about and in his own sensibility, and serve as an abiding source of his inspiration.

Collecting modern private press books is, if not worldwide, at least international. Tangibly connected with the movement of poetry into visual form, the modern private press tradition flourishes and grows, not just in England and the United States, but in continental Europe, as well, where the various modes of concrete poetry appear to be exploited much more diligently, and taken much more seriously, than in England and, especially, the United States. Books of concrete poetry, with their commitment to significant typographic design, strive to extend the horizons of page, book, and type; and they are therefore a natural interest for typophiles and other collectors of private press books and limited editions. But of course private presses do not limit their production to poetry—much less to the concrete poetry movement; and they do in fact bring out editions of classics as well as contemporary books of distinction.

With the internationalization of the rare-book market, a great many American collector–investors are drawing from European sources. Lately, because of the dramatic aberration of currencies, the careful investor will follow the adventures of the pound sterling, the franc, the mark, and the dollar with great interest. One factor that mitigates whatever disadvantage there might be for the American collector at any particular time is the fact that the modern private press movement—while indeed "modern"—has nevertheless been around for almost a century and a lot of their books have been assimilated into American libraries, private collections, and dealers' stocks.

While English and American private presses, with certain notable exceptions (e.g., Walpole's Strawberry Hill) are essentially a twentieth-century movement, on the continent the tradition is much older, the Dutch firm of Enschedé, for example, having a consecutive publication history of over two hundred years. Of course, Dutch printers, generally, have been famous longer than that, being especially influential in the seventeenth century when the Elzivirs prospered.

S. H. deRoos is considered Holland's greatest figure in modern book crafting, having designed various types—Erasmus, Grotius, Egmont, and Libra, for example—and having had a bibliophile society in Utrecht named after him. His fame notwithstanding, most of his limited editions are available in the $25 to $100 range. Such master-printers as Charles Nypels, A. A. M. Stols (of The Halcyon Press, which has printed editions of English and French authors, as well), and such presses as Boucher, Kunera, and *De Bezige Bij* ("The Busy Bee") have perpetuated the great tradition of Dutch printing. ·

Having relied upon Bertram Rota's *The Printer and the Artist,* for much of the above information, I can no do no better than quote verbatim from this solid and useful work in my brief reference to private presses in Germany:

> The Germans seem always to have believed in form nearly as much as in content, and this passionate dedication to the shape and feel of a book led to almost incessant experimentation with letter forms, layout, illustrations, papers and bindings. Even so small a matter as a specially designed or handwritten initial could acquire enormous importance in the mind of a typographer or printer or publisher. There are those who would dismiss this preoccupation as absurd, but it produced, as Stanley

159

Morison has argued, some of the most vigorous and exciting printing of the twentieth century. Happily that process continues and German artists and printers are working together to produce books of well-nigh unsurpassable quality.

Some of the more famous German presses are Bremer (possibly the best known of all), Cranach, Eggebrecht, Paul Cassirer, Ernst Ludwig (named for its founder, the Grand Duke), Janus (this and the previous were both founded in 1907, thus inaugurating the modern private press in Germany), Mainz, Klingspor, and of course many more.

While the Bremer Press edition of Tacitus' *De Situ Moribus et Populis Germaniae qui Fertur Libellus,* with a German translation by Rudolf Borchardt (Bremen, 1914) sells for $200 to $300, and the Cranach Press' *Canticum Canticorum Salmonis* (illustrated by Eric Gill) commands a similar price, most German press books are priced considerably below those figures. Along with the Dutch presses, they provide excellent opportunities for American collectors to acquire beautifully made fine press and illustrated books actively and at a reasonable cost.

The pseudonymous "Maximilien Vox"* once wrote: "The demands of the French bibliophile differ from those of the English or American booklover, who wants a perfect book. We require the grandiose book."

What he refers to is exemplified by a kind of book that is distinctively French—the *livre d'artiste.* This is more than simply an "illustrated book," or an "art book"—it is an individual performance, a tour de force, by an artist of reputation, who takes personal responsibility for the individual plates of a limited edition, exactly as he would preside over the quality of each print in a limited numbered edition. In the past, this has given the *livre d'artiste* something of a reputation for being little more than boards bound together to protect the art work, because of the strong emphasis placed upon it, an emphasis that was perhaps inevitable in view of the fact that most of the great masters of modern French painting interested themselves in the medium of the book. It is no wonder, therefore, that what might otherwise have been merely "illustration" of a text, more often than not dominated the book, traditionally thought of as the domain of print.

This reputation for neglecting the binding, paper, and type, thereby reducing them to means toward the end of displaying an artist's prints,

*Real name: William Théodore Samuel, *Typographe d'art.*

160

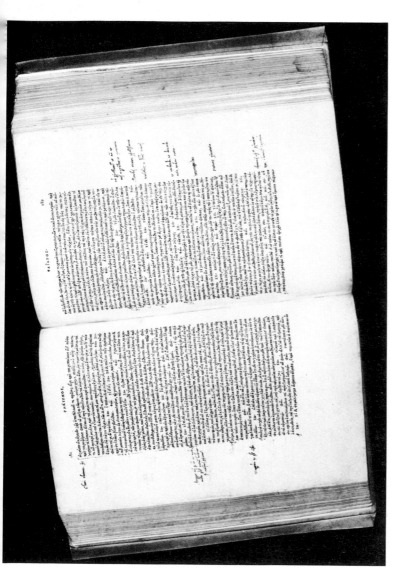

Plato. *Opera*. The first complete Plato, printed and published by Aldus Manutius of Venice, 1513. It is a folio volume printed in Greek letter.

Courtesy House of El Dieff

A landmark in fine binding: Cobden-Sanderson's *The Poetical Works of Percy Bysshe Shelley*, The Kelmscott Press, 1894–95. The binding is of natural pigskin, elaborately gilt-tooled.

Courtesy House of El Dieff

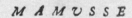

MAMUSSE
WUNNEETUPANATAMWE
UP-BIBLUM GOD
NANEESWE
NUKKONE TESTAMENT
KAH WONK
WUSKU TESTAMENT.

Ne quoſhkinnumuk naſhpe Wuttinneumoh *CHRIST*
noh aſoowesit

JOHN ELIOT·

CAMBRIDGE:

Printeuꝏp naſhpe *Samuel Green* kah *Marmaduke Johnſon.*

1 6 6 3·

John Eliot's famous Indian Bible, printed in Cambridge, 1663. A milestone in early American printing. A copy sold for $22,000 at Sotheby Parke Bernet in 1976.

Courtesy Sotheby Parke Bernet, Inc., New York

D. Gower

TRAVELS

INTO SEVERAL

Remote NATIONS

OF THE

WORLD.

In FOUR PARTS.

By *LEMUEL GULLIVER*,
Firſt a SURGEON, and then a CAP-
TAIN of ſeveral SHIPS.

VOL. I.

LONDON:

Printed for BENJ. MOTTE, *at the*
Middle Temple-Gate *in* Fleet-ſtreet.
MDCCXXVI.

Jonathan Swift's immortal *Gulliver's Travels*, first edition, London, 1726.
Two volumes. A copy sold for $2,500 in 1976.
Courtesy Sotheby Parke Bernet, Inc., New York

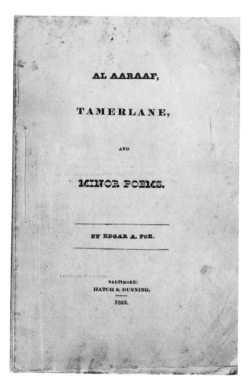

The second most important Poe first edition. Some copies appear in blue or reddish-tan boards; others stitched, without covers.
Courtesy Sotheby Parke Bernet, Inc., New York

Edgar Allan Poe's first published work and probably the most desired of all American literary first editions. It appeared in printed wrappers.
Courtesy Sotheby Parke Bernet, Inc., New York

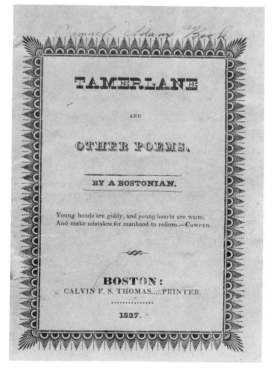

A N

ELEGY

WROTE IN A

Country Church Yard.

LONDON:

Printed for R. Dodsley in *Pall-mall*;

And sold by M. Cooper in *Pater-noster-Row.* 1751.

[Price Six-pence.]

Thomas Gray's great poem, first edition, London, 1751. A copy, rebound in Morocco, sold for $3,600 in 1976.

Courtesy Sotheby Parke Bernet, Inc., New York

Poor RICHARD improved:

BEING AN

ALMANACK

AND

EPHEMERIS

OF THE

MOTIONS of the SUN and MOON;

THE TRUE

PLACES and ASPECTS of the PLANETS;

THE

RISING and *SETTING* of the *SUN*;

AND THE

Rising, Setting *and* Southing *of the* Moon,

FOR THE

YEAR of our LORD 1 7 5 8:

Being the Second after LEAP-YEAR.

Containing also,

The Lunations, Conjunctions, Eclipses, Judgment of the Weather, Rising and Setting of the Planets, Length of Days and Nights, Fairs, Courts, Roads, &c. Together with useful Tables, chronological Observations, and entertaining Remarks.

Fitted to the Latitude of Forty Degrees, and a Meridian of near five Hours West from *London*; but may, without sensible Error, serve all the NORTHERN COLONIES.

By *RICHARD SAUNDERS*, Philom.

PHILADELPHIA:

Printed and Sold by B. FRANKLIN, and D. HALL.

Benjamin Franklin imprint. *Poor Richard Improved*, Philadelphia, 1758. Copies of this work list for more than $2,000 in good condition.

Courtesy Sotheby Park Bernet, Inc., New York

THE

President's Address

TO THE

PEOPLE

OF THE

UNITED STATES,

ANNOUNCING HIS INTENTION OF

R'ETIRING FROM PUBLIC LIFE

AT THE EXPIRATION OF THE

PRESENT CONSTITUTIONAL TERM

OF

PRESIDENCY.

PHILADELPHIA:

PRINTED FOR *J. ORMROD*, No. 41, CHESNUT-STREET,

BY ORMROD AND CONRAD.

1796.

George Washington's "Farewell Address," Philadelphia, 1796. This
23-page work, first edition, brought $13,000 at auction in 1976.

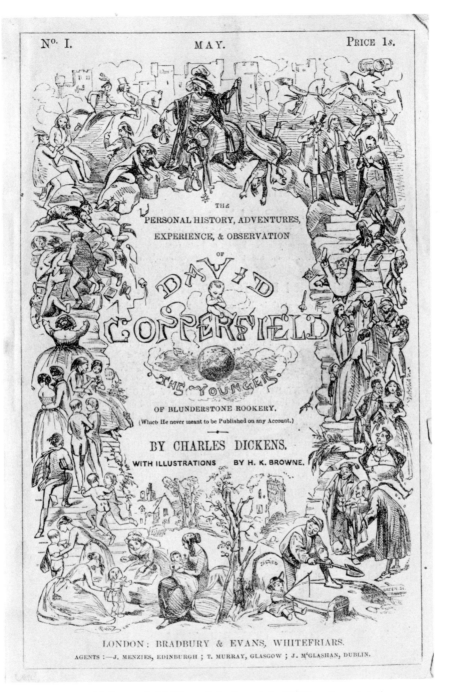

Dickens' *David Copperfield*. The original work in 19/20 parts, printed
wrappers. London, 1849–50. The copy brought $1,400 at auction in 1976.
Courtesy Sotheby Parke Bernet, Inc., New York

(Printed for private circulation only).

SCHOOLBOY LYRICS,

BY

RUDYARD KIPLING.

Lahore.
Printed at the "Civil and Military Gazette" Press.

1881.

One of Kipling's scarcest books. The first issue appears in either plain white wrappers or printed brown wrappers.

Courtesy Sotheby Parke Bernet, Inc., New York

TRAVELS

IN

MEXICO AND CALIFORNIA:

COMPRISING A JOURNAL OF A TOUR FROM BRAZOS SANTIAGO, THROUGH
CENTRAL MEXICO, BY WAY OF MONTEREY, CHIHUAHUA, THE
COUNTRY OF THE APACHES, AND THE RIVER GILA, TO THE
MINING DISTRICTS OF CALIFORNIA.

BY A. B. CLARKE.

BOSTON:

WRIGHT & HASTY, PRINTERS,

NO. 3 WATER STREET.

1852.

A rare narrative, of interest to all Americana collectors. A copy in the
original wrappers brought $400 in 1976.

Courtesy Sotheby Parke Bernet, Inc., New York

Walt Whitman's *Leaves of Grass*, America's greatest work of poetry. First published anonymously in Brooklyn, 1885. The first binding is dark green cloth with gilt and blind stamping, with edges gilt.

Courtesy House of El Dieff

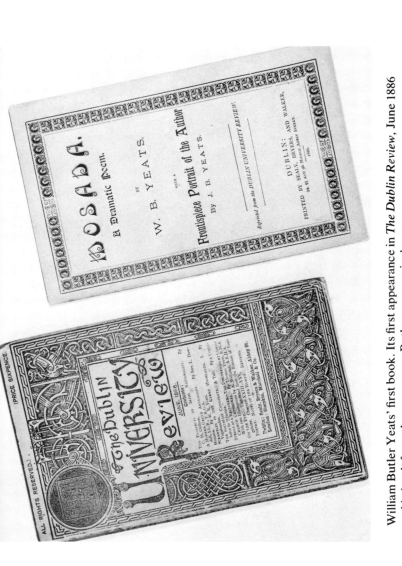

William Butler Yeats' first book. Its first appearance in *The Dublin Review*, June 1886 and in book form the same year. Both are excessively rare.

Courtesy Sotheby Parke Bernet, Inc., New York

Elinor Wylie's first book, printed in London, 1912. About 65 copies were issued, without author's name. One of the scarcest of all modern first editions.

Courtesy Sotheby Parke Bernet, Inc., New York

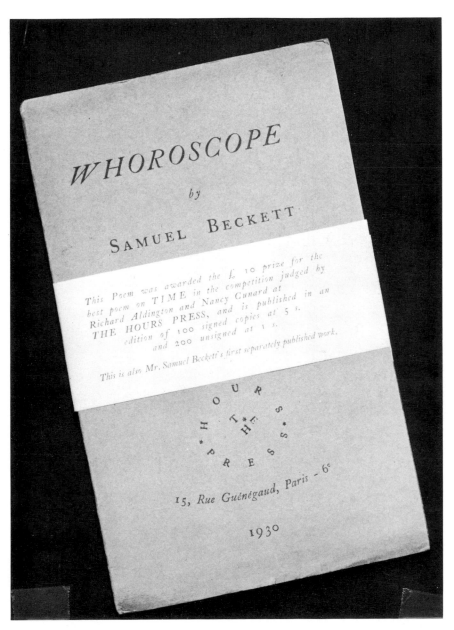

Samuel Beckett's first appearance in book form. It appeared in fragile wrappers and is the cornerstone of a Beckett collection.

Courtesy House of El Dieff

DEATHS AND ENTRANCES

Poems by
DYLAN THOMAS

LONDON : J. M. DENT & SONS LTD.

A key book in a Dylan Thomas collection. Published in London (1946). The copyright page must say "First published 1946."

is not really justified, however. Ambroise Vollard, whose historical importance in the development of the modern book in France is somewhat like that of William Morris in England, was from the very beginning of his career in the early 1890s concerned with the total book. And while he was enlisting the "illustrations" of Rodin, Bernard, Picasso, Dufy, Braque, Rouault, Chagall, and many others, he nevertheless gave his energies to matters of typography, paper, binding, and total design. Like the conductor of a symphony, Vollard's genius lay in his ability to create the final harmony of the book from the teamwork of individual artists, presiding over the total production as *maître d'oeuvre*. The June 25–26, 1975, auction at Christie's was rich in modern French rarities; and among them was a copy of Vollard's *August Renoir* (Paris, 1920), inscribed by Vollard, which sold for £65 ($156). Another copy sold at Christie's for £70 at their February 18, 1976, sale.

Under such passionate industry as Vollard's, the modern book in France has flowered into something that is, as Vox's quotation demands, "grandiose." It goes back farther than the career of Vollard, of course—already evident, for example, in the frontispiece etching made by Felix Bracquemond of Baudelaire, in the 1861 edition of *Fleurs du Mal*. And as for the premium given to such magnificence—it only awaited the great artists who were to accept the book as their medium; and by 1960, when the *Tauromaquia* of Pepe Illo was published, illustrated with twenty-six etchings by Picasso, there were customers lined up, waiting to pay $2,000 a copy, a price that doubled soon afterward. Picasso, of course, almost requires a separate and distinct category. In spite of his astonishing industry and the great number of productive years in his long life, his illustrated books demand booming prices, year after year. In a Sotheby Parke Bernet sale early in 1976, a copy of the limited edition of Balzac's *Le Chef-d'Oeuvre Inconnu* (Paris, 1931), containing twelve original etchings by Picasso (one of 240) brought $3,000. This sale consisted of a total of twenty modern French books illustrated by Bonnard, Braque, Degas, Chagall, Toulouse-Lautrec, Dufy, Matisse, and so on. The lowest price was $100; the highest was the Picasso mentioned above. Most of the books sold in the $300 to $800 range.

At a sale three months earlier, Picasso's illustrations for Buffon, *Eaux-Fortes Originales pour les Textes de Buffon* (Paris, Fabiani, 1942), brought $7,000. Limited to 226 copies and more exclusively one of 55 on vélin de Montval, the rarity of this copy was further increased by the fact that many of its siblings were destroyed by mildew while stored in a warehouse during World War II. It has been called "one of the great bestiaries of the twentieth century." Another book illustrated by Picasso, Tristan Tzara's *De Mémoire d'Homme* (Paris, 1950), one of 300 copies, went for $400.

The *livre d'artiste* exemplifies an attitude vastly different from the Anglo-Saxon world's traditional coolness toward the illustrated book. (There are still vestiges of the idea that "picture books" are exclusively children's books.) Philip Hofer points this out in this introduction to *The Artist and the Book: 1860–1960,* where he also tries to explain the reason for the "explosion" of success with such opulent productions when they are so staggeringly expensive. He was writing specifically about the exhibition of illustrated books at the Museum of Fine Arts in Boston, but his comments are relevant to the whole growth of the modern illustrated book as an art form:

> Another main purpose of this exhibition, therefore, is to demonstrate to the English-speaking world that during the last century *the book has, in fact, become a major vehicle of artistic expression:* that it is one in which the artist is not necessarily secondary to the author, but is often and rightly his equal. Indeed, in some cases, illustration is the major substantive factor in the book that finally appears. This is especially true in France, which possesses not only great artists, but also great technicians. Finally, the illustrated book usually offers the purchasers two values at once: an artist's designs and a text in words—a combined pictorial and literary expression of man's best creative talent. Inexpensive books with reproductive illustrations will also do this—but only at a loss of irreplaceable artistic values. The layman may be content with photomechanical prints. The connoisseur never is except for reference purposes.

In France, the great commercial publishers have somewhat eclipsed the private press movement, or rather have drawn it into their own orbits, producing a bewildering variety of special, limited, "prepublication" editions of novels, poetry, and nonfiction, along with the printing of the *livres d'artiste.*

Collectors of modern French first editions (not by any means limited to collectors in France) are confronted with more than the usual arabesque of points that bemuse and fascinate the collector. One such collector bewails the "French habit of making limited editions of virtually all their books . . . so that the unwary may think he or she has got the genuine first edition, when all he or she has is the first trade edition." But alas, this appears to be not so much a Gallic convention as it is a Gallic confusion, and not only will the editor of one firm understandably profess total ignorance of the time-honored habits of another, but he will sometimes profess ignorance of his own firm's practices, suggesting that his grasp of English is not sufficient to respond to a foreign inquiry so direct that it might lead to the breaking of his sworn oath to protect the hieratic trade secrets he has been entrusted with.

To explain the general French practice in this regard would no doubt be more complicated than explaining their foreign policy; but there is some light available, after all—and this from Jérôme Lindon of the firm Les Editions de Minuit, the publisher of Samuel Beckett's works, who writes:

> Two cases present themselves in the matter of the "original editions" of Samuel Beckett in French:
>
> a) When it's a matter of very short texts (for example, *Imagination Morte Imaginez, Assez, Bing, Sans, Pas Moi*) we proceed to a printing of some hundreds on deluxe paper. The whole, homogeneous, constitutes that original edition. The works in question are afterwards taken up again and regrouped in larger works (*Têtes Mortes, Comédie et Actes Divers*, etc.)
>
> b) When it's a matter of texts of normal size, we print, at the same time as the first edition on ordinary paper, a certain number of copies (usually less than a hundred) on deluxe paper, which constitutes the original edition, properly speaking. This is the case with *Molloy,* and *En Attendant Godot,* for example.
>
> The copies of this printing on large paper, authenticated by both the words "printing completed" at the end of the volume [i.e., a colophon] and the "justification of the printing" [*Justification du tirage*] have considerable bibliophilic value which results from both the reputation of the book and the reduced number of copies printed. Thus one of the thirty-five copies on large paper of the original edition of *En Attendant Godot,* put on sale for 1,000 old francs (10 present-day francs) in 1952, was resold two or three years ago for $3,000.

If the attention I have just given to twentieth-century private press books, limited editions, illustrated books, and so on (surely, there should be some generic term for all these!) seems disproportionate, it can't be helped, for collecting such books is perhaps one of the strongest trends in today's market.

Of course, there are numerous "trends" in collecting, and always have been, and many of these have been risky, from an investment standpoint. Black Sun's Harvey Tucker says, "Current popularity has always been dependent on media, and we find that the 'currently' popular author, unless competent and gifted, is subject to the fluctuating trends of our speeding culture." Tucker claims that books that have stood some test of time are a "better bet."

Black Sun's specialties include first editions, original art, and nineteenth- and twentieth-century illustrated books. "These have intrinsic merit as well as some aesthetic value," Tucker points out. "The modern collector is thus able to enjoy this type of item from more than one angle. There is also," he adds (not at all parenthetically), "the everpresent knowledge that good things increase in value."

Most dealers agree that high quality illustrated books, private press books, and signed limited editions of every sort are some of the most promising fields for modern collecting-investing; and most feel that the high appreciation rate of such books has been sustained so long that the danger of their eventually proving overinflated is slight.

Fine books have always been emphatic of good print, good paper, good binding. Books are, after all, things of this world, and capable of physical beauty and justified of being honored for realizing this beauty.

Probably America's greatest artist-printer was Bruce Rogers, who states the principles of aesthetic typography very simply and clearly:

> A perfect book is both easy to read and beautiful to look at. Pleasure in the reading matter itself is enhanced by pleasure in its suitable frame. An excellent balance of black and white lessens the effort of reading, and the eye unconsciously approves of both ensemble and details without being distracted by them.
>
> The art of printing abounds in subtle difficulties, in delicate nuances unsuspected by the majority of people. The masters of this art work with enthusiasm and devotion to satisfy a select few. One may reproach an author with meticulousness that cuts him off from appreciation by the masses, but not a printer. Stendhal quotes an exaggerated case—the great Bodoni, a mas-

ter printer, who spent six months looking for a single line of capitals to put on a title page of Boileau-Despreaux!*

There are a very few artist printers, and there are a very few scholar-printers—and Bruce Rogers is one of that still smaller class who can be included in both lists. His testament clearly demonstrates that while this sojourn through the realm of modern fine-book production and the typographic art generally may have seemed incommensurate, perhaps even eccentric, I have actually erred in the opposite direction, by treating so vast and complex a subject so casually, even omitting whole nations—such as Italy, Spain, Belgium, and the Scandinavian, and Latin American countries—in my attempt to give some coherence to that limited sampling of limited editions the focus and length of the present work require.

Nor should I leave the subject without comment upon what might have occasionally seemed an invidious comparison between the modern European (particularly French) and the American attention given to the book as objet d'art. Illustrated books have always been popular, everywhere. Such invidiousness will, I hope, be largely a matter of emphasis, rather than category. People who like illustrations in their books . . . well, like *illustrations* in their books. And this has always been the case. One of these people was Edmund Wilson, who wrote:

> I like picture books in general of the comic or fantastic kind: Gilray, Rowlandson, Fuseli, Spitzweg, Cruikshank, Phiz, Edward Lear, Beardsley, Toulouse-Lautrec, George du Maurier, Phil May, Max Beerbohm, Sem, Max Ernst, Marc Chagall, Peggy Bacon, Saul Steinberg, Leonard Baskin, Edward Gorey—to mention people of very different magnitudes.**

Not only of very different magnitudes, but of different times and places, and of course representing wonderfully different styles—from

*Letter publ. in *The Saturday Review of Literature,* October 29, 1927; reprinted in *PI: A Hodge Podge of the Letters and Papers Written During the Last Sixty Years by Bruce Rogers,* Cleveland, 1953.
**"Every Man His Own Eckermann," in *The Bit Between My Teeth,* New York, 1965, p. 583.

165

the heavy satire of Rowlandson to the delicate sadness of Toulouse-Lautrec; the sensible grotesquerie of Cruikshank to the tangled definitions of Leonard Baskin.

The marriage of picture and print is a felicitous one, and their progeny unforgettable. We all know that a picture is worth one thousand words, but of course it requires words to make that statement (although it could be approximated visually by means of a scale with a framed picture in one pan and a thousand words balancing out in the other, but which picture should be represented, and what words?).

The power and effectiveness implicit in type and the printed page as problems of visual design seem infinite. To express it, I can hardly do better than reproduce (that is, visually quote) a page from the fifth edition of Edward Johnston's *Writing & Illuminating & Lettering* (London, 1913). The specific effect under consideration is that of spacing; but the text of Johnston's sample is so telling in itself, and the tripartite message is so wise and so vividly transformed into the visual triad demonstrated for their several effects on the page, that I cannot but think this is a wise communication, applicable not only to the visible, particular page, but to life, manifold and general:

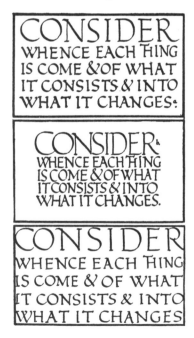

IX.

COLLECTING

THE KIDDIES

I t is hard to establish anything like a precise date for the invention of children; all we can be sure of is that childhood was, over a period of years, brought into being as a special entity, replacing that crepuscular apprenticeship for adulthood that once existed in its place. Speaking of the society in which Elizabeth Turner's *The Daisy: Or, Cautionary Stories in Verse* (Philadelphia, 1808) appeared, Max Beerbohm wrote: "Children were not then recognized as human creatures. They were a race apart; savages that must be driven from the gates; beasts to be kept in cages; devils to whose voices one must not listen." They may have been hated, but they were also just as often ignored. Earlier literature is virtually devoid of children *as* children; and even with the advent of the Victorian age, with the creation of a sentimental child image that seemed almost the personal monopoly of Dickens (Little Nell, Oliver Twist, and so on), there were still vestiges of the dark, unformed creature with the old Adam in his heart. The illegitimate Pearl in *The Scarlet Letter* is no doubt intended to be a somewhat vague and emblematic character; but she is also a believable one to a Victorian readership composed of people many of whom ate dinner seated, while their children stood. And still later in the century, Louisa May Alcott could write happily about children, and yet term them "little women" and "little men."

This momentous creation—like that similar one of a sentimentalized

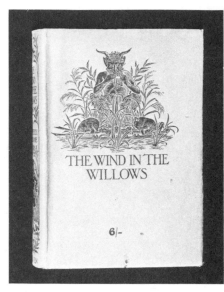

Courtesy of Sotheby Parke Bernet, Inc., New York

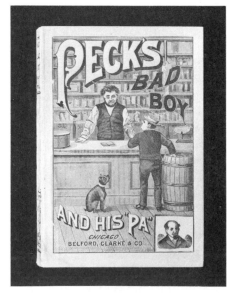

Nature—was the product of a long, slow change in attitude. It antedates the popular Victorian entertainment, for the seventeenth and eighteenth century had their version of children's books—the first that can be identified as a genre; the first *real* children's books—which is to say (in the good phrase of Charles J. Sawyer and F. J. Harvey Darton in *English Books 1475–1900,* Westminster, 1927), "books *for* children, not *at* them." The dominant figure of this movement is John Newbery, an eighteenth-century London publisher and bookseller, who also dabbled in the sale of patent medicines. He is best remembered for his Juvenile Library, which features such titles as *Tommy Trip and His Dog Jowler, The Twelfth Day Gift,* and *Goody Two-shoes.* The last is commonly believed to have been written by none other than Oliver Goldsmith, whom Newbery befriended early in his career. Goldsmith said that Newbery was "the friend of all mankind"—which seems probable, at least for that portion that are, or have ever been, children.

Goody Two-shoes was brought out in this country by the renowned early American printer, Isaiah Thomas, at Worcester, Massachusetts, in 1787. A. Edward Newton's copy was sold at auction in 1968 for $625; then sold again in January, 1974, for $1,000. The true first edition, published by Newbery, is one of the superb rarities among books. Sawyer and Darton claim that in 1900 only one copy of the first edition was known to exist. When the Singing Tree Press of Detroit brought out a facsimile edition in 1970, they reprinted the facsimile edition of 1881, which was, as the introduction states, from "the earliest complete copy that we have been able to procure." This copy was of the third edition, printed in 1766, a year after the first.

John Newbery began publishing in 1740, and one of his earliest authors was Sarah Fielding, first editions of whose *The Adventures of David Simple* (Two vols., London, 1744) are still available at prices between $200 and $500, at auction or over the bookseller's counter. Later, Newbery brought out another book by Sarah Fielding bearing a considerably heavier title: *The Governess; or, Little Female Academy, Being the History of Mrs. Teachum, and her Nine Girls.* This book was published in 1749, the same year in which Sarah Fielding's brother, Henry, had his novel *Tom Jones* published.

Children's books have always been collectable, but today their stock seems to be rising at a faster rate than ever before. Their charm is obvious, and always has been: they are little vessels of nostalgia, coming to us out of our own childhoods, regardless of their publication date, and richly laden with cargoes of adventure, magic, and early memories.

Their value has always been enhanced, too, by the terrible risks of their voyages in time—for, being children's books, they have after all been in the custody of little hands, motivated by all sorts of affection, no doubt, but murderous in the power to mutilate, tear, smudge, and destroy books. This fact helps explain why a copy of the first edition of *Tom Sawyer* (1876) usually sells for over twice that of *Huckleberry Finn* (1885). It is true that *Tom Sawyer* is older, and other things being equal, should have fewer copies remaining; but also *Tom Sawyer* is a boy's book in a way that *Huckleberry Finn* is not, and it has been read to destruction over the fastest route known—in the hands of young boys.

The true first edition of *Alice in Wonderland* (London, 1865) was suppressed shortly after it was run off, apparently because its author did not approve of the illustrations. Copies of this rarity are virtually all recorded somewhere by somebody, and their movements from owner to owner are watched over with the avidity of a well-behaved Airedale watching the family cat eat its dinner. Whenever one is next offered for sale, it will bring a price of five figures; even battered and defective copies have sold for two and three thousand dollars. As a collector's prize, *Alice* is obviously sui generis.

The Victorian and Edwardian periods were particularly rich in children's literature. And the price stability of books from these years is impressive. Robert Louis Stevenson's classic *Treasure Island* (First ed., London, 1883) has not only held its own, it has appreciated dizzily over the past decade. It is actually a fairly common book; in 1967, three copies were sold at auction, bringing an average price of $72. In 1970, there were three other copies of the first edition sold, averaging $90. In 1974, a single copy sold for $250.

Like *Alice,* Beatrix Potter's *Peter Rabbit* was written for a young child—a boy; and its publication in 1893 marked the birth of a child's classic. The authoress illustrated as well as wrote the book, and the blending of verbal and pictorial images has proved a source of delight for the generations since. Beatrix Potter's favorite of all her books was *The Tailor of Gloucester* (London, 1902). Bertram Rota offered a copy of the first edition for £150, or $360, in their Spring 1970 catalogue. Only four years later, another copy sold at auction for £220, or $520.

No account, however brief, could omit reference to A. A. Milne as an author of children's books. *Winnie-the-Pooh* suffered the whimsical indignity several years ago of being translated into Latin, in a spirit of scholarly play. Signed limited editions of this children's classic were printed in two series: the larger, consisting of 350 copies, Van Allen Bradley evaluates at $200 to $300; the smaller limited editions, consisting of only 20 copies on vellum, at $400 to $500.

Many of A. A. Milne's books have been published in limited signed editions, and the fact that they are widely coveted keeps their prices high. *The House at Pooh Corner* (London, 1928) in the limited signed edition also sells for as high as $500 (one of 20 on Japan paper) and *Now We Are Six* for almost as much.

It is evident that anyone with a child's bank account will be left out in the competition for these handsome rarities; but not all is lost—the trade editions are handsome investments, too, and available at much lower prices. Some will cost as much as a good sport coat or an inexpensive chain saw, but for a collector this will prove an easy expenditure. And some will crop up at bargain prices in catalogues or on dealers' shelves. A first-edition copy of *Now We Are Six* was sold by a dealer in 1970 for only five pounds, or $12. In just three years, a similar copy was sold for £24, or $58. Dealers' catalogues are bonanzas of opportunity, for those who have eyes to see, and the initiative to act upon the evidence revealed.

Children's books are traditionally illustrated, and sometimes the illustrations are a greater factor in establishing price of a rarity than the text. In the realm of the first edition, the ratio of values between text and illustrations in any particular title is impossible to know, since the illustrations are integral to the first edition, and there is no way to tell how much those illustrations are worth relative to the rest of the book.

The prevailing notion has always been that children can respond to pictures long before they can read; and that this response is developmental, so that by the time they can read at, say, the fifth-grade level, their ability to appreciate pictures has developed still further, up to the point where the meaning available from the printed page is thought to be so much greater than illustrations that the pictorial element is left behind as propaedeutic and therefore expendable.

This view should not shame the lover of illustrated books. It may be that there is a stage in our intellectual development where illustrations are no longer necessary for the visualization of narrative or ideational events; but that doesn't mean they cannot continue to enrich a reader's conception of the book, clear to the limits imposed by the artist's power and the reader's understanding. The fact is that sometimes the most austere text may profit from an exploitation of all the visual means implicit in the gallery of the page. Thus it is that even when illustrations are put aside as playthings fit only for childish amusement, they sneak back disguised as nonpictorial embellishments, as inessential charts and graphs, maps, headpieces, marginal designs, and a dozen other decorative minuets and filigrees.

The bias of the art of book illustration toward the young reader is only that, a bias, and not in the least necessary or categorical. Many older books were illustrated pretty much as a matter of course; and it is true that as one goes back in time, the literacy rate declines pretty steadily—which suggests that larger and larger percentages of readers read at a child's level. Still, there is no need to assume a superior attitude towards Victorian three-deckers because they were usually illustrated. And contemporary illustrated books are among the most expensive, most sought-after treasures. These will deserve a place for themselves, as will illustrated trade books, in spite of the fact that a goodly number of them will also be children's books.

Returning to the subject of children's books proper, it will be useful to consider a variety that has, in spite of years of contempt and ridicule, finally proclaimed something in the way of victory, simply by the fact that they are being collected today by an increasing number of people. I am speaking of all those various cheap-paper editions that have flourished parasitically upon the book industry for centuries, evolving from broadsides and chapbooks into dime novels and comic books. The emphasis in such productions has always been entertainment of the simplest, and often bloodiest, sort. The stories are epic, conventional, and grand; and when they are told in verse (as they originally were) they are calculated neither to furrow the brow of youth, nor let anything in the way of psychology or subtlety inhibit the sturdy progress of the tale.

One of the oldest of these "penny histories" (the word "history" is related to "story," and at one time made no particular distinction between the two meanings) is that of Guy of Warwick, which was born sometime in the thirteenth century, and put on the armor of print before 1500. The enormous popularity of this Medieval Romance lasted for centuries, enduring translations into verse and prose, and being illustrated by woodcuts of many descriptions. My copy of a late eighteenth-century chapbook in rhyme, titled *The Valiant Soldier,* and another with the jazzily abbreviated title, *K. William & The Plowman; or, Industry Reward-*

172

ed, both have cover illustrations of a soldier on horseback that is marvelously like that of the British Museum copy titled *The History of Guy, Earl of Warwick.* A few changes have been made in my soldier's equipment, however: instead of the pig's head fixed on a stake, which Guy carried, my soldier sensibly holds aloft a carbine, with another slung over his shoulder. He also wears a tricornered hat, although it rides so high on his head it appears to have been taken from the body of a small-headed enemy soldier. I have a small, badly-frayed-and-foxed collection of these little gems. Their titles are marvelous. While *The Valiant Soldier* is spelled correctly, I have another titled *The Sodger's Return.* Other titles are *Tars for All Weathers, My Colin Leaves Fair London Town, A New Song on Tobacco, The Rakish Butcher, The Distressed Sailor on the Rocks of Scilly, English Good Ale, Bessy's Haggies,* and (one of my favorites, though puzzling) *Blinkover the Burn Sweet Betty.*

Chapbooks and broadsides are very rare, and sell at dramatically different prices. Some can be gotten for as little as $25; others will cost many times that amount. While they are obviously very small (and size is pretty much a factor in rare-book prices just as it is in other things), they are also scarce. Their very cheapness contributes to their value, for they are fragile, often badly printed on poor paper, and conceived as a momentary entertainment, not as a lasting treasure. Also, though their literary merit is usually negligible, their value as curiosities and historical documents is considerable.

The factor of scarcity is always an important one in the history of cheap and popular literature. The inexpensively printed entertainments of the day fall like fat little soldiers in the march of time, so that their ranks are thinned awesomely within a few decades after their service. After all, these paperbacks of past years are the first things discarded, burned, or thrown into the rubbish; thus it is that many of the boys' adventure stories of the late nineteenth century have already become classics of a sort. It is not only book collectors who know about Beadle's Half-Dime Library, along with other imprints of the "dime novel" (which usually sold for a nickel, just as the former title claims). The most famous hero of these publications was Jesse James, who dominated the teen-age imagination of the dime novel audience. A first edition of *Jesse James, My Father* (Kansas City, 1899, possibly ghostwritten by A. B. Macdonald) is something of a printed-wrapper classic and in good condition sells for around $200. The catch is the usual one that juvenile paperbacks have a hard time surviving in any kind of condition. The later 1906 Cleveland imprint of this book also has a modest value, falling in the $10-to-$20 range.

Cops and robbers, as well as cowboys and Indians, serve as the meat and potatoes not only of hundreds of dime novel entrées, but of cheaply produced boys' books that became popular shortly afterward and flourished by their side. Among these heroes were the Younger brothers, Buffalo Bill, and scores of boyish paladins created by E. Z. K. Judson, whose famous pen name was Ned Buntline and whose fecund brain gave birth to such memorable figures as "Magdalena, the Beautiful Mexican Maid," "the Black Avenger," and "Navigator Ned"; he also gave William F. Cody his sobriquet of "Buffalo Bill," and contributed a population of some 500 books to the march of western civilization.

Books for girls were not far behind, if they were behind at all; but their productions were not generally of the "dime" variety, occupying that more polite and dignified stratum that a lingering Victorian propriety demanded. Girls' books were of the predictable, pietistic sort, at first; but soon they became sufficiently liberated to allow girls to have more exciting, physical adventures; and some of these heroines achieved that epic status of transcending particular stories, and becoming a "series" heroine. The most famous of these is Carolyn Keene's "Nancy Drew"; but there were many, many others, both of the transcendent, epic, series variety, and of the single-shot adventure sort. A few of the perpetrators of this genre were Mary J. Holmes, Edith Kellogg Dunton, Sarah Barnwell Elliott, and Kate Douglas Wiggin. The fact that many of these women sported three names may have inspired that cynical old commonplace that a woman writer with three names is not to be trusted (Willa Cather dropped her middle name, Sibert, early in her career). But this is unfair; the women writers of girls' books were probably just as good as their men counterparts, or at least, no worse.

The towering figure of popular American juvenile fiction was, beyond question, Horatio Alger, Jr. The prices of a handful of his first editions support this assertion—a good copy of *The Five-Hundred-Dollar Check* bringing close to a hundred dollars or one-fifth of the title; and one of *Seeking His Fortune and Other Dialogues* (written with August O. Cheney's collaboration) selling for around $400. Many of Alger's first editions in fine condition fall in the $25 to $75 range. As with all books—but especially with such popular books as these—the collector has to be cautious about picking up reprints; nine out of ten Alger books one finds in the slush have been published by Hurst, or some

174

other reprint house; and of course, most of *these* will be tattered and torn, bearing all the scars of mauling by urchins.

Some of Alger's inventions transcended their particular volumes and entered our folklore. The best-known is his eponymous hero, Horatio Alger. But there is also Dan, the detective—from the book of the same name, first published in 1884 in New York, and the first edition of which now sells for as much as $150. Detective Dan—like Sam Slick, Betty Boop, and other great American folk heroes—rode the tides of alliteration into the ocean of immortality, and appeared as late as 1933, simply as "Detective Dan, Secret Operator No. 48" in an edition that contains one story in comic strip form and another in narrative.

The influence of cheap adventure novels upon the generations of the late nineteenth and early twentieth century was incalculably great. Print is the medium of talking to oneself, and the voices of all those yarns—charged with moral and aesthetic notions and biases—were internalized by the passionate adolescent reading of future tycoons, journalists, bankers, and generals, subtly helping to create our national culture.

Some varieties of children's books fall into the category of specialist collecting and some, it must be admitted, verge upon the eccentric. Frazer Clark says that today there is an even greater trend toward specialist collecting, which has always been the most effective and reasonable game plan for most bibliophiles. Clark is referring to the sort that concentrates on "a single theme but with ample scope." Most of these "specialist" subjects exist very much in the mainstream of today's collecting—children's books, books on presidents, one-author collections, books on a particular war, collections built around particular subjects: rocketry, birds, guns, military vehicles, atomic weapons, and so on. But some of them are part of the pop-culture movement, and would have seemed outlandish fads to past collectors.

A midwestern dealer recently sold a small box of some fifty or sixty comic books for $1,100. This is impressive, even though it doesn't approach that fabulous $2,200 that was reportedly shelled out recently for the first issue of Superman comics. And apparently other vintage comic books from the thirties and forties are selling at high prices—particularly those featuring the first appearance of any famous series hero.

I remember buying Big Little Books for a nickel apiece back in the thirties, when I was a boy. One of the titles was *Tim Tyler in the Jungle*;

another was about Joe Palooka, and still another, Terry and the Pirates. Some of these squat little volumes made of pulp paper and covered with cheap cardboard bindings are now selling for $25 and more, in fine condition. The Mickey Mouse, Flash Gordon, Tarzan, Dick Tracy, and Lone Ranger titles are among those most sought after. I've read that one of these rarities—*Flash Gordon on the Planet Mongo*—goes for over $40.

It's hard to take such productions seriously, their inflated prices notwithstanding; theoretically, however, there's virtually nothing in this or any other conceivable world that can't be a legitimate object of interest, therefore of value, if we know how to regard it. And for those who need something in the way of scholarly authorization for their enthusiasm in collecting such ephemera, I quote the following from John A. Dinan's piece in an issue of *The Antiques Journal* (April 1975, pp. 36–38).

> With the acquisition of a complete set of Big Little Books by the University of Minnesota library, the Big Little Book has achieved respectability in the eyes of the public. If the fact of the purchase itself fails to impress, perhaps the price will: the 538 titles issued by the Whitman Publishing Company of Racine, Wis., between 1932 and 1949, sold for $3,200—up from their original cost of $53.80.

Like dust wrappers, advertising brochures, periodicals, campaign posters, broadsides—and in fact the whole inventory of those ephemeral productions that Lamb termed *biblia a biblia* ("bookless books"), from worthless gold stocks to brownie vouchers for *Liberty* magazine, all of these genuine relics of a past culture should be preserved somewhere, somehow; and no doubt, somewhere, somehow there is a spirited collector right this instant buying a copy of *Don Winslow vs. The Scorpion Gang,* or perhaps *Kay Darcy and the Mystery Hideout.*

There are many kinds of fad collecting, and if one is thinking only of investment, it's good to be in at the beginning and unload at the peak. I think the collector-investor is in a good position, given time, energy, and storage space, to accumulate as much trash as he wants with a view to some of it being all the rage in a few years. God knows what these things will be. Periodically it is reported that someone has paid a thousand dollars or more for a single comic book; and for all I know, someone may have, but here, we have gone beyond the limits of bibliophily, as most think of it; and anyone who wants to buy, or invest in, such maudlin fragilities is welcome to indulge as he wishes; my personal advice, however, is for him to stock up on John D. MacDonald paperbacks, available at the nearest yard sale at a dime apiece; then he'll at least profit by some good reading out of all that cheap paper. Not only that, John D. MacDonald—along with his nonbrother Ross—may prove to be a mightily collectable writer of detective stories within a few years, his hard-bound first editions conceivably joining those of Chandler and Hammett, a few of which bring a hundred dollars and more in today's market.

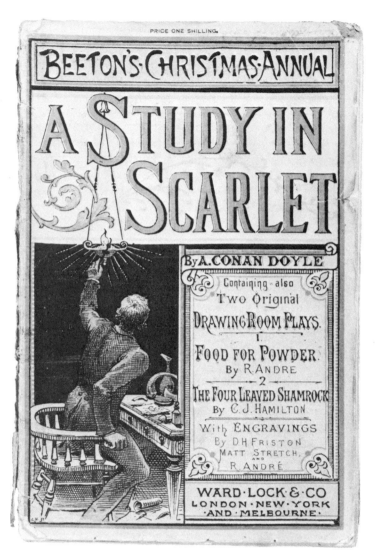

X.

DETECTIVE NOVELS,

SCIENCE FICTION AND FANTASY,

AND THE EVER-EXPANDING PRESENT

W hat a curious thing a 'detective' story is," Mark Twain wrote in his notebook.* "And was there ever one that the author needn't be ashamed of, except 'The Murders in the Rue Morgue'?" Whether or not Twain was ashamed of his own contributions to the detective story, those contributions were considerable. Some bear explicit titles: *Tom Sawyer, Detective* and *Double Barrelled Detective Story*. The latter has a detective named "Sherlock Homes," who has had books written about him; he appears in the wild west (time: the "present"—i.e., 1902) to solve a crime. Two of the local boys—named Wells Fargo Ferguson and Ham Sandwich—are in awe of the "scientific" detective. Ferguson wonders aloud:

> "I wonder if God made him?"
> There was no response for a moment; then Ham Sandwich said, reverently, "Not all at one time, I reckon."

Twain's fascination with the genre extends far beyond these two titles. There is the uncompleted novel, *Simon Wheeler, Detective*, that oc-

*Simon Wheeler, Detective, ed. Franklin R. Rogers, 2nd ed. (New York: New York Public Library, 1965), p. xii.

179

cupied him off and on for several decades. There are several detective short stories, and a number of ratiocinative motifs that extend throughout his work—some as indulgently satiric as the above, some more Juvenalian than Horatian, still others that are not satiric at all. One of the most interesting appearances of a detective story device is in *Pudd'nhead Wilson,* which contains the first reference in fiction to the use of fingerprints for identification.

It is no wonder that Twain is one of the most delightfully collectable of all authors. In addition to his major works as "high spots," there is his enormous range: if you want to collect western Americana, you must have *Roughing It* and *Life on the Mississippi;* if you collect fantasy, you will want first editions of *The Mysterious Stranger, Captain Stormfield, Connecticut Yankee,* and still others; if your interest is detective fiction, you'll need the titles mentioned above, plus others from Twain's work; and so it goes with such fields as humor, satire, semantics, philosophy, and of course, children's books. As if all this plenitude of excellence were not enough, there is the additional fact of Twain's enormous popularity, which—at least in all but his very earliest works—assured such huge printings that there still remain plenty of first editions of most of his titles at reasonable (in view of Twain's stature as a writer) prices. The first edition of *Double Barrelled Detective Story* is an interesting book, bound in red cloth, nicely designed, illustrated, and typographically distinguished. One can buy a copy for anywhere from $50 to $100; *Tom Sawyer, Detective* is collected in a volume titled *Tom Sawyer Abroad, Tom Sawyer, Detective, and Other Stories.* Illustrated by Dan Beard, published in New York in 1896, it goes at a higher price, having brought $325 at auction in 1974 and likely to continue rising. And there is Mark Twain's very first book, *The Celebrated Jumping Frog of Calaveras County* (1867) which crime-fiction collectors include in this genre. A first-issue copy may fetch in the neighborhood of $1,500.

It was not until the midtwenties of this century that crime and detective fiction (I lump them together to escape the futilitarian angst of reasonable distinction) began to demand the serious interest of critics and literary historians. Since that time, there has been an extraordinary growth in collecting such books, along with interesting interpretations of *why* we seem to need detective stories and, therefore, why we have to collect them. In England, the tradition is an older, more durable one—possibly because of the figure of Sherlock Homes, along with a hundred lesser, but still interesting, detective heroes.

What is this lasting appeal? Is the detective-protagonist a modern Faust, in search of Truth, even in its humblest guise of factual evidence—thus metaphorically engaged in a Quest for Knowledge? (Answer: sure.) Is the murder in a detective novel a projection of our own homicidal fears, and the identification of the murder a cathartic paradigm? (Answer: you bet.) Do we find in the intensification and simplification of the formulaic detective story a sop for our tyrannous fear of existential chaos? (Answer: no doubt.)

Now that we know why we need to read and collect detective stories, it will be useful to try to identify a few of the major opportunities that await us, for the field is still wide open to the enterprising and imaginative beginner. And it seems only right that the detective novel should provide unique challenges and opportunities that make particular demands upon those "detective skills' ' that are required in all phases of book collecting. According to the English collector, Eric Quayle, "One needs a flair for spotting books of mystery, crime and detection other than the high-spots that have become household names."

Just about everyone agrees that Poe created the detective story, in the form of his "tales of ratiocination," although some enthusiasts claim that Plato created in his Socrates the first detective; or that Greek drama generally, in its obsession with truth over appearance, is a forerunner of the modern tale. This is a little like science-fiction collectors claiming that Lucian's *Dialogues* were the first science fiction; but whoever wants to stretch whatever labels, the most sensible conclusion seems to be that Poe created this kind of tale just about as clearly and unequivocally as anybody can be said to have created anything.

Probably the first full-length detective novel was *Clement Lorimer: or, The Book with the Iron Clasps,* written by a Scot named Angus Bethune Reach, and published in 1849. Shortly thereafter, the Frenchman Emile Gaboriau began to publish his versions of the whodunit, and then in 1868, appeared Wilkie Collins' *The Moonstone,* which T. S. Eliot called "the first, the longest and the best of modern detective stories." The first edition of this classic should have the following points: the misprint "treachesrouly" (a truly exotic typo) on p. 129 of the second volume; and ads in both volumes two and three. If a copy possesses these points and is in fine condition, it should bring well over a thousand dollars. One such copy—inscribed by Collins—brought $2,500 at auction clear back in 1963. I own what appears to be the first American edition, published in one volume, but I am afraid the principle of "Fol-

181

low the Flag" obtains here with its usual authority, and this copy is worth only a small fraction of the true first edition in three volumes.

One of the most popular detective novels ever written was by another man with a Scottish first name: Fergus Hume. The title is *The Mystery of the Hansom Cab;* its locale is not Scottish or English, but Australian; and it appeared in 1886. Hundreds of thousands of copies were sold, and by 1900 it had been translated into twelve languages. Hume is said to have received less than £150 for his part in writing the novel, which amount would probably not buy a first edition, today, although it is true that *those* pounds had a lot more authority than their descendants.

Just around Time's corner awaits A. Conan Doyle, whose Sherlock Holmes entered the realm not just of legend, but of myth. It would be hard to explain the reason for Holmes' grip on our imagination. Partly, no doubt, he fulfills something of the trickster's role, partly that of unabashed hero in an age too much of whose antiheroism and sickly naturalism tends to sour the human spirit. Line by line, passage by passage, Holmes is a ridiculous figure; his celebrated logic is more often than not silly and arbitrary, and his posturing is hilariously arrogant. Part of his magic is no doubt attributable to Watson, through whose schoolboy mentality we are made to experience the revelations of genius in his idol. The other-self motif is evident in the relationship between Holmes and Watson, raising the function of the latter far beyond that of a mere narrative convention. The dialectic of the other-self is a very old and very strong one in literature: Don Quixote/Sancho Panza; Faust/Mephistopheles; Tom Jones/Partridge, the Barber; Boswell/Johnson; and yes, even Hopalong Cassidy/Gabby Hayes—all express a profound insight into our inner dualities, as well as into the dialectic character of human relationships.

But aside from all logical analyses, Sherlock Holmes bestrides his genre like a colossus, suggesting the genius of rational enquiry, even though he does not really embody it; and projecting a glamorous image of a disciplined, deadly intense intelligence (concealed in an insouciant manner) in command of situations threatening not only evil and destruction, but more importantly meaninglessness, in dozens of ritualistic "cases."

A defective rebound copy of the classic *Study in Scarlet* (London, 1888) was offered for $875 by a dealer in 1973. A fine copy should bring two or three times that amount, if it is offered in the near future. At Parke Bernet's sale of the J. T. Chord library in 1963, first edition copies of *The Adventures of Sherlock Holmes* (London, 1892) and *The*

Memoirs of Sherlock Holmes (London, 1894) were sold as a lot for only $110. The first of these copies was in slightly soiled covers; the second in somewhat better condition. Today, either copy in good condition would in itself, probably bring many times that combined price.

Agatha Christie (a first of her *The Murder of Roger Ackroyd* sells for as much as $200), Dorothy Sayers, Michael Innes, Edmund Crispin, and a whole scrum of others have continued, even enriched, the Holmesian tradition in England; and in this country, such writers as J. P. Marquand, Rex Stout, Mary Roberts Rinehart, S. S. Van Dine, and Ellery Queen have, in various and distinctly American ways, worked largely in this tradition—which may be thought of as the Mandarin, or sophisticated tradition. (That is the one whose detective hero smokes the philosophical pipe and mutters French or Latin to his Skye terrier, whose name is, well, maybe "Angus" or "Fergus." All things connect.)

While there are many other worthy novelists working in the Mandarin tradition in this country, that which distinguishes American detective fiction is the "hard-boiled" school, created by Dashiell Hammett and Raymond Chandler. A first edition of Hammett's *The Maltese Falcon* (New York, 1930) and the first of Chandler's *The Long Good-Bye* (London, which preceded the American; 1953) are offered at $100 each in a current catalogue—not an unreasonable price for either of classics of the *genre*. At Sotheby Parke Bernet's in Los Angeles, a first-edition copy of *The Maltese Falcon* brought $250 at auction on June 29, 1975. This represents an impressive contrast with the sale price of a similar copy for only £18 at auction in 1973.

The field of detective fiction is vast beyond the hope of reasonable, let alone tidy, appraisal within the pale of a single chapter. Already, in the half century of its admittance to the halls of respectability, detective fiction has acquired a retinue of commentary. Three of the more interesting books on the subject are Eric Quayle's —virtually priceless for the collecter of crime fiction—*The Collector's Book of Detective Fiction* (1972); Ellery Queen's *Queen's Quorum* (1953); and Howard Haycraft's *Murder for Pleasure* (1942).

One additional tip, useful for its simplicity alone: collect the first editions of any detective novel written by an author with the last name of MacDonald.

For years, science fiction has been a vital part of our popular literature. Most of it has been wretchedly written, no question. It has also, more often than not, been cheaply printed on shabby paper. It has indulged in the exploitation of interesting and even sophisticated scientific and technological ideas at the cost of sophomoric (or worse) philosophical and literary prejudices. However, in spite of everything, science fiction was *there*—these stories were being published, circulated, and read far beyond the immediate, popular influence of most better, more sophisticated works. Eventually, science-fiction novels and stories had to be acknowledged as an important, interesting, and vital part of our world, even if most of them were embarrassingly silly. The fact that many of the earliest were printed on pulp paper simply increased the natural attrition of the years, so that early works in science fiction— magazines and books together—in decent condition are hard to find, but increasingly sought-after and correspondingly rare to collectors.

The fact that science fiction has become eminently respectable is both cause and consequence of burgeoning interest. Today, there are an increasing number of *good* writers creating some form of science fiction, or "speculative fiction," as a few disciples like to call it. One writer, who can be considered collectable independently of any classification, is the internationally renowned Argentine, Jorge Luis Borges, whose intriguing blend of science fiction, fantasy, and philosophy has already greatly influenced contemporary literature. Borges' themes are often textual and bibliographical (he was once a professional librarian) and are likely to evoke a vital response from the book collector. Stanislaw Lem, from Poland, should prove to be another most collectable writer; his novel *Solaris* is one of the most powerful of any kind I have read in the past few years.

Fantasy is often associated with science fiction (to the discomfort of some and the delight of others), and it, too, has grown into an eminently collectable specialty. First editions of books by H. P. Lovecraft, Algernon Blackwood, Arthur Machen, August Derleth, and many others have soared in value during the past decade. Arkham House, founded by Derleth, and devoted to the literature of fantasy and the supernatural (and tirelessly promoting the works and fame of Lovecraft), published very actively from the 30s through the 60s. Today, most of these Arkham House imprints are pursued by collectors, in some cases bringing very high prices.

Lovecraft was an extraordinary man, a member of that long tradition of Anglo-Saxon eccentrics that includes John Dunton, William Blake, Erasmus Darwin, Jeremy Bentham, Johnny Appleseed, and Bertrand Russell. It is no wonder that Lovecraft—with his morbid inventiveness, eccentric manner, and odd name—should become a cult figure. I own a copy of *Something About Cats,* a posthumous collection of his stories edited by August Derleth. It is a strange and shabby little Arkham House edition (Sauk City, 1949) bound suitably in black, and with a frontispiece portrait of the author, *as a little boy.* (It also has Lovecraft's autograph on decorated paper pasted on a flyleaf.) In a way, Lovecraft appears never to have outgrown his childhood—a fact emphasized by one of the biographical essays in back of the book, titled "Lovecraft as I Knew Him," by Sonia H. Davis, who wrote with the authority of having been at one time married to him. But if he remained something of a child, that child was a febrile, "eldritch" (a Lovecraftian word) creature; such is eloquently borne out by the other biographical essays, the most laudatory of which is unequivocally titled, "A Literary Copernicus."

For many readers, the grotesque inventions and lugubrious fantasies of H. P. Lovecraft are a bit much; but for his disciples and defenders—and they are many and of an interesting variety of temperament and background—he is the creator of dreams and fantasies that are powerful and unique, and his morbidity—like that of Poe—is simply the obverse of genius. That Lovecraft collectors are quite serious about their commitment is evident in the fact that only recently a first-edition copy of his *The Outsider and Others* (Sauk City, 1939) sold at auction for $110; another, signed by the author, went for $250. *Beyond the Wall of Sleep* (Sauk City, 1943) and *The Shunned House* (Athol, Massachusetts, 1928) are still two other Lovecraft titles, whose first editions are likely to go into the hundreds of dollars as they appear in catalogues or on the auction block.

Unquestionably the two great modern masters of adventure fantasy are Edgar Rice Burroughs, and H. Rider Haggard, whose fifty-eight volumes of fiction include such genre classics as *She, Allan Quartermain,* and *King Solomon's Mines.* Nowhere has the influence of cinema been more apparent than in the gradual reevaluation of these popular writers of bygone times. It isn't simply that the Tarzan movies and the filmed versions of *She* and *King Solomon's Mines* have familiarized whole new generations with these one-time favorites, but films have schooled those very generations in a love for spectacle and melodrama, and the novels of Haggard and Burroughs are nothing if not spectacular and melodramatic. The causation is neither simple nor one-way; it can be well argued that Tarzan and his blood brothers have found their final home on the silver screen, and that the books they first appeared

185

in were mere transitional or larval stages; and that the very magnitude of their success as films derives from the fact that their emphasis upon the large and simple—if not always epic—actions can hardly be misconstrued by a crowd of popcorn eaters.

Whatever the cause, adventure fantasy is enjoying a lusty revival, and collecting the colorful novels that may be thought of as classics will prove a challenge to one's resources of knowledge and money both. In view of the heady appreciation of these books, many collectors will be happy to settle upon lesser-known (not necessarily less interesting or less skillful) writers. A first edition of *Tarzan of the Apes,* in fine condition with dust jacket, may sell for three or four hundred dollars. That's today; tomorrow, it may go for twice that amount. Many of Burrough's Tarzan first editions, as well as his Martian novels, sell in the twenty- to fifty-dollar range.

As for Haggard, his first editions range in the one- to two-hundred-dollar class—a price range generally proportionate to Haggard's being an older writer, whose first novel appeared while Burroughs was still a lad. But his first novel, *Dawn,* has an interesting history. Published in London in 1884, it is in appearance a typical Victorian "three-decker" (a three-volume edition). Also, it appears that a great number of copies were inscribed by Haggard, which fact naturally enhances their value. Auction records reveal that inscribed copies were sold in 1967 (for £90), in 1968 (£70), and 1970 (£130); these are hefty prices, to be sure , but while the general appreciation rate (i.e., between 1968 and 1970) is modestly favorable, there is nothing very exciting happening to the book's value, considered as a financial investment, alone. But a surprise was waiting somewhere, just around the corner in the early 1970s, for at an auction in 1974, a similarly inscribed copy of the first edition of *Dawn* sold for a whopping $1,100. If, by some chance, this copy was one of those sold from 1967 to 1970, it would represent an annual appreciation rate of from slightly more than 25 percent to slightly more than 35 percent.

How can one account for Haggard's popularity among collectors in view of his long-standing disrepute among scholars and critics? Henry Miller advances a curious explanation for Haggard's power over readers; in his essay on him in *The Air-Conditioned Nightmare* (no place of publication, no date; but Norfolk, Connecticut, 1945), Miller celebrates the grandiose powers of the boyish imagination and argues that Haggard was able to speak to this quality as more sophisticated writers cannot. Then he advances the curious theory that "His (Haggard's) method of writing these romances—at full speed, hardly stopping to think, so to speak—enabled him to tap his unconscious with freedom and depth. It is as if, by virtue of this technique, he found the way to project the living plasm of previous incarnations." Writing "at full speed, hardly stopping to think" hasn't helped many writers to success of any sort, Jungian or otherwise; when told that Jack Kerouac wrote without revising, Truman Capote is reported to have said, "That's not writing, that's typing." Evidently, Haggard had something else going for him.

Like that of science fiction generally, the publishing of fantasy is overwhelmingly a paperback enterprise. As "entertainments," rather than literature, such books are traditionally playthings of the moment, devoid of further pretension. Now that they are being taken more seriously, however, these paperbacks sometimes acquire collecting value. Some, in fact, are legitimate first editions—as stated quite explicitly opposite the title page of Arthur C. Clarke's collection of short stories, *Reach for Tomorrow* (New York, 1956): "This is an original publication—not a reprint—published by Ballantine Books, Inc."

Nevertheless, whenever the first edition exists in hard covers, the collector will want to possess that. There is a tacit assumption on the part of most collectors—a little less certain each year as the paperback industry grows and flourishes—that eventually most collectable books will find their way into hard covers. Some titles will come out simultaneously in cloth and hardbound copies; in which case, the collector will want both first editions. Ray Bradbury's most famous book, *Fahrenheit 451* (New York and Baltimore, 1953), appeared simultaneously in cloth and paper, along with a signed limited-to-200-copy edition that sells for $100 and more. Bradbury collectors want to possess all three of these editions.

The volatility of the rare-book market can hardly be better represented than by the collecting fortunes of books by J. R. R. Tolkien, whose rise to fame in the United States has been not just phenomenal (most things observable are) but, well, stupendous. Until the mid-1960s, few people on this side of the Atlantic had even heard of Tolkien, although he was obviously being quietly read and admired in England. Probably more American college students today read the books of Tolkien naturally (i.e., outside of assignments) than any other single writer. Is this faddishness? Will he last? Who can tell? His first-edition prices have not yet risen to the height that their popularity would seem to justify. In 1974, a dealer listed his *A Northern Venture* (1923) for £20; and another dealer listed the first American edition of *The Hobbit* (Boston, 1938) for $15. In 1967, the first edition (1937) had sold for £20 (about $50). E. R. Eddison's *The Worm Ouroboros* (London, 1922) is thought to have had some influence upon Tolkien's creations. A first-edition copy of this book sold in 1972 for $40. Independently of their price on the market, hardbound first-edition copies of all the works of these authors are very scarce indeed. Collectors who own any of them will want to hang onto them simply because of their great popularity, which—conjoined with scarcity—is an auspicious sign of a book's future collectability and cash value.

H. G. Wells has long been viewed by the academic literary establishment as something of a gifted hack. Possibly, he was stigmatized because of his jaunty optimism, his boosterish interest in science and technology, and especially—and as a result of this interest—his writing books that could in his day be labeled only as "science fiction." There are other causes for his neglect as a writer, no doubt; he did not do justice to his friend, Henry James; and Henry James was in truth a very great writer. But artists generally misunderstand one another. William Morris didn't think much of Baskerville as a printer; and look at what Blake had to say about Sir Joshua Reynolds, and what Dr. Johnson said about Swift and Sterne. Like forgiveness in Heine's God, intolerance can be an artist's métier.

Whatever the complex of causes for Wells' humble reputation as a writer, his stock has undergone a sharp appreciation in recent years (I speak at two levels of metaphor: both "literary" stock and "financial"). Not only is he being reevaluated because of his very great popularity during his lifetime (such evidence can never be totally ignored, especially when that audience has subsided, and the author can be listened to outside of the clamor of contemporary fame), but he is being studied in a new light, as one of the forerunners of science fiction, that very label that hung like a semantic albatross about his image, making it loathsome and unclean in the view of right-minded persons.

In the spring of 1970, the British firm of Bertram Rota—specialists in modern first editions—issued their Catalogue No. 164, that included two scarce Wells items: the first edition of *The First Man in the Moon* (London, 1901) and four separate early issues, including the first, of *The War in the Air* (London, 1908). The first (*Moon*) was offered at £8/10, or $20; the second (*War in the Air*) was offered at £15, or $36.

Two auctions early in 1974 saw copies of both of these titles go at substantially higher prices—the first at £19, and the second at £24, for the first edition only. In 1971, the same firm's catalogue No. 172 advertised Wells' *The Time Machine: An Invention* (1895), the first issue for $18. At auction in 1974, another copy of the first issue sold for £30, or $72; Bradley listed it at between $100 and $150 in 1976.

Here are some of the major writers in the science-fiction field who appear to be most avidly collected: Poul Anderson, Isaac Asimov, James Blish, Ray Bradbury, Angela Carter, John Christopher, Arthur C. Clarke, Edmund Cooper, Harry Harrison, Robert A. Heinlein, Aldous Huxley, Ursula K. Le Guin, J. T. McIntosh, André Norton, Frederik Pohl, Clifford Simak, Clark Ashton Smith, Theodore Sturgeon, A. E. Van Vogt, Jules Verne, Kurt Vonnegut, Jr., Donald Wandrei, H. G. Wells, John Wyndham. And some will wish to include William Burroughs for his *The Naked Lunch,* as well as the Italian writer, Italo Calvino, for his *Cosmicomics.* And of course there are many others.

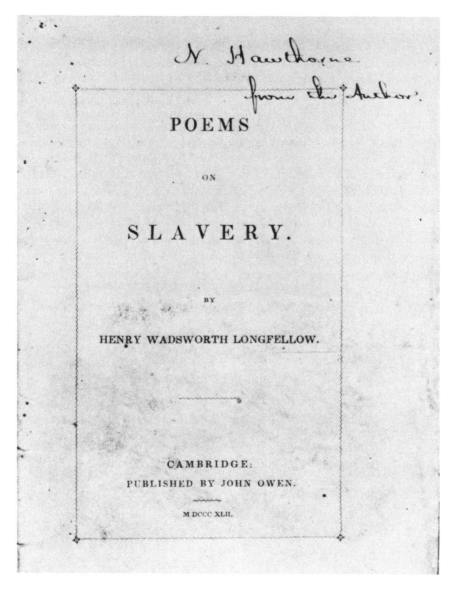

This fine association copy—inscribed by Longfellow to Nathaniel Hawthorne—fetched $5,000.00 at auction in 1975.   *Courtesy of Sotheby Parke Bernet, Inc., New York*

XI.

OTHER SPECIALTIES

FOR THE COLLECTOR - INVESTOR

ASSOCIATION COPIES
AND MANUSCRIPT MATERIALS

he reference to the three dropped lines of print in the Thoreau first edition, occasionally restored in the author's own handwriting, provides a good example of an association copy—a book that has been personalized in some manner by the author, or some other famous person. In the collecting of "associations," the book collector merges with the autograph collector, whose enterprise, in turn, extends from the enthusiasms of the most fatuous groupie to the austere labors of the bibliographer and literary scholar. Most collectors of association copies fall somewhere in the middle range, where sanity, of one form or other, is like enough to dwell.

The personal inscription, signature, or annotation of an author constitutes a "point" of a unique sort. If communication can be represented as essentially a coming or bringing together, then this proximity is vividly emblematized by the personal handwriting of the one who instituted that larger message of the book itself. The collecting of manuscripts, early drafts, notebooks, and personal letters of an important or interesting author is a lofty branch of bibliophily. It is also expensive (for the obvious reason that any holograph item is a one-of-a-kind rarity), unless one can come upon such personal documents before an author is famous. Signed or inscribed copies of books by living writers who are not famous crop up fairly often in the miscellaneous bins of used books, and if one honestly likes the work, he would do well to buy every association copy he can. Even if the writer in question does not become "famous" in the collector's (or anyone else's) lifetime, the assembly of personalized books is necessarily and in itself a testament of sorts, and likely to be a worthwhile communication.

Inscriptions can be telling in various ways: both in form and content. One does not have to believe literally in the principles of graphology to find significance of some sort in the careful, tortured, minuscule handwriting of Eugene O'Neill on the flyleaf of a copy of *The Iceman Cometh,* or in the flamboyant illegibility of Charles Dickens' autograph; what *precisely* these different styles might mean is debatable, but they are all interesting.

How much difference does an author's signature (or better yet, inscription) make in the price of a rare book? Sometimes, the difference is so great that the emphasis seems to have shifted almost entirely from the collecting of books to autographs. In a recent catalogue, two copies of O'Neill's *Marco Millions* were offered. Both were "first editions"; however, one was the first limited and boxed edition, signed by O'Neill, and the other was the first trade edition, but listed as a "fine copy," and of course with dust jacket. The price of the trade edition was $25; that of the limited (one of 440 copies), signed edition, $90. Signed limited editions of O'Neill's works are not extremely rare, and some can be gotten for $50; his other autograph materials, however, are very scarce and expensive. A signed photograph recently sold for $150; and his letters sell at $400 to $750.

The differential between signed and unsigned copies varies greatly, depending upon both the collectability of an author (usually, but not always, synonymous with his fame) and the scarcity of his autograph. Some writers are lavish with inscriptions, while others are as niggardly as the word will allow. This has absolutely no relation to talent or literary worth; nor, in any specific sense, does the supply of inscribed or autographed copies of a writer's books always affect their monetary value. Robert Frost inscribed and signed an enormous number of books; he also signed many Christmas pamphlets in limited "editions"; and, as if this supply were not plentiful enough, there are many Frost letters and manuscripts circulating at auction and among dealers. In spite of this rich and continuing harvest, the prices of Frost autograph materials remain high. In 1965 a packet of 27 letters written to his illustrator, J. J. Lankes, brought $11,500 at auction.

Some writers were so well appreciated during their lifetimes that many of their works were issued in signed, limited editions. Faulkner was one such author; and Faulkner collectors will naturally want to procure as many of these signed, limited editions as possible. And, naturally, they will have to pay for them. In a 1976 auction, two first edition copies of *Pylon* (New York, 1935) were sold; the signed, limited edition (one of 310) brought $475, while the unsigned, trade edition brought $175. This is perhaps not a just comparison in view of the fact that the trade edition was in somewhat less than desirable shape—the spine slightly faded, and the sides slightly scratched. Still, the presence of Faulkner's signature (independently of the higher price due to the better quality of any limited edition) accounts for between $100 and $200 in this difference of prices. His letters and manuscripts are very rare—a fact which helps sustain the prices of his many signed, limited editions.

Shortly before Yeats died in 1939, he signed 820 leaves for a special limited edition, but before they could be used, Yeats died; and then World War II erupted. After the war, a decision was made to bring out a variorum edition of Yeats' poetry. The task was undertaken by Peter Allt and Russell K. Alspach, as editors. Allt, who was renowned for his scholarship and wit, died tragically from an accident in 1954; but Alspach completed the task for Macmillan in New York, which had managed to buy those 820 signed sheets to tip into a special boxed, limited edition of the variorum. Thus it transpired that in 1957 a book published eighteen years after Yeats' death, bore his ghostly signature, and bravely entered the canon of his works. Falling into the category of artificial raries, as well as being a posthumous book, this title is not as expensive as one might think. I bought a copy for $95 from a dealer in 1968. In his next catalogue, he had the same title listed for $125—suggesting the possibility, at least, that my phone call had been followed by at least one other. And $150 to $200 would seem to be the price range for the variorum.

Yeats liked to sign books, and throughout his fairly long life managed to put his name in a great many. His stature in modern poetry, however, is sufficient to sustain the prices of this abundant supply, so that inscribed copies will seldom go for less than $200. Handwritten notes and letters will start at slightly more than that price and of course often sell for much more.

Even books by writers with sagging reputations will often be redeemed by the author's signature or inscription. The person for whom the book is inscribed obviously plays a lesser role, but may also figure in the worth of a book. Longfellow's enormous popularity during his lifetime, along with the fact that he was a very cunning promoter of his own works, and would bring out new "editions" consisting largely of works published in previous books, would seem to cheapen the supply of his first editions. Also, Longfellow's fallen reputation as a serious poet would seem to work against him. And yet, some of his titles remain very high, and even continue to appreciate. His *The Seaside and the Fireside* (Boston, 1850) is normally a somewhat humble book, which in good condition should not bring much more than $50 for the first edition; and yet a copy with "one joint worn" brought $325 at a recent auction—the difference in price attributable to the fact that this copy bore a personal inscription from the author.

In a 1974 auction, Longfellow's *Poems on Slavery* (Cambridge, 1842) sold for $225. A little over one year later, however, a copy of this same book, bearing Longfellow's inscription to Nathaniel Hawthorne, sold for $5,000. The difference is not all in the inscription, (and certainly not in that year's natural appreciation!), it is in this particular inscription to Hawthorne, whose great fame is sufficient to help lift the price of an inscribed book "from the wrong end," as it were. But also, this has to be a prime example of how wildly unpredictable auctions can prove. This unpredictability is part of their charm, after all; and representative of the opportunities they present for the astute and lucky buyer. Or seller.

The scarcest manuscript material is often, for obvious reasons, that of writers who died young. Among these are Poe (almost unobtainable, although according to Charles Hamilton, manuscripts and letters of Melville are even scarcer), Emily Dickinson, Stephen Crane, Dylan Thomas, and Thomas Wolfe. Long-lived writers seem compelled to produce great stores of autograph materials (taciturnity and longevity are somehow incompatible). Mencken did not attain an extremely advanced age and yet he was a prodigious letter writer, having produced an estimated 17,000 personally written letters over his career—many of them having to do with his monumental *The American Lan-*

guage. I have two such letters that were sent to me as an unasked-for substitute by a rascally Canadian dealer years ago when the books I'd ordered were found to be sold. Such unethical tactics cannot be defended, of course, but in this case I lucked out, and cherish these items of Menckeniana—even though that sporty, happy-go-lucky dealer had absolutely no way of knowing I might have any interest in them.

George Bernard Shaw, whose life almost bracketed a century, is beyond doubt the world's champion, all-time letter writer. Famous for his outspoken wit and cantankerous notions, Shaw cultivated the use of postcards for personal correspondence, and sent them out lavishly, in all directions, to a bewildering variety of people. A direct request for an autograph, however, infuriated him; but he had too much cheek to turn the other one very often, and his irascible responses to outrageous demands upon his time make hilarious and delightful reading. As incredible as it must seem, Dan H. Laurence, editor of Shaw's *Collected Letters* (New York, 1965), estimates that "Shaw, by conservative estimate, must in his lifetime have written at least a quarter of a million letters and postcards (squeezing as many as 200 cramped but completely legible words on a single card)." Whatever this number might be, it is certainly prodigious. The University of Texas acquired 3,000 letters in a single purchase, as part of the library of T. E. Hanley. On the market, these letters sell in the $100 to $200 range. The manuscript for his play, *John Bull's Other Island* sold in 1966 for $29,000. An inscribed copy of his delightful play *Pygmalion* sold for $350 as long ago as 1965.

Manuscripts and letters are an almost inevitable phase of collecting in its advanced stages; when one acquires most or all of a writer's printed works, he naturally turns to that much more difficult enterprise of procuring manuscript materials. The prices for signed or inscribed copies of books by authors of established collectability are very high, but their manuscript materials and letters are likely to be utterly beyond the reach of private collectors. A fair manuscript copy (not the original) of Eliot's *The Waste Land* sold for over $7,000 at a London auction. A corrected typescript of Tennessee Williams' *The Glass Menagerie* brought $6,000 recently; and a fragment of E. M. Forster's *A Passage to India* brought an almost incredible $16,000. The autograph manuscript of Steinbeck's *The Wayward Bus* brought $17,000 when it was sold in 1969; and Steinbeck letters are very high, going for as much as $1,000 each.

Part of the interest in letters, notebooks, memos, and other manuscript materials lies in the possibility that other, perhaps deeper, more natural revelations will appear in writings that are theoretically personal, perhaps private (at least not ostensibly directed toward any public). And often this is the case, regardless of the fact that no writer can achieve anything in the way of fame or recognition without an awareness that posterity—if not the living public—is looking over his shoulder. Some writers seem to be utterly devoid of self-consciousness, or at least possess a totally consistent and ever-ready persona. The letters of e.e. cummings sound exactly the way letters of e.e. cummings *should* sound—even those early letters from the "bad bald poet's" schooldays. Edward Dahlberg is a truly great epistler, and his hastily typed notes burn and coruscate with those very inextinguishable fires that ignite his printed works.

The unique "signature" of a writer's personal communications is both chirographic and stylistic, and it is what the collector desires in his manuscript acquisitions. Sometimes this metaphorical, psychological signature is present in the literal, autographed flyleaf of a book. Occasionally, writers sketch pictures and emblems to accompany whatever "best wishes" they convey. J. Frank Dobie drew the small figure of an "adobe" house—constituting a sort of rebus autograph—alongside his signature and a generous inscription in my copy of his classic of the southwest, *Coronado's Children* (Dallas, 1930).

Dobie is a fascinating writer—learned, imaginative, honest, and profoundly immersed not only in the land he knew and loved, but in the great ideas of western culture. He knew the Apache and the mule skinner, and in the words of Robert Frost, "savored of the land he came from." I cannot offhandedly think of a more dependably entertaining writer. In Fred White, Jr.'s *Western Americana* Catalogue No. 22, there are 36 Dobie titles listed, ranging from $9.50 to $550, with most costing between $15 and $100. The two most expensive books are a copy of the special signed limited edition of *Cow People* (Boston, 1964), for $550; and an original five-page typescript, with annotations and corrections in Dobie's hand—and "laid in superb leather folding box"—of his essay, "On Range and Trail in 1866," for $500.

Inscriptions always convey something personal, some momentary truth of mood, tone, situation. They possess a wonderful variety , and can be breezy, thoughtful, cynical, cold, friendly . . . each records the character of a moment. Sometimes there is sentiment, a reference to friendship and shared experience.

Some writers are uncomfortable signing a book, and are moved to an ironic and self-conscious reference to the act of inscribing. "What the hell can I say?" Charles Bukowski once wrote in a copy of his *Fire Station.* (Not a bad question for a writer any time.) Simply as a communication, this has more interest than Bukowski's clumsy autograph in orange paint on the blue end flyleaf of the Loujon Press' splendid edition of *Crucifix in a Deathhand* (New York, 1965). (This excellent book was issued as a "limited edition" of 3,100 and illustrated with etchings by Noel Rockmore. But in spite of that grossly expanded "limitation," this book is fine in every way, and its usual dealer or sale price in the $50 range is not in the least inflated or surprising.)

One of the most eloquent, and saddest, inscriptions I have ever seen was that of Vardis Fisher, in his book of short stories, *Life and Death* (Garden City, 1959). Inscribed near the end of his life to a young author, this inscription reads: "May you go farther as a writer than I have gone, and with more joy in doing it. Vardis Fisher." This one sentence, the name, and the date—that's all.

The most delightful personal anecdote I know about inscriptions concerns a young New York poet named Michael Waters, who was in London several years ago when Jorge Luis Borges gave a reading in Spanish (accompanied by an English translation) of his poetry and *ficciones.* Waters, who did not know Spanish, had recently purchased a translation of one of the Argentine writer's books and admired it so much that he decided to go to the reading and ask Borges to personalize the book with an inscription. Sensitive to the fact that a figure of Borges' stature must surely be tired of being asked for his autograph, he decided that the least he could do was learn enough Spanish to ask for the favor in that language. Accordingly, with considerable practice and a poet's ear, Waters memorized by rote a graceful, fluent, and colloquial request for a personal inscription in his book.

On the night of Borges' speech, Waters was nervous. He had assumed that the Argentine writer did not know English (which was not the case), but he had also heard that he was completely blind in one eye and almost blind in the other (which was quite true). After the reading, he gathered the necessary courage and approached Borges, who turned upon him kindly and politely received the young poet's request couched in proper and formal Castilian. Borges nodded his assent and took the book and pen held out to him.

Then it was that Michael Waters realized that he had neglected to re-

197

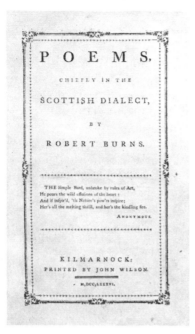

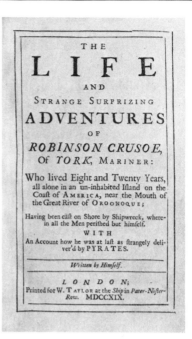

Courtesy of Sotheby Parke Bernet, Inc., New York

move the cap of the pen; and with growing anxiety he witnessed the old man before him scrawling a completely invisible inscription on the flyleaf of his book. Too embarrassed to call Borges' attention to what was happening, he simply stood there watching until Borges ended his ghostly inscription and, with a courteous smile, returned both the book and the still-capped ball-point to his admirer.

Then it was that Waters was visited with an idea of so exquisite and simple a delicacy that it borders upon genius: he thanked the old man before him, paused the merest instant, and then—removing the cap from his ball-point and holding forth the same volume—asked Borges if he would be so kind as to inscribe another book for him.

Which, of course, he did—capping a story that sheds a little grace upon both of the performers in this scene, one that is perfect in every respect, except for one small nagging doubt about what Borges' *first* inscription might have been, if he did not simply duplicate it the second time around. But that belongs with those other speculations concerning what song the sirens sang, and what name Achilles assumed when he hid among the women.

HIGH-SPOT COLLECTING

In 1902, the Grolier Club published a volume whose title page reads as follows:

ONE HUNDRED BOOKS
FAMOUS IN
ENGLISH LITERATURE
WITH FACSIMILES OF
THE TITLE-PAGES

And an Introduction By
George E. Woodberry

This volume was printed at the DeVinne Press, and was so handsome a production, and so valuable an aid to serious bibliophiles, that it itself

199

immediately became a collector's item, joining that delightful class of "books about books," whose titles almost inevitably attract good prices.

The Grolier list of high-spots is, in truth, breathtaking; and it has proved an inspiration for a number of similar lists through the years—most of these imitators suitably limiting their titles to a particular era, place, or kind of book. Their popularity and usefulness are easily explained: they provide guidelines for the beginning collector and touchstones for the veteran.

Here is the Grolier one hundred, as it appeared in 1902:

The Canterbury Tales (Chaucer), 1478
Confessio Amantis (Gower), 1483
Le Morte D'Arthur (Malory), 1485
The Booke of the Common Praier, 1549
The Vision of Pierce Plowman (Langland), 1550
Chronicles of England, Scotlande, and Irelande (Holinshed), 1577
A Myrrour for Magistrates (Baldwin, Sackville, and others), 1563
Songs and Sonettes (Howard), 1567
The Tragidie of Ferrex and Porrex (Norton and Sackville), 1570 (?)
Euphues (Lyly), 1581
The Countesse of Pembroke's Arcadia (Sidney), 1590
The Faerie Queene (Spenser), 1590
Essaies (Bacon), 1598
The Principal Navigations, Voiages, Traffiques, and Discoueries of the English Nation (Hakluyt), 1598
The Whole Works of Homer (Chapman), 1609 (?)
The Holy Bible
The Workes (Jonson), 1616
The Anatomy of Melancholy (Burton), 1621
Comedies, Histories & Tragidies (Shakespeare), 1623
The Tragedy of the Dutchesse of Malfy (Webster), 1623
A New Way to Pay Old Debts (Massinger), 1633
The Broken Heart (Ford), 1633
The Famous Tragedy of the Rich Jew of Malta (Marlowe), 1633
The Temple (Herbert), 1633
Poems (Donne), 1633
Religio Medici (Browne), 1642
The Workes (Waller), 1645
Comedies and Tragedies (Beaumont and Fletcher), 1647

Hesperides (Herrick), 1648
The Rule and Exercises of Holy Living (Taylor), 1650
The Compleat Angler (Walton), 1653
Hudibras (Butler), 1663
Paradise Lost (Milton), 1667
The Pilgrim's Progress (Bunyan), 1678
Absalom and Achitophel (Dryden), 1681
An Essay Concerning Human Understanding (Locke), 1690
The Way of the World (Congreve), 1700
The History of the Rebellion and Civil Wars in England (Clarendon), 1702
The Tatler, 1710
The Spectator, 1711
The Life and Strange Surprizing Adventures of Robinson Crusoe (Defoe), 1719
Travels into Several Remote Nations of the World (Swift), 1726
An Essay on Man (Pope), 1733
The Analogy of Religion (Butler), 1736
Reliques of Ancient English Poetry (Percy), 1765
Odes (Collins), 1747
Clarissa (Richardson), 1748
The History of Tom Jones (Fielding), 1749
An Elegy Wrote in a Country Church Yard (Gray), 1751
A Dictionary of the English Language (Johnson), 1755
Poor Richard Improved (Franklin), 1758
Commentaries on the Laws of England (Blackstone), 1765
The Vicar of Wakefield (Goldsmith), 1766
A Sentimental Journey Through France and Italy (Sterne), 1768
The Federalist, 1788
The Expedition of Humphry Clinker (Smollett), 1771
An Inquiry into the Nature and Causes of the Wealth of Nations (Smith), 1776
The History of the Decline and Fall of the Roman Empire (Gibbon), 1776
The School for Scandal (Sheridan), Dublin, 1780
The Task (Cowper), 1785
Poems (Burns), 1786
The Natural History and Antiquities of Selborne (White), 1789
Reflections on the Revolution in France (Burke), 1790
Rights of Man (Paine), 1791
The Life of Samuel Johnson, LL.D. (Boswell), 1791

Lyrical Ballads (Wordsworth and Coleridge), 1798
A History of New York . . . by Diedrich Knickerbocker (Irving), 1809
Childe Harold's Pilgrimage (Byron), 1812
Pride and Prejudice (Austin), 1813
Christabel, Kubla Khan, A Vision: The Pains of Sleep (Coleridge), 1816
Ivanhoe (Scott), 1820
Lamia, Isabella, The Eve of St. Agnes, and Other Poems (Keats), 1820
Adonais (Shelley), 1821
Elia (Lamb), 1823
Memoirs (Pepys), 1825
The Last of the Mohicans (Cooper), 1826
Pericles and Aspasia (Landor), 1836
The Posthumous Papers of the Pickwick.Club (Dickens), 1837
Sartor Resartus (Carlyle), 1834
Nature (Emerson), 1836
History of the Conquest of Peru (Prescott), 1847
The Raven and Other Poems (Poe), 1845
Jane Eyre (Brontë), 1847
Evangeline (Longfellow), 1847
Sonnets (Mrs. Browning), 1847
Melibocus-Hipponax: The Biglow Papers (Lowell), 1848
Vanity Fair (Thackeray), 1848
The History of England (Macaulay), 1849
In Memoriam (Tennyson), 1850
The Scarlet Letter (Hawthorne), 1850
Uncle Tom's Cabin (Mrs. Stowe), 1852
The Stones of Venice (Ruskin), 1851
Men and Women (Browning), 1855
The Rise of the Dutch Republic (Motley), 1856
Adam Bede (George Eliot), 1859
On the Origin of Species (Darwin), 1859
Rubaiyat of Omar Khayyam (Fitzgerald), 1859
Apologia pro Vita Sua (Newman), 1864
Essays in Criticism (Arnold), 1865
Snowbound (Whittier), 1866

Most of these titles would no doubt appear on a similar list made to-day. Some would be quietly dropped (not many would still have *The Rise of the Dutch Republic* represented), but truly there were some stu-

202

pendous bargains on that list—books that could have been purchased for practically nothing within the memory of its first readers. For example, Bernard Quaritch had printed the first edition of 250 copies of Fitzgerald's *Rubaiyat* as recently as 1859, and shortly thereafter dumped a number into his bargain barrow in front, because there simply were no buyers. The remainder price was four pence a copy. Some forty-three years later, the *Rubaiyat* was canonized by inclusion in this very Grolier list; and in 1927, a copy sold for £650—thousands of dollars in terms of the pound of that day, and that means thousands of *those* dollars.

In 1947, the Grolier Club published another high-spot list, this a catalogue of "One Hundred Influential American Books Printed Before 1900." Like all thoughtfully devised lists, this one is as interesting to the scholar as to the collector, for it presents a vivid image of American culture as it has been manifest in one hundred of its key testaments. Of course there are titles included that strike one as eccentric (e.g., Luther Emmett Holt's *The Care and Feeding of Children*) or pop-trendy (the first Montgomery Ward "catalogue"—a mail order broadside—in 1872), or campy (*Little Lord Fauntleroy*). But the fact is, all of these titles can be defended as "influential," and the majority of them are acknowledged masterpieces.

In 1928, A. Edward Newton published a book titled, *This Book Collecting Game,* in which he also includes a list of one hundred books— these called, simply and modestly, "One Hundred Good Novels." This has also had an influence on modern collectors, but while it is 26 years "more modern" than the first Grolier list, Newton's does not wear so well. Who today would include *Joanna Godden,* by Kaye-Smith, or *John Halifax, Gentleman,* by Mulock (to name two titles that appear one after the other) on such a list? Perhaps these (along with others) are excellent novels, conceivably approaching greatness—I wouldn't know, because one is only a name to me, and the other, outside of Newton's list, isn't even that.

Virtually all such undertakings are useful to the collector, however, and there is really no need at all to be contemptuous of their eccentricities. Most of the books on just about any list gotten together by someone who loves books and thinks enough about such things to take the trouble to *make* a list, will prove to have some value.

One of the more interesting, it seems to me, is that compiled by Cyril Connolly in *The Modern Movement* (Atheneum, 1965), subtitled "One

Hundred Key Books from England, France, and America, 1880–1950." Connolly was a thoughtful and superbly read man, whose criteria of "value" may well prove to be more dependable than most in the determination of books that will endure and thereby prove to be rarities of more-or-less consistent appreciation. "In preparing this list," he wrote, "I have tried to choose books with outstanding originality and richness of texture and with the spark of rebellion alight, books which aspire to be works of art."

Here is Connolly's list as he has arranged the titles, generally in chronological order:

1. Henry James. *Portrait of a Lady* (1881)
2. Gustave Flaubert. *Bouvard et Pécuchet* (1880)
3. Villiers de L'Isle-Adam. *Contes Cruels* (1883)
4. Joris Karl Huysmans. *A Rebours* (1884)
5. Charles Baudelaire. *Oeuvres Posthumes* (1887)
6. Arthur Rimbaud. *Les Illuminations* (1886)
7. Stephane Mallarmé. *Poésies* (1887)
8. Guy de Maupassant. *Bel-Ami* (1885)
9. Edmond and Jules de Goncourt. *Journal* (published from 1887–96)
10. J. K. Huysmans. *Là-bas* (1891)
11. Alfred Jarry. *Ubu Roi* (1896)
12. Henry James. *The Awkward Age* (1899)
13. André Gide. *L'Immoraliste* (1902)
14. Joseph Conrad. *Youth* (1902)
15. Joseph Conrad. *The Secret Agent* (1907)
16. Henry James. *The Ambassadors* (1903)
17. George Moore. *Memoirs of My Dead Life* (1906)
18. J. M. Synge. *The Playboy of the Western World* (1907)
19. E. M. Forster. *The Longest Journey* (1907)
20. Norman Douglas. *Siren Land* (1911)
21. D. H. Lawrence. *Sons and Lovers* (1913)
22. Guillaume Apollinaire. *Alcools* (1913)
23. Marcel Proust. *Du Côté de Chez Swann* (1913)
24. W. B. Yeats. *Responsibilities* (1914, Dublin, enlarged, 1916, London)
25. Thomas Hardy. *Satires of Circumstance* (1914)

26. James Joyce. *Portrait of the Artist as a Young Man* (1916, New York; 1917, London)
27. Ford Madox Ford. *The Good Soldier* (1915)
28. Norman Douglas. *South Wind* (1917)
29. Percy Wyndham Lewis. *Tarr* (1918, New York and London)
30. T. S. Eliot. *Prufrock and Other Observations* (1917) and *The Waste Land* (1922, New York; 1923, London)
31. Paul Valéry. *La Jeune Parque* (1917) and *Charmes* (1922)
32. Guillaume Apollinaire. *Calligrammes* (1918)
33. Gerard Manley Hopkins. *Poems* (1918)
34. Arthur Waley. *One Hundred and Seventy Chinese Poems* (1918)
35. Ezra Pound. *Lustra* (1916) and *Mauberley* (1920)
36. Wilfred Owen. *Poems* (published posthumously, 1920; ed. Siegfried Sassoon)
37. Lytton Strachey. *Eminent Victorians* (1918)
38. D. H. Lawrence. *Sea and Sardinia* (1921, New York; 1923, London)
39. Aldous Huxley. *Chrome Yellow* (1921)
40. Katherine Mansfield. *The Garden Party* (1922)
41. W. B. Yeats. *Later Poems* (1922)
42. James Joyce. *Ulysses* (1922, Paris)
43. Raymond Radiguet. *Le Diable au Corps* (1923)
44. Ronald Firbank. *The Flower Beneath the Foot* (1923)
45. E. M. Forster. *A Passage to India* (1924)
46. Wallace Stevens. *Harmonium* (1923)
47. e. e. cummings. *Tulips & Chimneys* (1923 & 1937) and *Is 5* (1926, New York)
48. Scott Fitzgerald. *The Great Gatsby* (1925)
49. Ernest Hemingway. *In Our Time* (1924, Paris; 1925 and 1930, New York)
50. Ernest Hemingway. *The Sun Also Rises* (1926, New York)
51. André Gide. *Si le Grain ne Meurt* (1920 onward in the *N. R. F.* magazine—published Paris, 1926)
52. William Plomer. *Turbott Wolfe* (1926, dated 1925)
53. Somerset Maugham. *The Casuarina Tree* (1926)
54. Virginia Woolf. *To the Lighthouse* (1927)
55. André Breton. *Nadja* (1928)
56. W. B. Yeats. *The Tower* (1928, London) and *The Winding Stair* (1929, New York; enlarged 1933, London)

57. D. H. Lawrence. *Lady Chatterley's Lover* (1928, Florence)
58. Evelyn Waugh. *Decline and Fall* (1928)
59. Henry Green. *Living* (1929)
60. Ernest Hemingway. *Farewell to Arms* (1929)
61. Robert Graves. *Goodbye to All That* (1929)
62. Jean Cocteau. *Les Enfants Terribles* (1929)
63. Ivy Compton-Burnett. *Brothers and Sisters* (1929)
64. Hart Crane. *The Bridge* (January, 1930, Paris; 1930, New York)
65. T. S. Eliot. *Ash Wednesday* (1920)
66. Ezra Pound. *Thirty Cantos* (1930, Paris; 1933, London)
67. Edith Sitwell. *Collected Poems* (1930, London and New York)
68. Antoine de Saint-Exupéry. *Vol de Nuit* (1931)
69. William Faulkner. *Sanctuary* (1931, New York)
70. Virginia Woolf. *The Waves* (1931)
71. Edmund Wilson. *Axel's Castle* (1931, New York and London)
72. T. S. Eliot. *Selected Essays* (1932)
73. W. H. Auden. *The Orators* (1932)
74. Louis-Ferdinand Céline. *Voyage au Bout de la Nuit* (1932, Paris)
75. Aldous Huxley. *Brave New World* (1932)
76. Nathanael West. *Miss Lonelyhearts* (1933)
77. André Malraux. *La Condition Humaine* (1933)
78. Dylan Thomas. *18 Poems* (1934) and *Twenty-Five Poems* (1936)
79. Scott Fitzgerald. *Tender Is the Night* (1934)
80. Henry James. *The Art of the Novel* (1934, New York)
81. Marianne Moore. *Selected Poems* (1935, New York and London)
82. Henry de Montherlant. *Les Jeunes Filles* (1936–1939)
83. Henri Michaux. *Voyage en Grande Garabagne* (1936; included in *Ailleurs,* 1948) and *Au Pays de la Magie* (1941; included in *Ailleurs*)
84. J. P. Sartre. *La Nausée* (1938)
85. Louis Macneice. *Autumn Journal* (1939)
86. Christopher Isherwood. *Goodbye to Berlin* (1939)
87. James Joyce. *Finnegans Wake* (1939)
88. Graham Greene. *The Power and the Glory* (1940)
89. Arthur Koestler. *Darkness at Noon* (1940)
90. W. H. Auden. *Another Time* (1940, New York and London)
91. Stephen Spender. *Ruins and Visions* (1942)
92. T. S. Eliot. *Four Quartets* (1943–1944, New York and London)
93. George Orwell. *Animal Farm* (1945)

94. Albert Camus. *L'Étranger* (1941)
95. Albert Camus. *La Peste* (1947)
96. Dylan Thomas. *Deaths and Entrances* (1946, London)
97. John Betjeman. *Selected Poems* (1948, London)
98. Ezra Pound. *The Pisan Cantos* (1948, New York; 1949, London)
99. George Orwell. *1984* (1949)
100. William Carlos Williams. *Paterson, 1, 2, 3, 4* (1946–51, New York; 1964, London)

Whoever undertakes a list of this sort has to be brave. For one thing, it is an invitation to cheat a little, by means of including two or three of an author's titles—or a whole series—as one "book." Also, it is a calculated risk for revealing one's own particular mixture of ignorance, prejudice, and obtuseness. Connolly's list is, in many ways, commendable; it is nobly enhanced by the author's annotations, many of which are worthy of the excellence they celebrate. For example, Connolly argues that George Moore is an undeservedly neglected writer, and concludes: "A man of such energy and imagination who gave up his long life to writing cannot still be ignored and surely awaits resurrection. Alas, he belittled James and Yeats and was cast into outer darkness." Also, consider this utterance about Hemingway: "No other writer here recorded stepped so suddenly into fame, or destroyed with such insouciance so many other writers or ways of writing or became such an immediate symbol of an age."

While such lists as these are usually careful to avoid the hubristic claim of being "the best," they are almost inevitably read as if they do, in fact, make such a claim. Whether they are called "influential" or "key" books, the simple fact of their titles being *chosen,* being honorifically isolated, the mere fact of their existence, implies that they are the *most* influential, or the most unquestionably deserving of being labeled "key" books. Otherwise, they should be replaced by those that are.

Thus it is that Connolly's shortcomings as a reader are revealed. As a critic, he is faced eastward, toward France; and he has a severe case of stiff neck. It isn't simply that American books are under-represented—possibly they are not; but one cannot defend listing a novel by Ronald Firbank, or *Eminent Victorians,* by Lytton Strachey, or Raymond Radiguet's *Le Diable au Corps,* while omitting *Huckleberry Finn,* and *The Red Badge of Courage. Pudd'nhead Wilson* and *All the King's Men* should also find a place among those listed.

But any list will reveal blind spots, distortions, prejudice. And in spite of their human frailties, they are nevertheless—most of them—of value to the collector. For one thing, they can provide a scaffolding for the beginning collector—a premise of order, upon which he can build. And one need not be imprisoned in any particular list: he may build his own, either by grafting parts of various lists together, or by independently devising his own. No collector, however, should be ignorant or inattentive to the information contained in lists of high spots. Aside from their intrinsic interest, they are fascinating and valuable guides for the collector-investor.

Actually, in one guise or another, high-spot lists crop up everywhere; they are likely to grow out of almost any kind of literary or historical discussion. In 1924, while he was in Sweden to receive the Nobel Prize for literature, Sinclair Lewis, in an iconoclastic revel, dismissed all "classic" American authors, only to replace them with his own list of modern authors, including Dreiser, Mencken ("our most vivid critic"), Sherwood Anderson ("my great colleague"), Willa Cather, Eugene O'Neill ("incomparably the best dramatist"), Robinson Jeffers, and Vachel Lindsay. At their best, such catalogs are almost works of art—as, for example, the "Golden Florins" section gathered by Christopher Morley in his *Ex Libris Carissimus*—a list which is virtually a poem of titles.

Every collector-investor should consult reading lists in establishing his own guidelines for collecting. Like their first cousins, the high-spot lists, they will vary enormously in their recommendations; and, unlike the high-spot lists, they will not have been gotten together with book collecting—let alone investment—in mind. And yet, their emphasis upon the "critically important" book, the essential text, the groundbreaking or near-perfect work of poetry or philosophy or fiction will likely prove to have some tangible relationship to value. In short, reading lists are intended to point to important books, and important books—particularly in first or special editions—are likely to have investment value.

One of the most recent high-spot lists is, in fact, quite explicit, and very much aimed at the collector of rare books: this is William Targ's selection (in his book *Indecent Pleasures,* Macmillan, 1975) of modern and contemporary authors who will in his opinion likely prove to be among the most enduring, the "classic" of the future; and whose books and manuscripts will therefore prove most valuable from an investment standpoint. Targ's list is a personal one, which is exactly as it should be, and one of its more helpful features is its inclusion of authors very much alive and kicking. These living authors represent a real opportunity for the collector-investor who likes what they do and wants to stock up on their first and limited editions now, when the buying is good and easy.

Reading lists by prominent literary figures are especially worthy of attention. Referring to Charles Olson, Robert J. Bertholf wrote: "Supported by borrowings from Whitehead's philosophy (in fact Olson read extensively in all fields) his *Bibliography of America for Ed Dorn* (San Francisco: Four Seasons Foundation, 1964), takes its place alongside of Pound's letter to Williams (printed in *Paterson: Book III*)—in which Pound tells Williams to read the Loeb Classical Library—as the grandest reading lists of modern poetry."*

Some reading lists are not overt, as in the learned poetry—not only of Pound and Olson, but of T. S. Eliot and David Jones (in Jones' *Anathemata*). Commentaries, footnotes, exegeses will always provide rich information, not only for the scholar, but for the collector-investor as well.

Do high-spot collectables make good investments? Unquestionably, most of the titles they include are among the best, thereby proving to be the most dependable of all rare books over the long haul of years. This is especially true of those titles that "make" more than one list, or that claim some kind of universality by inclusion in such lists throughout the years. The principle here is a little like that of all-American selections or media awards: being chosen by more than one selection committee is a powerful recommendation. Some kind of popularity is, after all, essential to the operation of the market. When Galton decided to write a book on genius, he went to all the encyclopedias he could find and counted the words devoted to famous people in order to arrive at an index for those who might deserve the label. Galton's premise is vulnerable as a theoretical approach, no doubt; but as a basis for extrapolation in the market it is valid.

Most high-spots are, in the nature of things, older books. They have proved themselves in catalogues and auctions over the years, so that their values are often more predictable than the values of more topical

*From "The Key in the Window: Kent's Collections of Modern American Poetry" in *The Serif*: Quarterly of the Kent State University Libraries. Vol. VII, No. 3, September 1970.

collectables. The great titles of literature obviously figure strongly among them. When John Howell listed the first American edition of *Moby Dick* (New York, 1851) at $1,250 in a 1971 catalogue, some buyers were scared away by the price; but whoever bought that copy spent his money wisely, for at the Stockhausen auction three years later, the price had more than tripled, with a copy going at $4,250. The English first edition is a three-decker that preceded the American first, but lacks 35 passages that appear in the American; simply titled *The Whale,* the English first is a much sought-after book, whose next copy at auction is likely to bring a stunning price.

A first-edition copy of Swift's *Travels into Several Remote Nations of the World,* by Lemuel Gulliver, (2 vols., London, 1726) is, in spite of its greater age and longer history as a classic, a more accessible book. In 1963, a mismated copy (volume one, the second edition; and volume two, the first) sold for only $60 at auction. In 1970, two copies of the complete first edition sold at auction for $525 and £170. In 1974, however, the auction price for a first edition was $1,100, and "a fine copy" has been offered in a catalogue for $2,000. A still more readily available high spot on many lists (although not on the Grolier) is Sterne's *Tristram Shandy,* the six-volume, London, 1760–1762 first edition of which sold at Christie's November 26, 1975, sale for only £240—a modest enough price, to be sure, but a significantly higher price than past sales records for this whimsical and knotty-brained classic show.

References elsewhere to the dizzying rise in sales prices of the scientific classics of Vesalius, Harvey, and Newton indicate a trend that is of recent acceleration, even though it can hardly be called recent as a collecting field. One of the most splendid sales histories is that of Darwin's epoch-making (here, the term is deserved) *Origin of Species.* The first edition (London, 1859) sold at auction in 1970 for $700. Three years later, there were three copies offered at auction which sold for $1,400, £500, and £700. The mean dollar price for these 1970 sales is approximately $1,600. At Sotheby Parke Bernet's November 19-20, 1974, sale, however, a copy of the same book brought $2,100.

Not all high-spots accelerate all the time, of course; and as with rare books generally, there are more or less natural periods of leveling off. A first edition of Newton's *Optics* (London, 1704) sold for £340 in 1975; but a copy had sold six years earlier for almost exactly the same amount. No two copies of any used book are alike, and no two auctions are alike. A copy of the first edition of *Tom Jones* (London, 1749) sold at a 1963 auction for $225. In 1975, two copies were auctioned, the first selling for only $550 (just more or less holding its own, with reference to the 1963 sale), but the other bringing £310, late in the year, only a few months before the sharp drop in the value of the pound.

Some high-spot rarities are so nearly impossible to obtain at any price, that they force compromise upon even the most austere collectors. Burton's *Anatomy of Melancholy* is one such title, so inaccessible in the first that its second edition has acquired a lusty sales record at auction. In 1970, two second-edition copies sold for $375 and £95; in a sale at Christie's on November 26, 1975, a copy sold for £200. In 1969, however, a first edition of Burton's classic went up for auction, where it brought £1,900. Speculation about what the next first-edition copy might bring requires considerable imagination, but on the basis of past records and the general appreciation of the market, one might predict a good copy will go for well over $10,000. The popularity of this masterpiece among book people is legendary. It has something for everyone. Whole populations of scholars and writers have exclaimed over its dazzling heterogeneity of whimsical and solid learning, its discursive brilliance, its encyclopedic breadth. People look in it and see what they want to see, or what they require—it has this spontaneous universality. It has been thought of as a beautiful philological monstrosity and a tour de force; and yet, Sir William Osler—a bibliophile and writer (Morley includes his *The Student Life* among his "Golden Florins") as well as a world-renowned physician—termed it "a great medical treatise, orderly in arrangement, serious in purpose."

Occasionally, leaves are removed from the greatest high-spot rarities and sold independently, or bound into fine press editions of works that have critical, biographical, or bibliographical relevance to the high spot. Leaves from a Gutenberg Bible, or from a Shakespeare First Folio have often been dispersed in such a manner. The extreme rarity of the 1478 *Canterbury Tales* is another example, a single leaf from "The Parson's Tale" selling at a 1970 auction for $300.

Later high spots do not suffer such benign indignities. The first edition of Poe's *The Raven and Other Poems* (1845) is virtually unobtainable, more scarce in fact that most high spots two and three centuries older. A copy did appear at auction in 1970, selling for $1,250—which price will be eclipsed whenever another copy appears on the auction block. Since Poe's classic comes from a relatively modern period, it is unlikely that it will ever be separated and sold in leaves; the print and paper are not in themselves distinguished or emblematic of typographic antiquity, as are the leaves from books made by Gutenberg and Caxton.

High-spot collecting obviously presents an enormous challenge to any collector. Today, older high-spot lists—such as the Grolier—can be undertaken only with considerable hedging. And once this happens, the purity and authority of the list is destroyed, and all kinds of substitution and compromise are invited. Thus, there is the flourishing of collectors who boast of "having 83 of the Grolier Hundred," or "91 of the first editions on Newton's list," and so on. There is also that other compromise of settling for crumbs from the table in the form of a single leaf from a Gower's *Confessio Amantis* or a wildly sophisticated copy of Donne's *Poems*.

Old fashioned collectors would have been appalled by such concessions, no doubt; but as time and institutions take their toll, and as the population of collectors naturally increases, such adjustments will be increasingly sanctioned. One adjustment that has not been elaborated upon is that of making one's own list of high spots. If this is done in a totally self-centered way, it will be meaningless; but if it is done responsively and eclectically, drawing upon those Visions of Titles that the best lists of the past afford us, the project of making your own list can be not only a defensible, but a most absorbing and useful undertaking.

ONE-AUTHOR AND FIRST-BOOK COLLECTIONS

Once upon a time there was a man who gathered about him an astonishing collection of books. This collection was not astonishing because it was large; on the contrary, it was quite small. In fact, it consisted of only 650 books, which most collectors would not even allow to be worthy of consideration *as* a collection. What made this collection astonishing, however, was the fact that all of those 650 books were simply copies of different editions of *one book*. Not a single passage differed significantly (to the common eye) from its coordinate passage in another edition. The words were the same words, arranged in the same order. The book was *Robinson Crusoe*.

If you were to choose one book to possess in the form of 650 copies, what would that one book be? I confess that this seems to me a fascinating problem; it is more telling philosophically, more austere, more *critical* than that similar problem about what ten books you would want to have washed ashore with you if you were to be stranded on a desert island. Think of the consequences of such immersion in a single text! Might one conceivably *read* every one of those 650 copies? If he were to do so, would the differences in type, paper, format, and binding all eventually have their say, and reveal once and for all their tangible importance in the character of what we like to think of platonically, as an idea, a "literary" experience?

But aside from the theoretical dimension, *what book would you choose?* Many people, no doubt, would choose the Bible; and if it were the King James version, they would emerge from their libraries sounding like Increase Mather, no doubt. But a reasonable choice, a rich one. Others would choose a favorite imaginative work: *Alice in Wonderland, War and Peace, Moby Dick.* I would give thought to a novel like *Tom Jones,* anticipating the joys of basking in the warm sunlight of Fielding's commodious intelligence. But if one were to choose *Tristram Shandy,* would he emerge whimsically learned, mad, and impotent? Already, as you can see, I conceive of the issue in terms of the "desert island" problem, because after all, one's library *is* an island, but it is "desert" only if that collector does not read his possessions and thereby becomes as hubristic as a mad king who does not believe in the realities of his subjects.

The one-title book collector is an extreme example of those who have been somewhat inscrutably called "Lone Lamb Collectors" ("Lone Lion Collectors" seems more honorific, and more accurate, somehow). While there have been people who have limited their active collecting to the various editions of *Robinson Crusoe, Don Quixote,* Boswell's *Life of Johnson,* and other widely reprinted classics, most collectors possessed of the self-discipline and instinct to collect within a strictly defined subject confine themselves—*as* collectors (it may be assumed that they possess other books)—to a single author.

One of the critical decisions one makes when he begins to collect books of any kind is whether he will choose depth or breadth. It may be that a kind of madness waits at either extreme. No one has ventured farther into breadth and the unsettled territories of sheer, exuberant acquisitiveness than the fabulous Sir Thomas Phillipps (1792–1872), who at one time dreamed of possessing at least one copy of every book in the world. As an antiquary and bibliophile, he carried the passion for breadth to, and beyond, the limits of sanity in an enterprise that is not too neurotically intent upon observing such limits. When Phillipps became godfather to Sir Frederic Madden's second son, his ceremonial gift to the babe was a copy of the *Cottonian Manuscripts Catalogue* by Joseph Planta—a gift which so appalled Sir Frederic (who was Keeper of Manuscripts at the British Museum and could never be accused of bibliophobia) that he wrote in his journal: "He certainly is crazy! What mortal ever heard of such a present before?"

Phillipps' hoard was colossal. It is reported that he would simply fill a room in his mansion with books, floor to ceiling, and then seal it off. His antiquarian passion was focused primarily on the collecting of manuscripts, (he referred to himself as a "vello-maniac"), but he also collected printed books in great numbers. His furious energy was expended at a time when the supply of collectors was relatively low, and the store of rarities still plentiful. In view of this fact, it was inevitable that Sir Thomas should gather into his keeping a few items of almost priceless value. His possessions included 60,000 manuscripts, and were still being sold at auction a century after his death. In 1974, Sotheby's sale of a portion of Bibliotheca Phillippica included a magnificent late sixteenth-century illustrated Persian manuscript that sold for £48,000.

Somewhere near the pole opposite Sir Thomas' frenzy, in the region of depth collecting, will be found those one-author collectors, accounts of whose careers are likely to sound like parables of self-knowledge, industry, and unswerving dedication. Often, because of his scholarship and dedication, a one-author collector will eventually become identified with his subject. Thus, when one thinks of Michael Sadleir, he thinks of Trollope; when one thinks of Wilmarth Lewis, he thinks of Horace Walpole.

To be a one-author collector is not necessarily a limitation, but a focus. It was through his study of Trollope, Sadleir claimed, that he first began to love the three-decker Victorian novel "as a material thing." And out of his study of Trollope—who is often thought of as the *typical* Victorian novelist—Sadleir built his vast bibliographical knowledge of nineteenth-century British literature. Similarly, Wilmarth Lewis, through his long years' fascination with Horace Walpole's work, acquired an extensive technical and scholarly knowledge of eighteenth-century printing, literary and political fashions, and social life.

Matthew Bruccoli's F. Scott Fitzgerald collection is probably the best most comprehensive private collection on Fitzgerald in the world. Naturally, it includes virtually all the editions and printings of all Fitz-gerald's books, along with letters, inscriptions, and other manuscript materials. Bruccoli's concentration on Fitzgerald is scholarly as well as bibliophilic, and out of this concentration have grown a number of projects and opportunities, including the editing and publishing of similar publishing enterprises, as well as an association with the Detroit businessman, Frazer Clark, whom Bruccoli unhesitatingly designates as the greatest one-author collector in the world.

Clark's major specialty is Nathaniel Hawthorne, and his collection of Hawthorniana consists of some 30,000 items, including books, manuscripts, letters, peripheral materials, and memorabilia. *The Scarlet Letter* is included in Newton's, as well as almost any conceivable, high-spot list; and it has gone through a total of 289 different printings. Clark possesses at least one copy of each. In spite of its secure claim to being a classic, *The Scarlet Letter* has been, until recently, an underpriced book. As late as 1972, a copy of the first edition sold for only $85. Its price has been rising, however, and a fine copy of the first edition sold at auction in November 1975, for $650, which is a much more realistic price for this masterpiece.

Among Clark's memorabilia is the stencil Hawthorne used when he worked in that famous Customs House in Salem. The story of Clark's quest for this stencil, which required imagination and a perseverance extending over the years, is a fascinating one. He first sniffed his quarry while looking through some old auction records from the 1920s. The man who had bought it then was dead, but after considerable detective work, Clark located a grandson of the purchaser, who still happened to possess the stencil. Eventually, Clark wore him down and got what he wanted. This little episode is only one of countless examples of how much knowledge and opportunity are packed into dealers' catalogues. An ardent student of the chase, Clark reads catalogues the instant they arrive so that he can have a shot at the choicest items.

Two contradictory factors influence the value of one-author collections, and they are referred to elsewhere, in other contexts, but will bear repetition: such a collection must necessarily, in the name of completeness, have a lot of worthless books (most of those 289 printings of *The Scarlet Letter* have no bibliophilic worth); on the other hand, the work, care, and extensive bibliographical knowledge required to build such a collection can be of almost immeasurable value, and the scholarly importance of a complete one-author collection may inspire active competition among institutional libraries to possess it, running the price higher than the collector's hopes.

There are always interesting options available to the booklover who would like to start a one-author collection, but is discouraged by the difficulty of collecting his chosen author successfully, because of the popularity of that author's works as collector's items, and a consequent inflation of first-edition prices. Or perhaps the enterprise may seem to be lacking in adventure, simply because of all the heavy traffic and the *obviousness* of that author's collectability. One option is, of course, to go simply to another author and begin to collect his or her first editions. This can be a liberating experience and an adventure: it can be enormously interesting and challenging to specialize upon a reputedly "minor" figure; sometimes one will see this "minor figure's" stature grow under the light of close and sympathetic attention. And it is possible that there will be a corresponding growth in that author's reputation, thereby vindicating one's own taste and proving that the dollars spent in the deflated market of that author's deflated reputation were a good investment.

But it isn't necessary to abandon one's first choice, no matter how heavily a writer is collected, and no matter how banal it may seem to concentrate upon him. Instead, it is possible to consider building a satellite collection—an option that has been suggested elsewhere in other contexts. If you can't afford to collect Trollope three deckers in the first edition, collect his American firsts (three of these are actually *the* first, preceding the London editions); or collect the appearances of his work in periodicals; or books about him (perhaps focusing upon American reviews of his works, reflecting his own commentaries about his travels in this country); or collect the Barset novels, alone—the first editions will prove expensive, but most of the reprints will be very cheap, and when they are all collected, they will constitute an interesting, solid, and worthwhile unit.

Satellite collections are within the reach of all collectors, and they possess the additional interest of embodying an idea or expressing a unique insight into a writer's works or personality. Whoever launches upon the project of collecting the plays, handbills, theater programs, notices, reviews, and so on, of Henry James; or collects all the books and articles (perhaps including manuscripts and letters) of Rufus Wilmot Griswold, with a view to gathering a whole testament for the understanding of this man who had so great and insidious an authority in creating the popular reputation of Poe—whose own first editions are classically rare and expensive—such a person is engaged in an enterprise that requires inventiveness, knowledge, skill, and a flair for luck. And as his collection approaches that always receding goal of completion, it will begin to increase its value at a faster and faster rate: those last few titles that keep eluding your grasp will probably be the greatest rarities, and it is when you are closing in on them that the chase, like the ideal of the collection itself, reveals the fullness and roundness of its meaning.

There is another kind of specialty collection that lies at the opposite extreme from the satellite collection: this is the first-book collection, which is not meant for the timid or impoverished. First books of famous or classic (or possibly just collectable) authors are often feeble productions, hardly worthy of their name; and because of this, their mortality has often proved staggering. Sometimes the first published effort is a juvenile enthusiasm—"juvenile" in both a literal and figurative sense; so it is not surprising that authors have tried to have all traces of these first faltering attempts obliterated. If the author does not become highly collectable, such a first book will likely pass through the hands of whole populations of browsers without exciting any interest. But there are some that carry a voltage of association and rarity, and these are the quarry of the first-book collector.

The appeal is understandable. If the life work of an author is considered as a unit, as a single testamentary volume, then his first book is the first edition of that lifework. The classic rarity of this sort in American literature is the first book of a classically difficult author to collect, who (also classically) tried to have his first book suppressed. This is *Tamerlane,* "by a Bostonian"—who wasn't a real Bostonian at all, but Edgar Allan Poe. This volume is so majestic a rarity that the next copy (if there ever is one) may determine its own price almost unresponsively to the criteria of the market. This seemed to be the situation in 1974, when a copy termed "the finest known" brought $123,000 at auction. (The buyer was John F. Fleming.)

Most first-book rarities are expensive and difficult to obtain, but they belong to a whole different scale of value. Frost's *A Boy's Will*—his first book of poems—has been cited as one of the great rarities among modern books, bringing prices in the $1,000 range. Even a copy of the second issue brought £70 at Christie's on November 26, 1975. Stephen

217

Crane's *Maggie* in the famous yellow printed wrappers is a greater rarity, having already exceeded $3,000 at auction, and destined to go higher. Willa Cather's *April Twilights* (Boston, 1903) brings close to $500; Hemingway's *Three Stories & Ten Poems* almost four times that amount. Robinson Jeffers' *Flagons and Apples* (Los Angeles, 1912) sells for around $500. Occasionally, the price of a first-book rarity will transcend an author's general reputation. Elinor Wylie's first book, *Incidental Numbers* (London, 1912) was printed anonymously in an edition limited to only 65 copies, and it remains not only a great rarity, but a very high-priced book. Two years ago, a copy brought an incredible $3,750; and early in 1976, another copy was auctioned off at $2,300. Possibly at this date (1977) it is a $4,000 or $5,000 book.

Not all first books are scarce. While most famous authors eased into the literary scene from some back door (often anonymously or pseudonymously), some entered with fanfare and applause, thereby easing the purse of future collectors. Thomas Wolfe's first book was his magnum opus, *Look Homeward, Angel.* It was hotly promoted, lavishly praised, liberally printed, and remains today a somewhat accessible first edition of a first book at a price range from $150 to $300. Other first books—though highly collectable—are reasonably priced because of their limited appeal. Wallace Stevens' *Harmonium* (New York, 1923) can be gotten for under $200, in spite of its beauty and excellence, and in spite of Stevens' commanding stature in twentieth-century letters. But people who take on the collecting of first books of famous authors should be a hardy lot—disciplined, durable, and happily able to write checks for big, meaty sums of money.

XII.

THE FACTORS OF

COMPLETENESS, CONDITION,

CARE AND PROTECTION OF BOOKS

I t is everywhere acknowledged that condition is a prime factor in the value of a book. Occasionally, some bookman will give token resistance to the neurotic extremities of bibliophilic concern over condition. Most, however, are pragmatic. "I think condition *has* been overemphasized," Matthew Bruccoli, says. "But realistically, condition means almost everything in the price of a book. A mint copy will bring, not just a *little* more, but a great deal more than a bad copy."

But of course, one does what he can; and with the great rarities, a book in excellent condition is sometimes virtually impossible to obtain, especially with a limited budget. Here, you have to compromise, and each has to establish his own criteria for compromise. "First I get a copy," Bruccoli says, "and then I worry about improving it." This seems to me a much more sensible and intelligent attitude than the Olympian advice of a prominent New York dealer, who says, "Only buy the very best in whatever interest you have." For a lot of people, this would mean not collecting at all; and that would be a great pity.

"The more common a book," Roderick Brinckman, of Monk Bretton Books, points out, "the more repairs decrease its value. Obviously, if it's a rare book not usually found in good condition, repairs matter less." Replaced pages hurt a book's value, Brickman believes, but he acknowledges that "rare books ought to be made good in this way, if it can be

219

done expertly and, it goes without saying, if there is no intention to deceive." Frank Walsh, of Atlanta's Yesteryear Book Shop, states that, "any lost/replaced pages shoot at least 50 to 75 percent of the retail value out of most books." Walsh specializes in Southern Americana, as well as illustrated children's books. Another dealer in Americana, Bob Hayman, acknowledges the critical importance of good condition, but points out that it is a less important factor in Americana than in, say, first editions or illustrated books.

As for the prudence in rebinding rare books, there are almost as many views as there are collectors, librarians, and dealers. Since there are people who collect bindings, almost independently of the content, you would think a simple arithmetical compounding would result in an accurate judgment that a good first edition or antiquarian book would be enhanced by a tasteful and expensive new binding. Obviously, this is not always the case. If one collects first editions, he is in search of the original, the *Ur* book, the book "as it first was"—original binding and all. However, if that original binding is disgustingly shabby, why might one not reasonably argue that it would in fact be enhanced by a superior, artistically wrought *new* binding? After all, it wasn't *published* with a shabby binding.

One might be as reasonable as he likes, but of course not everyone will listen. Most collectors still cling superstitiously to the idea that the whole book must be "original" at all costs, even at the expense of neanderthal ugliness or antediluvian decay. I accuse such people of superstition because I am of another taste, and believe that my copy of the 1695 edition (the fifth) of Dryden's *Tyrannick Love* is enhanced by its full-leather Sangorski and Sutcliffe binding, and that my first edition of Trollope's *Phineas Redux* is similarly ennobled by the red, half-leather Riviere binding that some anonymous collector judiciously had it clothed in many years ago.

But I must admit that while *I* cherish these books for such embellishments, and feel that they should prove more valuable at auction than their original-binding counterparts (assuming only very good to fine condition) would be, I am forced to admit that I seem to be in the minority, believing as I do; and thereby take comfort only from the righteousness and good sense of my stand.

Obviously, a book whose basic appeal is that of its fine binding (sometimes itself ornately decorated, or even illustrated) will not be enhanced by a more recent binding, no matter how splendid. And some bindings, such as the brown cloth of many American literary classics (most first editions of Emerson and Hawthorne, for instance), are interesting and handsome, in their way, if they can be found in good condition. But such bindings did not wear well, and today, over a century later, they are more often than not sullen, shabby, and drab; and it is hard to believe that such a book should not be considered more worthy in a strong and elegant new binding than in the bruised and dirty integument of its long-departed youth.

Before deciding upon having any book rebound, however, one should be certain that it will be worth the cost, either in usefulness, personal satisfaction, or resale value. "I have found that a book should be worth at least twice the rebinding cost," a dealer advises, "or it's a waste of time even to fool with it."

Art books, private press books, and illustrated books whose value is basically that of their appearance (and to a lesser degree, texture of paper and binding, along with the heft, the "feel" of the book) will obviously be required to be in superb condition. There are virtually no exceptions to this rule, not even the hedging that is allowed in other sorts of rare books, whose values are perhaps somewhat more nearly those of the spirit, rather than the body. A supremely rare first edition of *The Vicar of Wakefield,* with a broken hinge on one of its two volumes, or the rebound copy of the first edition of an early novel by Smollett will be forgiven; but no such lapses from perfect form are allowable in the world of the private press editions and illustrated books. And of course these comprise some of the most exalted figures in catalogues and at auction sales.

The heroic presences of this realm are the illustrators and designers. Books designed by William Morris, T. J. Cobden-Sanderson, Bruce Rogers, D. B. Updike, and any of a number of other famous type-and-book designers bring premium prices that seem never to peak. Even books on the *subject* of type styles and designers are avidly sought after, as are books on almost any subject directly or indirectly related to the making of books, especially such extraordinarily valuable treatises as Dard Hunter's on the subject of papermaking.

In modern times, there has been a drifting away from illustrated books (except in children's books and those expensive press editions that flamboyantly wear the colors of conspicuous expense). Fortunately, the illustrator's art seems to be returning, precisely as more and more expensive private press books and special illustrated editions from the large commercial publishers are printed. The old and venerable art of Walter Crane, Sir John Tenniel, Arthur Rackham, Kate Greenaway, et al, is also enjoying—not a comeback, for their work has never been really neglected—but a popularity that has lifted prices for the books they've illustrated to lofty and majestic heights.

One aspect of the twentieth century illustrator's and designer's art that was never allowed to disappear, however, is the dust jacket. Surely, future historians of literary practices will be amused by our attitudes toward the thin paper cover that was initially intended to protect the book's binding, but quickly became an almost fetishistic object to collectors of first editions.

If the binding is the hide of the living book, then the dust jacket is the epidermis; and the tattoos it bears can make the difference between a book that is practically worthless and one that is worth a great deal of money. Perhaps this is logical, in a way. The value of rare books, like that of all objects of beauty, is ultimately dependent upon two factors beyond their personal excellence: scarcity and ephemerality; and these are of course related, the latter constantly at work in creating the former. The most ephemeral part of a book is obviously the humble dust jacket, whose original purpose was that of protecting the valuable part, the essential book, at the same time providing a place for a little harmless promotional hoopla.

But a first edition is always an emblem of its time and place, and a considerable part of its value derives from this fact. And even though the ardent pursuit of the dust jacket may be considered fetishistic, it is nevertheless undeniable that the collecting of first editions generally is vulnerable to the same charge; and anyway, who cares, in view of the fact that fetishes can prove very interesting, not to mention the logical and psychological systems of proprieties that surround them. So let's not call them fetishes at all; let's call them, well, *talismans.*

The dust jacket, as the term states, is the outer clothing of the book, not really the epidermis at all; and as Hawthorne somewhat primly stated in his notebook, clothing is now (or at least *then*) part of the human body. And dust jackets can be fascinating: the blunt-nosed biplanes cavorting on the blue and gray cover of Faulkner's *Pylon,* for example. Or, on the dust jacket of *Mosquitoes,* the stylized expatriate foursome gathered around the deck table of a yacht (one ashtray, one martini glass, and a scatter of playing cards on top), with a pincurl ocean peak-ing in the background *with only one eye in all those four faces;* and with only the letters "erver" showing upon the life preserver at the left margin of the picture. All these features are fascinatingly present to the whole context of the book as a social (i.e., printed) event. And those figures speak more vividly of that time than Faulkner's prose does, for the dust jacket was a work of what is now known as "pop art," whereas it is not at all idolatrous to claim that Faulkner's art transcended his time in important ways that neglect to show how rooted, in some ways (even if largely in his contemporary readership), it was in the values of the 1920s—as specifically as Fitzgerald's writing, for example; and this radical connection is conveyed with superb immediacy by the anonymous creator of those four well-dressed sophisticates, sharing one martini glass, one ashtray, and one eye.

Dust jackets are essentially a product of the twentieth century, and while their original purpose was to "protect books from dust," this function was soon absorbed by their providing a relatively inexpensive medium for promotion and advertising on cheap paper. As such, they are interesting not only for their conventions of style and their reflection of a communicable visual response to the content of the book, but for the literary conventions they reflect. The rhetoric of "sophistication," of regionalism and the proletarian return, of literary liberalism, and so on, phasing in and fading out, from the twenties through the thirties and forties, and up to the present day. And yet, these commonplaces of dust jacket praise, while more or less distinguishable, do not possess the identity that the visual designs do. One would have to work at identifying the period in which a particular dust jacket puff was written; but the design of a dust jacket is known immediately, and like the telltale qualities of bindings Seymour de Ricci mentioned, can announce the decade of a book's publication three times out of four.

Apparently the premium given to dust jackets has inspired at least one minor specialty. A collector of modern first editions reports that he knows of a dealer who salvages all the dust wrappers that are taken from newly published books and discarded by a large institutional library. This dealer then sells the dust jackets to other dealers throughout the country to place on their "minimal-value, dustwrapper-less first editions."

Some publishers (among the university presses, for example) are experimenting with the publication of books *sans* dust jacket. With university presses—especially scholarly and scientific works—the dust jacket is surely expendable insofar as a book is directed to specialists who, it may be presumed, will be less interested in, and influenced by, the visual belly dance the dust jacket affords in order to sell the patent medicine within. Even though the cheapest and flimsiest paper was originally used, there have been more recent books whose dust wrappers are of the highest possible quality, featuring handsome designs that almost qualify as works of art in themselves, rather than mere curiosities or period decorations. Still, even cheap paper is now costly: the owner of a printing company told me recently that cheap paper was harder to get than the finer grades because of an overcompensation to the problem of scarcity among the quality grades.

It appears that the dust wrapper is here to stay; for a while, at least. And it is very much part of the whole book, and therefore very much part of the first edition. And if it seems ridiculous, well, that's all right, too; for in the world of proprieties (regardless of those *other* worlds), Hamlet's meditation on relativity, that nothing is good or bad, except thinking makes it so, still obtains.

Gary Lepper says it well: "For all intents, the book without dust wrapper is shunned, and the book with appreciably damaged dust wrapper is avoided. Silly, really. I suppose it's overemphasized, but then why unhinged stamps, unchipped porcelain, uncirculated coins, and so on? If you're going to collect, you're going to try, inevitably, for as presentable (read: admirable) a collection as possible. You can't *explain* why people collect things; one either knows or doesn't—it's like trying to explain *why* a joke is funny; you either get it or you don't."

The physical care of books is a very important but often neglected aspect of collecting. Clothbound editions should be kept dusted, and leatherbound books should be cleaned periodically with saddle soap or a mild solution of white cidar vinegar in water, and oiled with one of several acceptable preservatives—a half-and-half solution of neat's-foot oil and untreated lanolin, for example, or a commercial leather preservative, such as Lexol. All books should be kept from direct sunlight and extremes of temperature as well as extremes of moisture or dryness (central heating and air conditioning both tend to be harmful to leatherbound books).

It is appalling to see how wretchedly some otherwise conscientious collectors house their books. I have seen rare and valuable books jammed together on shelves not fit for anything but mason jars and monkey wrenches—shelves consisting of number-three pine (neither planed nor sanded), or resting on cement blocks rough enough to scar metal. Running out of shelf space is, of course, one of the inevitable crises a collector must face; and when this happens, he *may* have to resort to crating his less valuable books and storing them someplace. When he does, he should obviously take care that, (1) the crates or cardboard boxes are clean, firm, and strong; (2) the books are put in carefully, with an abiding realization that they are after all, essentially creatures of paper and glue; (3) packed in a dry (but not *too* dry) place, away from the foraging of roaches and mice.

As precious objects go, books are relatively durable; but the travails and misfortunes an old book is likely to have endured during even a single century of use, misuse, and storage is awesome to contemplate. Proper care of books is, after all, a fairly simple business, providing one knows a few elementary facts about their construction.

Most hardbound books today are made of cloth, paper, and glue. Usually, the cloth is cotton or linen, and the colors water colors, which means that water is just about the worst enemy a book can have. Cloth-bound books may be satisfactorily cleaned in many instances, however, with a special preparation—such as Goddard's Book Restorer, whose odor suggests it is an ammonia compound. I have used this with good results on all but the grimiest and filthiest specimens.

There are other enemies almost as noxious as water. Sunlight, dirt, rough handling, and jamming books too tightly on shelves or in boxes are among the most common. One of the chemicals most disastrous to paper is the kind of acid used in the sealing compounds of most transparent tapes. To the average person, nothing could be more innocent than applying a strip of Scotch tape, for example, to a dust wrapper tear. But if that same person will remove the tape a year later and see how brittle it has become, and how it has browned the paper underneath, he will know something about its toxicity, and he will no longer be quite so innocent in this regard. The effects of these transparent tapes are equally deleterious to leather.

Possibly the most common defect of hollow-back, clothbound books is being "shaken"—which means that the paste or glue at the very rim of the spine, crucial in holding the front and rear boards together, has lost its adhesiveness. A book is badly shaken if it wobbles when you handle it. A good firm copy will be known by the fact that if you take it by the outer rim of the front and back boards, one in each hand, and lift it slowly so that the spine is up, the opening revealed by the sag of the bound pages away from the spine (the "hollow back") will be either a crescent, closed on either side, or two facing parentheses, closed on either side. This latter will be the case if the book is relatively thick and heavy; however, if the book is obviously in bad condition and *very* heavy, this test should not be made; and in any case, it should be made very carefully. If the crescent shows a sag at the edge (a small vertical wall, before it joins the board), or if in the case of larger books the parentheses are apart at the edge, then the book is shaken.

Most book people caution against doing anything to a book, unless you're a professional; but I have found a shaken book easily reparable. All that is needed is a small amount of Book Saver, Sobo, or some other nontoxic glue that dries flexible (a skilled binder I know recommends Elmer's); hold the book vertical, by the boards, so that the gap shows, and dribble a little glue down the inside of the crease, so that it covers the separation (only be careful not to get any on the middle portion of the spine, for that part is meant to hang as loose as the coolest philosopher); then after all the shaken joints have gotten an inch or so trickle of glue down the inner crease, close the book and let it dry under pressure. I now use a book press, but in the past I've used barbell weights, or even a stack of heavy books, with perfectly satisfactory results. One of the little pleasures of bibliophily is buying a shaken copy of a worthy book, gluing it under the arms, as directed above, and then putting it under pressure, and occupying your mind elsewhere, perhaps with reading from an unshaken copy purchased on that same day, bathed in the realization that, hour by hour, that shaken copy is being mended, and thereby renewed.

A special box or covering for a rare book functions in protecting the book not only physically, but symbolically; a book that is boxed is not in as great a danger of being casually pulled out by the top of the spine, cracked open, page-flipped, and dropped (all disasters to a book) as one sitting on a shelf or lying on a table. Solander cases were first designed for the protection of botanical specimens; they were invented by a man named Solander, who was a pupil of Linnaeus. Soon, these boxes—which feature a fall-down front or back—were adapted for the protection of prints, and eventually made their natural progress to housing rare and delicate books. They are very efficient, no doubt; but most collectors want *most* of their possessions to be visible, and a book ensconced in a solander case is very much out of the way for good, as well as bad.

Most rarities are adequately protected by any one of a variety of commercial transparent plastic or Bakelite covers.

There are companies that specialize in materials for the repair and conservation of books. Most of these will be found under some such listing as "Library Supplies," but their products are of great usefulness and value to the private collector-investor. One such company is the Talas Company in New York City, whose inventory of bookish materials even includes a variety of vellum, for those whose spirit is strong enough to venture into the touchy problem of rebacking or recovering some old volume—an undertaking recommended only for those thoroughly trained in such matters, and therefore, so far as most collectors are concerned, best left entirely to professionals.

Most collectors naturally acquire their own variations upon these methods, but the variations are for the most part simply matters of the trade names of supplies and equipment, kinds of paste or adhesive compounds, and tolerance for disrepair and/or rebinding. Whatever his methods might be, decisions regarding repair, protection, and safekeeping face every collector in a variety of ways. (In making such decisions, one might well keep the following meditation of William Dean Howells in mind: "The mortality of all inanimate things is terrible to me, but that of books most of all.")

In conclusion, badly damaged books should be restored by professionals or left as they are. This is the consensus of book collectors everywhere. One of the controversies that exercised past generations was over whether or not a gentleman collector should have his books rebound. Some collectors did so as a matter of course, "wanting their friends to be well-dressed," as one of them put it. Today, if the original binding of a rare book is in good condition, virtually no collector would want to see it rebound. If a fine binding, alone, is wanted, then have a reprint edition, or a lesser book rebound, rather than destroy or detract from the original value of the first edition.

Henry Wagner is reported to have said that "Every great book may be expected to turn up once in seven years." But the truth is, we don't always *want* to wait those seven years, especially in view of the fact that we don't *know* that *that* good book will turn up again (it may be eight years), and even if it does, it will likely cost two or three times what it costs now, even in the same condition. All of which means: most of us will be tempted, in spite of all advice to the contrary, to buy a poor copy of a very desirable book anytime it is available for a price we can afford.

"Please do not include my address in any printed material," a wealthy collector asked in his response to my inquiries for this book; and then he went further and asked that I even avoid mention of his name altogether. "Our book collection and other objects of art are woefully under-insured," he explained. "When we travel every year, as we have done, our items are vulnerable to knowledgeable theft. Many of the very rare incunabula I store in our bank vault when I leave for trips."

"Vulnerable to knowledgeable theft" is a good phrase; but it would be insensitive to pause too long over its stylistic felicity, for its reference is a grim and fearful one to the bibliophile. It is also a familiar one; and the above request was echoed in several ways by others whose knowledge and expertise I have drawn upon.

Fire and theft are, of course, the great dangers to a private collection. In the case of fire, damage is more often caused by the water used to extinguish the blaze than by the fire itself (the books being caught in the cross fire, as it were). Theft is somewhat a function of fame (of the collection, the collector, or both) and locality (some geographical areas being almost beyond the reach of an insurance company's willingness to take a risk).

Protection of his private library is obviously a matter of great concern to the bibliophile who spends so much care, patience, and money on his acquisitions. The danger of fire is something of a constant for most of us who do not have books of so breathtaking a value that they require safekeeping in a fireproof vault. Deterioration from extremes of temperature and humidity is probably a greater danger, statistically, than fire. Nevertheless, fire presents one of the most fearful threats to one's collection, and a consideration of one's library—how valuable and how vulnerable it is—should be added to those normal considerations of fire insurance for the home.

The problem of theft, which in the case of rare books will almost certainly prove "knowledgeable," is a quite different one. Most bibliophiles, like most art and antique collectors generally, are protected by the cloak of anonymity. It will prove to be a very special sort of thief, after all, who undertakes to steal rare books—especially in view of their being cumbersome and heavy to transport (especially in any significant number and compared to jewelry, and even furs), and being awfully hard to dispose of. We have all heard of fences for stolen furs and jewelry, but fences for stolen Elzivirs, Ashendenes, Kelmscott, and Doves Press editions? The knowledgeable book thief, like his victim, is faced with the very tough problem of selling rare books profitably. Books just aren't all that liquid; and while a collector may shop around for buyers, and perhaps even put out his own catalogue, of sorts, your average thief, before he reaches such extremities, is likely to turn his attention elsewhere, to other kinds of loot.

Still, as was just stated, a book thief will prove to be anything but average. He'll have to know a valuable book when he sees one, even under somewhat inhibiting conditions (bibliography by flashlight *has* to be an uphill crime), and he'll have to have some fairly practical idea of how to turn rare books into cash (criminals may be visionary, but they're seldom less than pragmatic in their profession).

Back in 1971, Miss Frances Hamill, of Hamill and Barker in Chicago, bore witness to the expertise of at least two book thieves, posing as priests of the Russian Orthodox Church. Finding both of the men "rather charming and very bright," she bought (1) seven atlases from them for $7,000, and (2) their story about planning to use the money to help establish a monastery on Long Island. One of the volumes sold was the superbly rare *La Atlas del Mundo o el Aquado,* printed in Amsterdam in 1665. According to Peter T. Chew's account in *The National Observer,* early in 1972 Miss Hamill approached the Yale Library about the atlases, and was told that Yale already owned *La Atlas del Mundo.* This was surprising, since only three copies were known to exist, so she asked if their copy had any distinguishing marks, and of course found out that their copy and hers were one and the same, having been spirited from one place to the other by those bright and charming, if larcenous, men of spirit.

The theft of rare books is a very specialized and somewhat highfalutin kind of larceny. Institutions are probably more vulnerable than the private collection because of three factors: they're likely to have more valuable holdings, these holdings are likely to be well known, perhaps even famous, and they will be accessible (in spite of every precaution) to a great number and variety of people. For the private collector whose possessions are so valuable that they invite "knowledgeable theft," there are a number of precautions, all of which will, alas, prove incomplete, since it is a truism that a totally theft-proof device or place is, along with the perpetual motion machine and a totally just society, unlikely.

On a recent visit with the rare-books curator of a small liberal arts college, I was discussing the problems I faced in cataloguing my private collection for insurance purposes. In fact, as I explained to him, my collection at that time was covered only by an extension of the coverage on our household goods—which seemed to me a practically worthless sort of coverage, since individual items were neither appraised nor listed. He agreed with me (we were both right); and then went on to speak of their institutional problems in having their collection of 35,000 rare books insured for 2.5 million dollars. This was a special policy that was improvised by the underwriters after they first questioned the college's application for so much coverage. In fact, they were downright suspicious ("Two and a half million dollars coverage for a collection of *books?*"), and sent two representatives to investigate. Within fifteen minutes, they were convinced—awed by the age of the books they pulled at random from the shelves; and their suspicions of fraud or put-on were laid to rest.

"People like that," the curator mused sadly, "don't know the first thing about rare books, so anything they do in the way of policy is pretty much a gamble, a calculated risk."

"I suppose I'll face some of the same problems when I try to have my private collection insured," I said.

"You won't have any luck at all," my friend said. "When I tried to have mine insured, all they would do is just add fifty dollars coverage for what they considered a bunch of worthless old books."

I found the curator's story a little depressing, but thought it would be wise to check it out on my own, so I brought up my problem with a neighbor who is in insurance. He took my inquiry pretty much in stride, and seemed confident that some kind of policy could be worked out for my own collection. And in fact, within a few days he got back to me with the gratifying (and a little surprising) news that—not only could I get a fine arts policy on my books—but the cost for such policies is very reasonable—$25 annual premium on the first $10,000 valuation, and $23.50 for the next $15,000, and so on, with a minimum premium of $25.00.

Naturally, one's collection should be catalogued and appraised before insuring it. There is some flexibility in this, but essentially, what the insurance company should have is an inventory of the books insured, some sort of item-by-item valuation, and an explanation of the principle by which this valuation was arrived at. However, one collector I know has by-passed the detailed valuation, with the theory that any book can be evaluated precisely if and when it is stolen or destroyed, by simple reference to current catalogues and auction records.

Another factor is, of course, how and where the books are housed. As for the "how," there is little likelihood of a problem if one's private library is part of, and therefore just as secure as, his residence. Location is another matter: if you live on a country estate five or ten miles out of town, and depend upon relatively distant county agencies for fire and police protection, you will naturally pay a slightly higher premium. (The rates given in the last paragraph are "city rates," for the area where I live.) Geographical location is an even more critical factor; if you live in Manhattan or Miami, my agent informs me, you may have considerable trouble getting good coverage; in less-crowded places, with a lower average income and a correspondingly lower crime rate, the problem is no greater than that of general insurance.

In working with an insurance company, there is more room for negotiation than people tend to think, especially when you stray from the well-worn paths of standard protection for home, auto, personal liability, and so on, where the issues are all pretty much cut and dried. Rare books represent a very special kind of valuable, and it is likely that a good policy will grow out of some kind of dialogue, or at least mutual adaptation, between the collector's needs and the company's resources for protection.

If you have really thought about your collection, and have arrived at a clear idea of what you want, you'll stand a much better chance for developing meaningful and effective protection. Consider the case of one wealthy collector, who reports:

> You need something like a fine arts policy on the collection in which you list every item insured worth over a given sum, say $50 or $100. You need this specificity. Also, most important, and something which may be unique to me, I think you need a clause which stipulates that the title to an insured item stays with the collector. That is, if a claim is paid and the item later

231

turns up (as is likely with rare books), I have the right to repay the claim and retain the item. Otherwise, the title usually reverts to the insurance people and you risk losing something irreplaceable.

By the time a library grows even to a modest thousand volumes, it should be catalogued in some way that is, (1) efficient, (2) convenient, (3) suitable to the specific collection the catalogue is intended to map, and (4) clear to outsiders. The reasons behind all these principles are obvious; and yet, there are many collectors whose "catalogues" grow more-or-less spontaneously (if at all), and because of this fact, omit or neglect one or more of the above principles.

For example, in the early days of his collecting, one may decide not to list values for his books, either in the way of listing what was paid for them or what their market value might be. The reasons for such an omission might be good ones—the collector may not yet feel he has sufficient grasp of the market to assign monetary values to his books; he may want to wait out a period of rapid appreciation, until prices stabilize; he may not want to list the purchase prices of books he got very cheaply, lest these depreciated prices influence an outsider brought in to liquidate his stock in the event of an emergency; and so on. Whatever his "good" reasons are, however, the fact remains that a rare books catalogue without values—no matter how tentative—assigned to the titles is an incomplete, therefore inefficient catalogue.

Exactly how one's cataloguing is done is not too important, with certain obvious exceptions. Circulating library procedures obviously don't apply, because some of their data are irrelevant to a rare-book collection, and, even more importantly, the code designations on the spines of books—Library of Congress or Dewey Decimal—would be unthinkable in any form for use with rare books. The collector has to rely on his memory and a general classification according to cases and shelves to locate his volumes.

One of the most interesting and simplest methods for cataloguing a small collection of hundreds, rather than thousands, of books is that used by an old lady I met several years ago, who was gradually liquidating the books collected by her father-in-law, a lumber dealer back in the 1920s. This was an interesting collection, and I owe a half dozen of my choicest items to it, which the lady in question sold to me for the identical price her father-in-law had paid for them. Having gone through the shelves of her house and pulled out the books I was interested in, I took them to her, and she opened a huge old-fashioned business ledger that contained the information she needed. Consulting a number marked by pencil on the front paste-down leaf, she then found that number in the ledger, after which were listed the author, title, edition, issue, state, and so on, followed by the purchase price. Needless to say, I was the beneficiary of all that half-century's appreciation in value; and as happy to make my purchases as she was to sell the books, since she had no interest in keeping them, nor was she in particular need of money. Obviously, this long-dead lumberman did not "invest" in his books at all; and for sentimental reasons I would like to think he didn't look upon his books in that way, since he had evidently not taken any precautions about disposing of them at their true appreciated value. But, of course, that doesn't make any difference now to anyone.

Basically, cataloguing one's collection need be neither complicated nor fancy. Robert L. Wilbur, of New York's Gramercy Book Shop, gives this simple advice, which also happens to point to the best method for cataloguing a private library: "Get a batch of 3 x 5 slips or index cards and start at the top, left-hand corner of the room, and, working to the right, enter the following for each book on a card: Author, title, place & date of publication, where and from whom the book was bought, the price paid and the date of purchase. If you want to be fancy, you can add details about size, binding, number of pages, and so on. When you finish, sit down and alphabetize the lot, and then put it in an old shoe box, and you have your catalogue. Or buy LC cards for each book. Or hire a professional cataloguer."

Good advice, succinctly stated. And when your catalogue is finished, you will possess a map of your library, which is itself a map of your mind and heart, whose individual moods and features are more specifically mapped by the individual volumes. Therefore, your card catalogue may be thought of as the map of a map of maps.

XIII.

SOME STRATEGIES AND TACTICS

FOR BUYING AND SELLING

ou need not be a dealer, nor have the intention of becoming one to take up the sport of bibliophilic scouting and scavenging, thereby occasionally finding yourself in a position to buy books in huge lots. Once they are sure you have a genuine interest in books, want to buy them, and show some acquaintance with them as theoretically marketable commodities, people are likely to fasten upon you with an almost hysterical resolve, and point you to a cache of books in the shed or attic, or their great uncle's library that has been stored in the loft above a garage for eleven years.

For the collector, there is a natural inclination to shy away: after all, he's not looking for *that* many books. What will he *do* with all of them? Since he is not a dealer, he doesn't have any business in buying a whole library.

Such an opportunity has come to me upon occasion, and there is a thrill in it that is undiminished by either time or repetition. Did the fact that I was not a dealer mean that I shouldn't buy a thousand, or even ten thousand, books? Buy them and relieve some anxious soul? Why not? The burden of so much possession weighs heavily upon the custodian or owner of all those books. Where will he *store* them? How could he ever find *shelf* space? He or she does not know where to turn to investigate their value, if, indeed, they have any. He or she throws himself or herself upon you, exasperated by the populous ignorance that insulates him or her from knowledge.

They are, in short, asking for it. Because, well, how do they think anybody else *found out?* Isn't there a public library nearby, in which reside some, at least, of the tools of reference necessary for finding out? (There always is: but even the local civic librarian will likely prove ignorant of even the most elementary considerations concerning rare books, for rarity is an impurity in her, or his, domain, that is not accounted for in the courses of library science, and consequently, best not even thought of.)

Recently, my wife and I stopped at an auction in a small town some thirty miles from our home. A few tattered music books (circa 1900) and a few old Ray's arithmetic books, a Methodist hymnal, and a graying clutter of sad and defeated old paperbacks were all that were displayed. Of course, I asked if there were any other books to be offered for sale. I have learned to ask such questions in a loud-enough voice that others might hear, for there are a lot of people who have heard of a cache of old books stashed away somewhere.

A woman heard my question. She had an antique shop, and she made the obvious inquiries; and after a few ceremonial dodges (always having to do with someone who wanted to sell some books, but the name is forgotten), she told us about a huge old house, only two blocks away, that had just been sold, and the housekeeper was still living there, and there were a lot of old books that she didn't think they had gotten rid of yet. And so on.

She told us where to go, and of course we went there—not terribly excited, for the cousins and brothers of those music books, Methodist hymnals (a trillion must have been printed), and a whole covey of limp and livid copies of Ray's *Arithmetic* might be lying in wait.

But such was not the case. A very gracious and cultured woman (she used the word "pragmatic" casually and with felicitous accuracy) greeted us, showed us into the house, and then immediately informed us that she had to go for a hairdresser's appointment and would be leaving in about five minutes, but please make ourselves at home. This made me a little uncomfortable, because—as I told her—I wasn't a thief, but if something should turn up missing later on, would it not be natural for *them* to wonder?

"Never mind," she said breezily. "We in Appalachia are friendly that way." (That's exactly what she said, and exactly the way she said it.)

Then she showed us upstairs to a grand central hallway, flanked by four huge bookcases, filled with good old books in good condition. There were also books downstairs, in two bookcases in the huge living room, which was of truly manorial proportions, and furnished with at least a dozen excellent pieces of antique cherry and walnut furniture.

Cheerily, she bade us good-bye; whereupon I made a survey of the library. It had belonged to a scholarly attorney, with a special, if somewhat predictable, interest in Lincoln and the Civil War. Almost all the books were handsome and in good condition; at one time, they had been expensive. Now, all but a few (say twenty-five or thirty out of a thousand) were devoid of bibliophilic interest, but those few were very nice indeed.

I have phoned the owner, who lives in a city two hundred miles away, and she informs me that her son intends to rent a truck and bring the furniture and books to the city, where he is convinced everything will bring a better price. Probably, he's right. Certainly, he's prudent to work at the idea. All I said to his mother is that I am willing to make an offer; I think (but did not mention) that it is one which will likely match the offer of just about any rare-book dealer (although I cannot be sure of this), and will save that young man the trouble of hauling all those books and the eventual frustration and anxiety of having one dealer choose a handful from the stock, another dealer take a still smaller handful from those remaining, and so on.

In short, these people are in the position of trying to dispose of a modest, if respectable, collection of books, some few of which deserve the label "rare." My particular advantage is that, first, I have taken the trouble to look at the books (no dealer would travel to this small town, probably not even if he had sworn evidence that there were first editions of Stephen Crane and Ambrose Bierce awaiting him); second, I am not in a position where I have to worry about "turnover" as a dealer would; third, I can pretty well predict how much any one of several dealers I know will pay me for some of the books in this collection, which amount will probably cover the cost of the books plus my expenses; and fourth, which is best of all, this calculation will leave several books for my own library that will enhance it. As for the remainder: they can be traded, sold, stored, and given away.

This episode is still not over; and it is interesting to me, not only for the suspense that remains, but because I find it instructive, in its way, and representative of a general attitude toward books. And this atti-

237

tude adds up to still a fifth, quite subtle advantage in my having visited that house at just that time.*

If someone pays two hundred dollars for a single copy of a book, people are naturally impressed. But in a quite different way, there is something even more impressive in someone's paying the same amount of money for a thousand books. The former has simply "invested" heavily in an object that he obviously believes or knows to be valuable; the latter, however, has committed himself in a way that the former has not. He has, in the lexicon of many people, "bought a whole library." He has, therefore, taken on a mysterious responsibility that cannot be measured by the mere expenditure of two hundred dollars. Not only is there the physical problem of hauling and storage, or the practical one of marketing and selling, but there is a deeper, more mysterious obligation—that of assuming the custody of objects that are, even to some of the most benighted and ignorant of people, not *simply* objects at all. There is, in fact, a cultural residue (perpetuated and subtly cultivated by the schools) of the idea that books are something apart, something special. (I naturally agree with this idea, and proclaim it more fervently than most, but the object of this reverence is the book as ideal, the book as it is best exemplified, not simply any sad sheaf of bound papers.) That invisible line drawn around any and all books represents a kind of taboo. Even if uneducated people don't read, and even if they have no conscious feeling for books, they nevertheless are likely to stand somewhat in awe of them. And the fact is, most people—educated and otherwise—just don't know *how* to possess books.

Here, of course, we enter the domain of symbol and superstition. Having run off his first "copies" of the Bible in the late 1400s, Johann Fust displayed them, and was immediately suspected of witchcraft. Half a millennium later, we still marvel secretly at the miracle of bookmaking, and are uneasy in our sense of the ideals that we find implicit, everywhere, in the mere fact of a book's existence. Book burning is such an egregious sin, in our thinking, that the very thought makes us uncomfortable. There are few books most of us could personally, thoughtfully burn (dousing them with gasoline, say, and dropping a lighted match onto the cover), regardless of how despicable or worthless the contents may be. This is not only superstitious, it's silly: the fact

---

*Since this was written, my offer was accepted and all has transpired very much as predicted.

is, we would all be wondrously cleansed if, after announced deadlines (to allow all booklovers a chance to buy everything they want), all the books in every Good Will and Salvation Army store in the country were periodically taken to dumps and burned. What a spiritualizing experience! What a relief to have the world purged, at intervals, of all those dismal textbooks, dollar book-club editions, legal codes from the early 1900s, real estate question-and-answer primers, twenty-year-old how-to manuals, psychology self-help tomes, and all of the marvelously varied, but dismally familiar, once-relevant dreck that discourages all but the most ardent biblioscope from ranging along those aisles. Within a week, all the shelves would be filled with similar trash, no doubt, but there would be *some* unexpected books among them; and after all, this would be a constant rebirth and renewal, as well as a graduation of quality.

Whenever one buys two or more boxes of books at one time, he is providing another, more lasting pleasure for himself. In selecting from hundreds of books, one is challenged to focus very clearly upon the particular book at hand, which—like all abstracting and memorizing—is connected with a simultaneous forgetting (blocking out the background in order to concentrate more effectively upon the "figure," the immediate object). Thus it is that when you return with your haul, you can indulge yourself in long and leisurely moments of rediscovering your treasures, picking your books one by one from their boxes, checking the points against the bibliographies, palpating the bindings and hinges for weaknesses, reading the dedications, prefaces, introductions, copyright information, notations, tables of contents, and all those other harbingers of the book itself.

The opportunities for making large purchases are everywhere. There is an elderly lady who lives in our town—a very active and spirited woman, with bright blue eyes and a pile of white, spun-glass hair. I have encountered her at many yard sales and auctions. Her specialty is the collecting of dolls. She loves them, I would guess, as I love books. And of course, it is good to trade information—let others know what you collect and find out what they collect.

Several years ago, when I bought a three-faced doll (whose head pivots in and out of a cloth bonnet), I mentioned it to this lady, and she professed to be mightily interested. We talked about it, and I promised to show it to her. And during each conversation we had, we became more and more vivid to the other, and our interests were more and more deeply fixed in each other's memory. So it was not surprising, one day, when she informed me of a lot of books scheduled for sale that very evening at a nearby auction house. For some reason, I had missed the announcement.

Of course, my wife and I attended. There were exactly fifty-two boxes of books, all stacked near the back wall in dim light. After sorting through several boxes, I discovered that this was the library of a professor of psychology who had recently died. (I hadn't known him.) Many of the books were technical, some scholarly, and some were very interesting, perhaps valuable.

Shortly before the auction began, I went to the auctioneer and asked how he planned to dispose of them. He, in turn, asked if I would be interested in giving him an opening bid for all of them. "Yes," I said. "Twenty dollars."

He frowned. "That's a lot of books for twenty dollars. I don't think I'd like to start at that. How about thirty?"

"I'll open at twenty-five," I said.

He thought a moment, and then nodded.

An hour and a half later, when he got to the books (I had already bought a stupid and wobbly little Victorian table by then), we were ready. He announced that there was an opening bid of twenty-five dollars, and he asked for thirty. He asked for it again. The audience merely stared. (I don't think there were many who had even noticed the books stacked in back.) He asked for thirty again. He asked for it slowly, with feeling. He asked for it in a shrill voice. He told the audience they weren't listening. He told them that those books represented the professional library of a scholar, a professor, a man of science. They listened. He asked for twenty-seven-fifty. They listened respectfully. His vision glided over those sitting before him, and then—with professional poise—he knocked the books down to me, for twenty-five dollars. The audience stirred with the release of tension; and the sale went on.

What do you do with fifty-two boxes of books? Well, first you look through them. My wife and I started, right then, far enough away from the bright lights of the auction so that we wouldn't disturb the progress of the sale. I lifted box after box out from the stacks to where we could get to their contents and see all that we had just purchased in a moment's glorious madness. Some of these boxes were filled with slick-paper periodicals, and as heavy as blocks of salt for livestock. (You need a strong back and a firm resolve for this sort of business.)

We labored for over an hour in that dark and dusty alcove, serenaded by the chant of the auctioneer, as he offered a motley of new and used items involving weed killers, table lamps, footstools, kitchen stoves, antique mirrors and garden hose to his listeners.

With each new box of books we opened, there was a revelation. The signature of the man who had once owned all these books was becoming clearer and clearer, for one's library is, after all, a unique testimony to what he is. Here, in addition to all the scientific and scholarly texts, was revealed a lively interest in literature. Particularly, the avant-garde of the 1930s and 1940s. There were two Obelisk Press editions (one in the classic plain brown wrapper) of Henry Miller's works. There were editions of Freud, Jung, Adler, and all the canon of the modern thought-thinkers. There was a liberal scattering of the modern literary classics—Joyce, Thomas Wolfe, Lawrence, Faulkner. None of these was a first edition, but some were early enough to be worthwhile. One of the most interesting surprises was a box filled with early copies of science-fiction magazines. (Later, I traded this with a dealer for a first edition of Henry James' *The Real Thing,* superbly rebound in red half-leather by Brian Frost.)

It was, in short, a rich collection, gathered by a thoughtful and interesting man. It is a pity that it was disposed of so ineffectively, so cheaply; but of course, given this fact, I am pleased that I was the one to get it. Of all the books this collection contained, I remember one most vividly, for its retail value alone is almost twice the amount I paid for all those fifty-two boxes; this is the first edition, in dust wrapper, of course, and in excellent condition, of *Paterson (Part 2),* by William Carlos Williams. Most of the remaining books—the vast majority, indeed—I gave away. With, as they say, a full and happy heart.

Time, the old adage says, is money. But it's a lot less money for some than for others. Or to put it another way, if you are lucky enough to have spare hours during the week, you will have the opportunity to indulge in such shenanigans as I have been reporting upon. Many of my friends who are professors have said they would like to collect books, but they just don't have the money. I have always tried to point out the error of their thinking: they may not be able to pick up the phone and order first editions of Swift or Blake, or the edition of Tacitus put out by the Doves Press in 1900, autographed by T. J. Cobden-Sanderson, but they can collect; and once they accept certain rational and obvious compromises, they can collect significantly and well. (I do not imply that "professors" work fewer hours than other folk—I know better; but I do know that we usually have more flexibility in our working hours than most vocations allow.)

Whether you call it scouting, dealing, or wheeling and dealing makes absolutely no difference: the best way for most people to collect is to place themselves as often as possible in the flow of books. "Read lots and lots of catalogues," Matthew Bruccoli advises the beginning collector; "handle lots and lots of books. Nothing can replace years of handling, looking at books. Try to get a job—even if you have to work for free—in a rare-book library. Nothing can replace the experience of being exposed to lots and lots of books, of handling them, memorizing them."

Bruccoli grew up in an area where there were plenty of bookstores, and he figures that in those early days of his collecting he was actually handling—physically handling fifty thousand books a year, possibly more.

If much of the advice given above appears to be prejudicial against those potential collector-investors who have considerable money to invest, but little time, well, perhaps it is, in a way. This doesn't mean that collecting rare books—long thought of as a game for the super rich—is now somehow stacked *against* those folks; not at all. As mentioned previously, the wealthy investor in rare books (as in every other kind of investing) has distinct advantages: he can buy the "top ticket" items that are so obviously valuable, so immediately salable, that if and when they are resold dealers are willing to pay higher percentages for them than for their humbler brethren, and auction houses will eagerly accept them in their consignments.

Adventuring among books can be enormous fun, no doubt, if you have spare time, or at least a flexible schedule, and if you have the temperament for prospecting in basements, attics, barns, and cold garages. But for most people the best method of collecting with an eye on investment is working with and through one or more dealers. Beyond question, this is the most efficient method for you, even if you have a small budget, but little time to spend in learning the rare-book market. If this is your situation, you should happily put your fate in the hands of dealers pretty much as you would your stock broker or financial adviser—always observing the fact of the special quality of books, however, for if you don't, the unique charm of rare books against any other kind of investment is forfeited. One will naturally, and one should, collect out of a feel for a particular kind of book, out of an interest in a subject; because whatever collecting interest one develops will have a built-in investment potential, and somewhere there will be a dealer who can help you achieve this potential.

Working with a dealer is not advisable for the wealthy collector only. Anyone who can put aside a monthly sum of as little as twenty, thirty, or forty dollars—the price of an installment loan for an inexpensive television set—can collect meaningfully and invest actively with that sum. Ideally, a little of this money will be reserved for your own scouting, while most of it should be allowed to accumulate for those special purchases your dealer can look for if you will let him. Most long-established dealers of any reputation can be trusted, of course. They'll want your continued business. A few may not like it if your approach is solely that of investing in books, rather than collecting them for yourself; but I suspect most will be found willing to sell to you without too close a scrutiny of your motives, if you have the cash.

The affluent collector-investor, as well as the less affluent, can work well with a single trusted dealer acting as a sort of agent. Like a real-estate agent, a book dealer will work a lot harder if he has "an exclusive listing," and knows a customer has put the growth of his collection in his hands. He'll look for hard-to-get items in all the obvious channels, plus a few of his own. "If a collector selects a dependable dealer," Jake Zeitlin (of Los Angeles' Zeitlin & Verbrugge's Booksellers) claims, "he will do better than if he plays the field." And of course, most people simply don't have the time to play the field; and even if they did, they would very often find themselves at a disadvantage, for they would be forced to enter the arena with dealers—who, it may be assumed, usually know a lot more about what they're doing than the average, passionate, well-heeled amateur.

As for scouting on one's own, there are all those strategies I have mentioned, and all the satisfactions in following the chase with the hounds, rather than with the riders. Here, especially, the tactics that relate to the expanding market are available—and of these, one of the most fruitful and interesting opportunities lies in the rich lode of future rarities that one can find in today's new book offerings, or even in the huge miscellany of remaindered books. "By some kind of stale iro-ny," Edward Dahlberg wrote, "books that were once remaindered fre-quently become deluxe collector's items."* In this quoted passage, Dahlberg was alluding to the books of Randolph Bourne, but the truth of what he said is also evident in the fact that some of Dahlberg's own books have been remaindered—and quite recently—in spite of the fact that he is a deep, passionate, and learned writer, and one who is more and more obviously "collectable" with the passage of years. I came upon the boxed limited edition of his *Sorrows of Priapus,* recently, on a dealer's shelf for $150; however, *this* edition, you may be sure, was nev-er remaindered.

Although I have referred to some of the various arts of procuring books, here and there, these principles deserve repetition. It is impor-tant to study as many dealers' catalogues as possible to be the first to discover bargains, to be sure, but also to grow constantly in book knowl-edge—knowledge of prices, trends, bibliography, and collectable titles, authors, and presses. Nowhere does the axiom "Knowledge is power" prove itself more directly than in book collecting. And there is no other undertaking so rich in details of nuance and information than collect-ing: truly, you can never know enough about books.

Also, one should learn the best sources *he* has for procuring books. This will always prove somewhat an individual thing, dependent upon such personal factors as one's geographical location, budget for book buying, temperament, employment and social contacts, travel habits, and so on.

The alert collector will be responsive to a great variety of facts; and if his approach to collecting is like those well-advertised liniments—deep and penetrating in his mind—he will discover opportunities where oth-ers would not dream they exist. Take, for example, the fluctuations of the dollar in international exchange—a subject that most people would assume to be pretty much the exclusive interest of financiers, bankers, corporation executives, and currency speculators.

But of course, the international rare-book market is, like all markets, sensitive to the up-and-down adventures of national currencies. Books, along with diamonds, gems, works of art, and antiques, increase in val-ue simply by virtue of their relative stability as measured against a wild-

*Alms for Oblivion (Minneapolis: University of Minnesota Press, 1964), p. 79.

ly inflating dollar. And of course the career of the dollar is intimately related to monetary policies. A wealthy Midwestern collector writes:

> In recent times book prices have risen due to the unwise monetary policies adopted by our Congress since 1960, in pursuing planned economy goals, that required a constantly rising price level, which is to say, a deliberate depreciation of the value of currency by increasing the outstanding money supply.
>
> As the money supply increased in the United States, and bank deposits and loans grew rapidly, reflecting growth in credit outstanding, and the speed-up of the rate of money velocity, the net effect of the inflationary atmosphere was felt everywhere, world-wide. Since the price of rare books is determined by the supply vs. the demand, in general, all book prices rose. The supply of old and rare books is absolutely limited. Of these kinds, all have been produced that will ever be produced. There is no increasing supply overhanging the market; but there has been a constantly increasing supply of available money ready and willing—and seeking—genuine objects of art, such as old and rare books, manuscripts and missals.

The recent history of the dollar in the European market has had a profound effect upon the international rare-book trade, and the loss of stability in the dollar has brought about within the past few years a reversal in the long-standing American policy of raiding Europe with checkbook and pen, and skimming off thousands upon thousands of its bibliophilic treasures. Now, more and more, European dealers are buying books in the American market for their affluent customers.

The role of the international money market in the establishment of book prices isn't really anything new; and of course it has a political as well as economic dimension that is more visible in some situations than in others. The collector just quoted (who wishes to remain anonymous) gives this interesting account of his modus operandi through the years:

> Many of my acquisitions are really examples of speculation in foreign exchange. Those experiences started more than forty-five years ago. During the great depression and through the pre–World War II period, I acquired many books out of Germany and Austria, as well as Holland and France, because of the need by numerous individual European book owners for a

245

way to secure funds to be deposited to their account in American banks—as they saw social and political disorders increase daily and the specter of war on the horizon. They could not transfer funds out of Europe but they could sell items into the United States for United States currency.

Many of my incunabula were paid for by checks sent to domestic banks in money centers to be deposited to the seller's account. Thus were funds secured in the United States when no funds could be sent out of Germany and Austria. The local book dealer—or an individual—could spend his available national currency to buy rare items and offer them for sale by mail; and ship them to the United States. This was a way of transferring wealth; and a wave of rare books came here before World War II.

After the war ended in 1945, many books which had been looted by soldiers and others, found their way to the United States because of foreign exchange needs. People and institutions sacrificed national treasures to get United States currency, so goods and services which were desperately needed could be bought in the United States and shipped to Europe.

In my collection is one volume of a three-volume Koberger Bible of 1483, which was probably stolen out of an East German Abbey during the war. I got it from Copenhagen in 1946.

Foreign exchange rates (prior to our 1971 suspension of gold redemption of American paper dollars and bank balances, and the subsequent two devaluations of the American dollar in 1973 and 1974) made book prices extremely high for the European owner in terms of his currency and very cheap to an American buyer. Many of us took advantage of this opportunity to buy real treasures. With the depreciation of the dollar, a reverse flow has commenced.

Some kinds of books are obviously more affected by the international money dance than others. These include most of the greatest rarities— namely the very oldest books, which are necessarily of European origin and therefore necessarily of European interest. Or they are fine press books, most of which it so happens, have so far been printed in Europe.

Of course, some of the very oldest and most valuable Americana possess European as well as American interest, and in fact, many of these are printed in European languages (e.g., *Relations des Jésuites,* Prince Maximilian's *Reise in das Innere Nord-America,* Luis Sales' *Noticias de la*

Provincia de Californias). One's language is as intimate a possession as his land, so the proprietary feeling expressed by European collectors and institutions in buying up very early and rare Americana printed in European languages is understandable.

The American collector is not necessarily forced to bide his time, however. There is plenty of Americana—most of it, in fact—that is virtually his own exclusive province, even though the prices may seem more and more prohibitive each year. And of course, the American collector has not been priced out of the European market by any means; maybe in today's rare-book market there is actually a better price balance between Europe and America than there ever has been. Maybe we've just been spoiled too long; but then again, maybe European ascendancy in certain areas is only a short-range phenomenon. Whatever, there are still plenty of areas in which to collect, and plenty of books within the range of every collector's budget.

Most treatises on book collecting begin with some such reasonable advice as, "Choose a subject and stick to it." No doubt, there are arguments for such a strategy, but if the decision were to be forced, yea or nay, I would vote against it. For one thing, I don't think anyone ever chooses a deep subject: I think it chooses him.

There is no doubt that a focused and well-defined collection possesses an aesthetic, scholarly, or scientific integrity; no doubt such integrity is sometimes reflected in the sale price, if the collection goes to the auction block, or is sold intact to an institutional library. However, most rare-book collections will possess most of the books in any other collection of the same type and the owners or curators will not want to buy the whole business, but will want to fill in the gaps of their own— which means, the integrity of that patiently and thoughtfully gathered collection of books will be destroyed the instant it begins to be sold.

Unquestionably, one should collect with some kind of focus, some sort of system. And yet, if you yourself are not hopelessly, pathologically confused, every book you honestly want will be reflective of yourself—a system of sorts, after all. Like all good thinking, one's collection should represent a responsive, dialectic collaboration of deduction and induction.

"The collection should fit the person," Glen Dawson, the Los Angeles dealer, says. "Build on strength. If you have a treasured family heirloom, build a collection around it. Collect on ethnic background, place

247

or residence, profession or vocation, special talents or interests, friends and connections. However, many doctors do not collect medical books, because they want something entirely removed, as a relaxation and change." The best part of this salubrious advice is its emphasis upon growth outward from the solid truth of what one is.

Even though a collector should be responsive and somewhat flexible, he should nevertheless have his head together; which means, he should enter a field of influence with a pretty good idea of what he is and what he wants; and the importance of certain deductive principles is implicit in the very act of giving advice.

Here is a bibliophile who conceives of building a collection of rare books as an exercise in the most difficult art of all—self-knowledge:

> Try to have knowledge as well as interest in your collecting. Know why you want something, why the item is important, know your subject, be an authority. If it is important enough to invest in, it's important enough to know all you can about it.
>
> A couple of simple rules—on your first visit to a dealer you hope will find you things, buy something, even if you don't need it—make yourself a customer. Never quibble about price—reject an item if you feel it is overpriced, but don't challenge the position of the dealer who set the price. Things will even out—you will get bargains as well as toppers—that is, if you pay more than you think you should for a good letter, you will find one that's a bargain and you can consider that you have both for a reasonable sum. You will only regret the good things you turn down. And, buying an expensive item, even if it pinches, can be a good investment . . . if only in that it may insure you of first refusal on the next item to come along.

R. and L. Wilbur, of the Gramercy Book Shop in New York, believe that, before a booklover decides to collect, he should take sober and deliberate counsel with his purse. Also,

> He should try to find a field in which there is some room to work, if this can be reconciled with his tastes. He should then find out as much as he can about the books he wants to collect by buying the available bibliographies in his field and reading booksellers' catalogues. He should also remember that if he tries to get his books at the lowest prices, he won't have much of

a collection. He should try to establish good relations with as many booksellers as possible. News travels in the book trade and if a collector gets a reputation as troublesome, he'll get short shrift and few books. By troublesome, I mean trying to bargain, returning books for whimsical reasons, taking too long to pay his bills, expecting too much service for too little return, and playing dealers against each other. Even if he is an expert in his field, wearing his knowledge with grace will do him no harm.

Several years ago, I visited an antiquarian bookstore and after an hour or two scanning, probing, even palpating the books swarming on the long sagging rows, I finally turned to a dark and cluttered corner, filled with a motley of dirty and dispirited tomes, and, as you knew would somehow be the case, my eyes fell upon an astonishing sight; an old leather volume, in good condition, with "Lewis' Journal" clearly imprinted upon the spine. I withdrew it, thinking naturally of Meriweather Lewis—not just *thinking* of him, but *thinking mightily,* of him, for the appearance and heft of the book clearly betokened the early nineteenth century.

Opening the book to the title page, however, I saw that it was not Meriweather, but Matthew G. ("Monk") Lewis, whose journal this was. Probably the proprietor had also thought of Meriweather when he'd first picked up the book. I am sure he did, in fact, for he is knowledgeable in Americana, and an early nineteenth-century edition of any journal of William Clark's sidekick would be a prize, indeed. Unfortunately for this dealer, however, he did not care for literature at all, and therefore didn't know it worth a damn; and therefore did not know about the recent "rediscovery" of "Monk" Lewis in the form of the 1952 Grove Press edition with an introduction by John Berryman.* If he had known this, he would also have known that any contemporary edition of anything by Monk Lewis should bring a whole lot more than

---

*The quotation marks are often appropriate when using the word "rediscovery" in a literary context; the fact is, *The Monk* was never really lost or forgotten. I have a small, handsome, three-volume edition published by Gibbings, in London, with illustrations by R. C. Armour; this was published in 1913—presumably at the height, or depth, of Lewis' eclipse as a writer. His reputation may have been almost as great then as it is now, twenty years after his most recent "rediscovery."

the three dollars he had marked in this particular copy. As a matter of fact, since I was a good customer, he sold the book to me for $2.50. And since I like and respect him (nobody wins all the time, cousin), I didn't tell him what a smashing bargain he had given me. For such a copy, the first edition in very good condition (excepting one badly frightened hinge) should bring something like $150 at auction or in a dealer's catalogue. All, or pretty much, because of the reevaluation of Matthew Lewis' stature in literary history.

It would be useful to be able to distinguish between a genuine "rediscovery," and a simple peak in the periodic fluctuation in the reputation of a writer; but these are simply matters of degree. No author is *ever* rediscovered in the sense that he is pulled out of absolute anonymity, for how could he be found at all? Considering this, it is evident that as an alert and interested collector, you, spend your time well when you browse among the lost authors of yesteryear. If one honestly strikes you as good or interesting, you should buy his works, read them, read about the writer, read about his works, seek them out until your enthusiasm is eased. Then at the very least stash those books away somewhere, for that mood will surely return. At best, give those works a proud and honored place on your shelves, and thereby know you are enriched by their presence.

The fact that one can respond to the unknown works of a generally neglected writer always means that there are others who can respond, too. "You are not alone in the world." The directness and pointedness of this therapeutic cliché seem brilliant when one considers the socially centrifugal tendency of most psychological problems. This insight is also central to the belief of the artist, as well as the collector, and, well, the human being. So it is, and should be, with the collector of rare books: collect what you personally believe is good and fine and powerful. There is a pretty good chance you will be vindicated. And if in your harvesting you come upon duplicates, well then buy them, for these may become trading stock for rarities otherwise beyond your hope of possessing. Or just store them away with the realization that if your hunch was right, then the few dollars you spent will prove to be most handsome investments, and these duplicates you can trade, then, at their giddily inflated prices, or possibly sell for cool cash, leaving your basic collection undisturbed in its Olympian calm far above the dust and smoke of the marketplace.

It is endlessly fascinating to see how often our "new horizons" are really discoveries of things that are either explicitly or implicitly part of the past. Marie Antoinette's philosophical maid was right. If the totality of human existence is seen as a finite inventory of facts—comprising all ideas, events, emotions, attitudes, and so on—then the overwhelmingly largest percentage of this totality belongs to what must be called the "Past," by any conceivable definition. This idea is at the heart of the antiquarian impulse, one of whose basic motivations is the acquisition of knowledge.

No one is in a better position to explore the past, and thereby to rediscover it, and reevaluate its productions, than the collector of old books. One of the reasons he is so eminently qualified is that he is not "professionally" obligated to master a particular period or area, and is therefore exempt from what Thorstein Veblen called "trained incapacity," which is too often the curse of those titular scholars who can "get by" merely by amassing great stores of information, without being challenged to renew their insights and overhaul their preconceptions. Like most things in this imperfect world, professionalism is both a benison and curse, and it is sometimes practically impossible to separate the two in their living state.

Gathering a valuable collection of books is only part of investing in them; the other part is disposal, which can prove difficult and even disastrous, if one proceeds ignorantly or impatiently. For every lucky collector who gets a rare book for a bargain price, there is a seller who is obviously not getting the money he might have gotten from that book. This is an instructive and sobering fact. The best way to get a just price for a rare book is to know both that book and the market generally, which is to say, to "be in the business" in a way that the mandarin collector-investor, with a dealer or dealers acting as his agents, will not necessarily have to be. Of course, anyone—regardless of his wealth—is obligated to be attentive to the rules and principles of his investment.

To the extent we consider rare books an investment, we tend to think of the disposal of a rare-book collection as the moment of truth. After all, this is the negotiation that brings to an end all those other negotiations that eventuated in the collection. And yet, that "moment of truth" may have very little to do with the "true" (i.e., potential) value of the collection, for the books may have been disposed of very carelessly or stupidly, they may have been practically, or actually, given away.

Basically, there are three options (including combinations thereof)

251

for the disposal of a private collection of books. They may be sold outright to a dealer or rare-book collection of an institutional library; they may be offered for sale at auction; or they may be sold directly to collectors. Since the disposal of one's collection is a subtle and interesting art, every collector should give thought to it, and should, of course, discuss every detail with those who are likely to be his heirs; someday, they will probably have to translate his plans into action.

As do all of these scenarios, selling a collection outright to a dealer or library has solid advantages. For someone who is too busy (especially in view of the probable value of the collection) to preside over the disposal of books, there is ideally a quick, clean, neat way to solve the problem: call in two or three dealers or librarians, ask them each for an offer for the entire collection, and then sell to the highest bidder. Most dealers and librarians can of course be trusted, but naturally they will want to buy at a low price, so it never hurts to let them know individually that other bids are being solicited.

This may seem to be the simplest and most direct method, but real life isn't all that neat and tidy. For one thing, it won't always be easy to get three dealers to come and look at a collection, let alone make a bid. This will be a special difficulty if you live in a small town, or otherwise outside the main channels of the rare book trade. Some dealers, especially the smaller ones, depend pretty largely upon buying "accumulations" of books, rather than collections, which means, they buy them at a nickel or dime apiece, or like to make the "fifty dollars for all the books in the attic" sort of purchase. Obviously, they are profiting from the unwary—which doesn't seem all that ugly when you consider that many of those fifty dollar lots aren't immediately worth over a hundred dollars, the likelihood of which is proved by the fact that such dealers seldom if ever get wealthy from such tactics; and of course, they are performing a worthy service in taking all those old books off someone's hands, and giving them *something* for the lot, even if it's only fifty dollars.

For a *rare* book collection to be disposed of in this way, however, is a sad and ruinous failure. If one wants to sell a valuable collection to a dealer or library, he has first to know how to present the information. Usually, this will involve some knowledge of bibliography. No dealer or librarian will want to buy a lot of books without seeing them, but the trouble of arranging to see them is such that they will more often than not decline any vague, idle, or ignorant inquiries. Ninety percent are worthless, misrepresented, or both. On the other hand, if a dealer is consulted by someone who has a library to sell, and this library contains many titles germane to that dealer's interests and specialities; and if accurate bibliographical descriptions are given to him—or perhaps a sampling of the books themselves, if this is convenient—then the dealer or librarian is in a position to decide upon the next step: going to examine the books and making an offer for them.

The bibliographical part need not be complicated; name of author, title, where and when published, and any information given on the title or copyright page about the printing or edition. More sophisticated bibliography can wait; the above information will convey enough, statistically, for any large number of books. One old lady recently consulted a dealer and gave him a fistful of legal-sized yellow sheets torn from a pad, filled with the names of authors, titles of the books, and the dates. This was a more intelligent and efficient approach than most, but the omission of the place of publication was an important one, and—since the titles did not suggest great value—the dealer hesitated before going to look at them. After looking, his suspicion was confirmed, and he found he could offer so little for the books, that the good woman was insulted, pointing out—quite correctly—that such a small amount of money would hardly compensate her for all that secretarial work. A much easier and more efficient method is simply to make Xerox copies of the title pages of those books which seem to be most valuable. But this method presents problems of two kinds: one has to know a lot about books to cull out those that are likely to prove valuable; also, for old and fragile books—particularly leather books with cracking hinges—the act of Xeroxing may prove fatal, if the book has to be spread wide and flat, as is normally required.

Above all, the prospective seller of a lot of books has to let the dealer or librarian know that the books being offered *are* valuable, and that they are being offered *as valuable books.* Even then, there may be problems. If three dealers come to look at a collection, it is probable that dealer A will want some books, dealer B will want others, and dealer C will want still others. Probably, all these will share an interest in buying some, which *may,* by that fact itself, indicate that these are the cream of the collection. Nevertheless, dealers tend, like all of us, to develop serious cases of tunnel vision, and will often ignore astonishing rarities, because their heads are elsewhere, or they feel insecure when faced with buying outside their specialties.

It is instructive, and very interesting, to find out how often the needs of dealers or librarians will not coincide; this fact is not surprising in itself, for obviously they specialize pretty much as collectors do, but it *is* surprising that dealers do not buy "trading stock" more often than they do, which they can always convert to their special needs at the next book fair if not by letter or over the phone right away.

Given the problem of three different dealers who want to buy three different selections from a stock of books, what does the seller do? He can offer the whole lot to dealer A, but he should realize that dealer A will not want to pay top price for those books he hasn't culled out, whereas dealer B or C will find many items among those books not chosen by A that he will pay a good price for. If the collection is broken up, so that each dealer can pick out what he wants, there will probably be a residue left, some of which will in turn be salable to still other dealers and, of course, libraries. Already it can be seen that the seller of the collection has become a dealer, of sorts, selling his wares, bit by bit, at "wholesale" to dealers and libraries. Obviously, then, he should know his stock well before approaching them; obviously, too, he might well consider selling some of those books at "retail" prices through other outlets—by advertising in *AB Bookman's Weekly,* for example, or in one of a number of antique trading journals.

When the owner of a collection decides to sell it at retail, he is of course becoming a dealer in every sense of that word. His best course is to face up to the implications of his decision, study and learn as much as he can for this new undertaking (perhaps not so difficult for the collector himself, but a tremendous challenge for an unschooled heir), get together a catalogue, anything from mimeographed to letter press, listing the books with correct bibliographic descriptions, and attaching realistic prices to them. This doesn't even *sound* simple, and it is not: to do it well requires years of study and experience—such knowledge is, after all, what one pays a dealer for possessing.

Still, it doesn't hurt to try, if one is ambitious, something of a gambler, has plenty of time, and wants to milk the last dollar from the collection. Surely, he will learn a lot; he will also make some mistakes, if the collection has any complexity at all, but, of course, dealers make mistakes, too; although they don't generally make them of the size and frequency that will surely mar the undertaking of the amateur with a rare-book collection to sell.

If one decides to dispose of a collection at auction, he must first of all be assured that the items he offers are not of the ten- and twenty-dollar class, for the auction houses will not be interested in handling them (unless, in a very few cases, they are groupable in bundles of eight or ten books). Also, he will of course abjure the local auction houses that cater to buyers of general antiques, or—even worse—general merchandise: a fifty-dollar book may get lost among books that sell for seventy-five cents a box at such sales; and what happens to a whole box of fifty-dollar books in auctions like these is a spooky thought, if your sympathies are with the seller.

The specialists in rare-book auctions are, with certain exceptions, the only good outlets for selling rare books at auction. However, books having some local historical relevance—old promotional tracts, county atlases, county and local histories, city guides, and so on, will very likely do well, perhaps best, at a good local auction (i.e., one for which the books are well advertised). Also, certain kinds of large, handsome picture books (the large two-volume edition of the Gibson girls, for example), almost any costume book, along with books about the early local frontier, homecrafts, furniture, firearms—all that relate tangibly, in some way or other, to antiques, will often sell respectably, sometimes handsomely, at your neighborhood auction house.

It is possible to approach a dealer on an advisory basis, rather than with a request for him to buy the collection outright: he will then, for a special percentage or fee, either find individual buyers for books (retaining a smaller percentage than if he buys them, since he has no cash investment in them), or handle them all on consignment, disposing of them on a percentage basis, selling various books to libraries, collectors, and other dealers among his clientele, and perhaps choosing still others for sale at auction, taking a slight fee from the sale price, after the auction house has subtracted its regular fee. This may seem like a compounding of costs, especially with the sale of those books the dealer finally decides to have auctioned: but the seller should realize that such a decision itself may prove critical in getting the top price for books, and a good dealer will likely have a pretty good knowledge of book prices, bibliography, and the best method for selling each book.

When one considers, not just time and effort, but the likelihood of receiving the most money for a collection of rare books, the last-mentioned method is probably the best. Most dealers I know enjoy selling books on a contingency basis, and enter into the task with industry and enthusiasm.

255

Implicit in all the little scenarios that I have sketched out is the familiar principle that, like the individual books that comprise it, a collection is more salable the more valuable it is. In a very real sense, it is more difficult to get a just price for a thousand-dollar collection than for a ten-thousand-dollar collection; and as personal collections rise in value above that latter amount, they are more and more famous, more sought after, more salable, and of course, *as* investments, more profitable. The thousand-dollar collection will consist largely of books that will trickle into the libraries, bookstores, and private collections at a more-or-less predictable rate; and because of this, most buyers are not terribly excited by thoughts of purchase when they gaze upon them.

To summarize: as adventures happen to the adventurous, and as good luck happens to the lucky, so do riches multiply upon the heads of those who neither sow nor reap, but spend their worry counting tokens in the cool grove of the counting house. And yet, in that granary of wealth, there are little holes and cracks between the boards, through which many an assiduous mouse can crawl, and feed himself largely and to his full satisfaction.

XIV.

CONCLUSION

There is a renaissance in book collecting today. This is a fact that cheers the heart of the older collector for several reasons, not the least of which is that natural gratification we all feel in witnessing our private enthusiasms endorsed by some degree of public accord and to have the rituals of so much pleasure perpetuated. Also, there is the more mundane satisfaction of having the enlistment rate in these invisible bibliophilic armies sustained to the degree that one can be assured that rare-book prices are solidly based upon a foundation of assured demand, and that he is accumulating wealth as he builds his own collection.

Back in the days when the wealthy connoisseur seemed to have a virtual monopoly on collecting rare books, it was also thought of as the preoccupation of one's feckless, if opulent, old age. The picture is clear. Breathing stertorously into his bent meerschaum and wearing a velvet dressing gown in his chair before a gas fire, this old dude lifts his recently acquired first edition with uncut pages; with trembling hand he picks up his silver dagger-style opener (given to him by loving grandchildren on his eightieth birthday) and slowly deflowers that virginal tome.

The enactment of this grotesque ceremony is a minor part of the folklore of book collecting; and whatever validity it might have had in the past has now pretty well vanished. If there is no specific, vivid im-

257

age of today's collector, it is a result of the thorough democratization of collecting. Books have proliferated so relentlessly for so long that there is plenty for everyone. Most of this plenty is utterly worthless, to be sure, from a collecting or investing standpoint—at least, *now*; but of course, the instant a circle is drawn around some hitherto unrecognized domain of collectables, and it is pronounced good and even interesting, why, then something else is already happening.

Today, not just rich old men, but rich *young* men, and rich old women, and poor old women, and poor young men, and poor young girls and boys . . . God knows who is collecting. But of all this marvelous and healthy heterogeneity, there is no more inspiring segment than the young collectors. I have never discussed collecting with college students without feeling a responsiveness that is almost electric. Part of this is good old-fashioned greed, I don't doubt; but it is more than that, because when you think of collecting books—even as a means for accumulating wealth—you can't really ever forget that it is books you are collecting, and they, in all their infinite variety, are like nothing else in the world.

Intelligent young people who begin to collect, or even deal, in books, bring fresh ideas with them, and they look upon the landscape of collecting with new eyes. Sometimes these people live far away from the channels in which rare books normally circulate; but, of course, this shouldn't and doesn't inhibit them.

One such young collector has just "turned dealer." She is married, the mother of two children, and yet, with her husband's help, manages to conduct a modest book business by mail and in nearby flea markets. Her printed cards have the following somewhat incoordinate, but very interesting "Want List" on the back:

> Books on aircraft—anything before 1930
> Autograph Books, before 1900
> Book covers—beautiful or colorful
> Bookmarks—silk, pretty, unusual
> Children's Books, including books of toys and games
> Christmas Books, with Ornaments, etc.—the older the better
> Civil War—Books, letters, Diaries, etc.
> Books on Clothing—Adult and Children, the older the better
> Color Plate Books—especially before 1900
> Cookery & Housekeeping books
> Curious, Unusual books, any subject

Doll Books (Furniture, Clothes, etc .)
Books of Herbs, Nostrums, Home Remedies
Hobby & Craft Books
Indians (American)
Miniatures—Dolls, Toys, anything
Needlework & Quilting Books
Poetry—anything
Post Cards before 1925
Presidential documents, campaign posters, etc.
Private Presses & Printings
Sheet Music
State, County, City, & Local Histories

Want lists such as this are always interesting and informative. They show very tangibly what that dealer knows to have a predictable cash value.

One of the more comprehensive, therefore simpler, lists of wanted books appears in an ad run in *AB Bookman's Weekly* by Ximenes Rare Books, Inc., of New York:

—all English books printed before 1700
—all American novels printed before 1875
—all American poetry printed before 1830
—all English novels printed before 1895, especially those in two or more volumes
—all English poetry printed before 1830
—all English and American plays printed before 1830

The ring of that splendid word "all" creates a music in the mind. Not just collecting rare books, but life itself should be this simple.

One of the most famous lists of collectable books is that gathered by Randolph G. Adams in 1938, in response to an enquiry by Lawrence Clark Powell. It, along with Adams' cautionary remarks, should be quoted at length:

WHAT MAKES A "RARE BOOK" is a matter of taste, connoisseurship, scholarship, aesthetic appreciation, sentiment, as well as the numerical analysis of surviving copies. It is obvious that this job of deciding what constitutes a "rare book" cannot be delegated to a person lacking in the above qualities, however much "library training" he or she may have. The following are useful classifications but are only a few of the norms we employ:

- Any incunabulum.
- Any book printed in England before 1640.
- Any book printed in America before 1800.
- Any book printed in states west of the Appalachian Mountains in accordance with McMurtrie's schedule, e.g., a Wyoming book of 1863.
- All "association" books.
- All books originally printed in an edition of 300 copies or less.
- Any book which has an auction record of $25 or above. [i.e., in 1938.]
- Any book which the proper official having all the qualities mentioned above believes, subjectively, to be a "rare book." (The emotional reaction of the connoisseur is the best of all measurements.)
- Any book which cost more than $25 [in 1938] when the library acquired it.
- Any book which for any reason a professor asks be considered a rare book; or any bookman in whom the librarian has confidence . . .
- Any other reason a qualified bookman can think of.

. . . Every general principle has a hundred exceptions, and these can never be reduced to rules . . . No amount of the writing of books nor rule-making can tell the story to people who are congenitally unable to understand what it is all about. It is too much like taking a person who is stone deaf and trying to teach him to play the piano in the course of one afternoon.

The fact that this list is almost forty years old would seem to italicize the principles stated therein, for whatever could be judged rare in 1938, must surely be considered "forty years rarer" today. For example, consider the second and third categories (the first, incunabula, being an unchanged category): one could reasonably add forty years to these listings, and assume that today, any book printed in England before 1680 may be thought of as rare; and any book printed in America before 1840. But rarity is a factor that—recently, at least—has been increasing disproportionately to time; and I think it is unquestionable that those watershed dates have outdistanced the forty years of the calendar, so that Adams' criteria would now be: "Any book printed in England before 1700," and "Any book printed in America before the Civil War." And here the term "any book" means *any book,* providing, of course, it is complete and in good condition.

Implicit in such lists as these just given is the idea that no one, no matter how sanguine or enthusiastic or wealthy, is going to want to collect all these eminently collectable books; therefore, he will always keep alert for bargain purchases in the areas mapped, knowing that all he manages to buy at a good price might be sold or traded to dealers (some dealers do not like to trade, however) or other collectors . . . and if he trades, rather than sells, or sells with the view of adding the profits to his book-buying budget, he is pursuing a strategy that will enable him to build a much finer and more valuable collection than he would be able to do in any other way, with the same investment of money.

In its year-end issue of 1975 (December 29), *Business Week* took a reading from a cross section of investment authorities, and the results are interesting, if not altogether telling. Following the charts that show heavy emphasis on the more popular and conventional investment areas, there was a section titled "Alternatives to Common Stocks," which listed recommended investments in order of preference. Corporate bonds led the list (recommended by 50 percent of those consulted), then municipal bonds (38 percent), treasury bills (33 percent), and a little father down the pike, a category labelled "art, antiques," which was recommended by only 15 percent of the people consulted. This was, in fact, near the end of the list, although I was interested to see that it led "farmland" as a recommended investment, which got the nod by only 7 percent of the experts.

Books were not listed separately, of course; therefore they must be thought of as belonging somewhere in the "art, antiques" category; and they would probably constitute a relatively small portion of *that,* trailing well behind such popular art and antique investments as paintings, gold and silver artifacts, glassware, porcelain, and so on. (And also, as an individual investment category, trailing well behind farmland.)

This would all add up to pretty discouraging news for the collector-investor in rare books, if it were not for several things. First, the list is simply a list of recommendations, and is therefore generally composed of the obvious, the simplistic. If you are making blanket recommenda-

261

tions, you speak of treasury bills and corporate bonds—which are all pretty much of a muchness in the *kinds* of profit and risk they invite— rather than Nonesuches and first editions of Joyce, even if you know about the latter. The rare-book market is made up of a staggering heterogeneity of titles, each one with its own, specific, built-in investment factor, as unique as a genetic code. As if this were not enough, different copies of the same title will have wildly different values because of their condition, and this is independent of the vacillations of the buying market, which is of course every bit as impetuous and fun-loving as that of stocks and bonds. In short, what "Peregrine Pollen" (that's right) advised the investor in art (quoted elsewhere in that same issue of *Business Week* just referred to) might very well apply here, *mutatis mutandis*: investors should buy "what's not in fashion." And no doubt there are many investors in today's market who no longer feel safe riding with the trends. In bullish times, this might be devilish fun; but in bearish, one might perish.

But *nobody really knows.* And if investing in books can be criticized as dangerous and speculative, there can nevertheless be found interpreters of Wall Street who urge their customers in common stocks to be *more* speculative, *more* imaginative, *more* willing to risk capital in nontraditional ways. (See Chapter Six of Gerald M. Loeb's *The Battle for Investment Survival,* where Loeb leads some cheers for Speculation, which in this context has to be considered the Visiting Team.) I understand there is even something called the "Random Walk" philosophy, which emphasizes the disjointedness and randomness built into the very character of stocks. (See "Adam Smith's" interesting *The Money Game* for an account of this approach.)

If the rare-book collector-investor feels intimidated by the colossus of the stock market that bestrides the world beyond his library window, he should probe the mentality of those folks who make it walk and talk and smile like Frankenstein's monster, pretending it is alive and ticking. Because, that colossus is not only vast and powerful, it is also a bit kooky, full of jumpy nerves striating its seemingly gelatinous mass. This is just a fancy way of leading into the account of something that happened to me recently.

Having read in a number of places that banks and other large investment corporations had taken to rare books as a new and interesting investment, I decided to follow through on this idea, not to verify it, specifically, for some of the sources were unimpeachable; but simply to gather whatever additional information there might be lying around in the minds of people who know.

So one morning I telephoned two internationally known investment companies in New York, and asked for someone who could tell me if their firm was investing in rare books. My calls were passed from department to department, leaving a wake of almost audible perplexity. (Excitement is often revealed by, and productive of, a mixed metaphor.) I soon got the feeling that neither of these institutions was investing in rare books. (One officer hedged a little, saying that *so far as he himself knew,* none of their people were investing in rare books.) My calls were passed around like chip dip at a party, and with almost as much polite interest.

The fact is, however, people *were interested.* And herein lies the point of this digression. Approximately an hour after my first call, I was talking with a very pleasant and helpful woman, who—upon learning of my problem—seemed a little less surprised than the others had been. She seemed almost prepared, in fact. And then I found out why. After explaining that her firm did not invest in rare books, she said, "But you know, I heard of another call just this morning, about investing in rare books, and I asked myself, '*What's happening?*' "

Her question was out before she quite realized that this previous call must have been one of my earlier ones; and I could almost hear her snap her fingers, as she said, "Why, that must have been *you!*"

I agreed that it probably had been me, although of course I couldn't be sure. And after hanging up, I brooded for a while over the implications of this huge Kafka-esque institution that is at once so marvelously efficient, and so vast, and yet had trembled like a gigantic spider web at the insectival weight of a mere phrase dropping from the telephone receiver.

Thousands of others have noticed the same phenomenon and a few have tried to make this morbid sensitivity to rumor serve them in their construction of a fortune. My scenario would take some such form as this: I would gather a dozen friends about me, coach them briefly, and then start them making long-distance phone calls for the next three weeks, asking if it was true that people were now buying up first editions of so-and-so's work for investment purposes. But before doing any of this, of course, I would have cleaned out all the remainder houses of every one of so-and-so's titles, at a dollar apiece. Then. . . .

But I guess it wouldn't work quite that simply. And anyway, as I said, it's probably been tried before. Many times.

Here in the valedictory posture of the last section of the last chapter, I should be expected to say something about the future of collecting-investing in rare books. After all the idea of investment focuses upon the future as clearly and unequivocally as any idea can. This is no doubt part of its charm, for—no matter how sophisticated the intellectual tools used to promote it are—there is something that is starry-eyed and wishful at the heart of all investment.

There are a number of good and vital signs that investing in rare books will prove to be a happy commitment for the right sort of person—which means, the person who genuinely loves books, and would gather them about him, anyway, independently of any hope for financial appreciation. Some of these signs are simply the obverse of negative signs regarding more conventional investments—the feverish behavior of stocks in the early seventies has inspired many people to look elsewhere for other kinds of investment opportunities.

The general economic recovery in Europe—in spite of periodic fluctuations and the dance and counter dance of crisis—has been an invigorating, even inspiring factor in the growth of the rare-book market on both sides of the Atlantic. (Europeans seem to be readier than we to buy book rarities; London alone supports some 350 antiquarian bookstores.) Also, more and more young people are collecting books, which fact helps assure that substructure of demand that is essential for the support of any market.

In spite of what seem to be sensationalistic claims, there really *are* incredible stories of great book finds, extraordinary profits turned over with the casual effort of flipping a card. We all know a lot of these stories and love to hear them. Gary Lepper writes: "Last month a dealer stumbled upon a review copy of *Go Tell It on the Mountain* (James Baldwin's first novel). Bought it for ten cents. He sold it to another dealer, who sold it to a collector. Three sales in twelve hours; from ten cents to $125."

It would be cruel to lead young collectors to believe that this sort of thing happens often or as a matter of course. It is cruel to lead them to suppose that, even if they come across this same book tomorrow, they could sell it for $125. But the *possibility* of such a find is always there—

just beyond your reach, on the next shelf; and this possibility lends an enchantment to collecting that is unique. No doubt, collectors of rare books—whether they are scholars, or professional men, or the supermarket carry-out boy who visits the used book or Salvation Army store three or four times a week, thumbing through the latest arrivals from attic or barn—all are dreamers.

And of course, those stunning finds *are* made; they *do happen*—just often enough to keep the true booklover digging. To quote Gary Lepper again: "There are better ways to invest money, but as a combination of the aesthetic and financial, collecting books is hard to beat." No collector would disagree with the latter part of this statement, but there are a few—and their number may be increasing as the stock market careens and sags—who may not entirely agree with the first.

After tracing the escalating price of the limited 100-copy edition of *Ulysses* that Joyce signed in 1922, which in 1968 had shown a fifty-fold increase, Frazer Clark wrote:

> This kind of spectacular increase in the market value of rare books and manuscripts is not limited to certain "highspots" but is general not only in literature, but in modern illustrated books, private press books and limited editions, color plate and natural history, Americana, atlases and travel—and is even more energetically reflected in scientific and medical antiquities. [from *Among Friends,* No. 52–54, Fall–Winter, 1968; Spring, 1969, published by the Friends of the Detroit Public Library, Inc.]

To be sure, this was written in 1969, and people were still scratching their heads over the sudden, brief, incredible escalation in rare-book prices in 1965, when Pick's *Word Currency Report* listed investing in rare books as second only to buying unimproved land bordering on large cities in growth rate. (Question: would that "unimproved land" have fallen in the category of "farmland" that only seven percent of *Business Week*'s experts recommended buying in their year-end report?)

It is no doubt wise to point out that this was over ten years ago, and nobody in his right mind should expect it to happen again. At least, soon. But of course, the same thing could have been said (and *wisely* said) in 1964. Still, I doubt if anyone actually made a fortune in that sudden, bewildering appreciation of rare books. But if no one did, it is at least possible that this was because no one at that time was seriously thinking of rare books with regard to their investment potential. If someone had, he would obviously—according to the simple facts—have been in a position to make just about as much money as he liked. And given today's market, and in spite of prices that seem fantastically high by yesterday's standards, a judicious collector-investor can reasonably look upon every dollar he spends for rare books as being an investment.

This is a far cry from quoting Pick, citing some such story as that about Baldwin's book, and then advising a stockholder to sell twenty or thirty thousand dollars worth and reinvest it in rare books.

Because that's not the *way* to invest in rare books. That's only the way to invest in stocks or corporate bonds. The way to invest in rare books is to learn about them, look at them, think about them, read them, and— gradually as opportunity presents itself—buy them and care for them. Then, if you're good and smart, and a little lucky, they'll grow for you in all the good ways, and keep on growing.

GLOSSARY OF

BIBLIOPHILIC TERMS

ADVANCE COPY. A copy the publisher has distributed before publication date to reviewers, critics, selection committees for book clubs, or people of renown, whose comments may promote sales. Often, such copies are made of what are in effect page proofs specially bound in paper.

ADVERTISEMENTS. Pages of advertising bound in at the end, or sometimes, the beginning of a book. Often the number of advertising leaves, along with dates and titles listed, are important clues regarding the particular issue of a copy.

ALL EDGES GILT. (Abbreviation a.e.g.) The outer edges of the leaves on all three sides cut smooth and gilded.

AMERICANA. Books dealing with some aspect of American social, political, or military history; usually Americana is limited to nonfiction, although in such areas as folklore, social customs, local legends, and so on, the distinction is often blurred.

-ANA. A suffix indicating a loose and comprehensive inclusion of material about a given place, thing, or person. Thus one may speak of *Ohioana* as well as *Americana*; one may speak of *railroadiana* and

267

Custeriana (material relating to Gen. George Custer). In his *ABC for Book-Collectors,* John Carter says that the term *Hardyana* "is repugnant to Latinity"; but did he ever consider *Indiana-ana?*

ANNUALS. Bound books issued annually, for the most part in the nineteenth century. Often these books are handsome productions and sometimes contain important original material.

ARMORIAL BINDING. Stamped leather binding with a coat-of-arms either blind stamped or stamped in gilt.

AS ISSUED. This term calls attention to the fact that some apparent anomaly of binding or printing is, in truth, essential to the book as it was first issued (e.g., "Library half leather binding, as issued").

ASSOCIATION COPY. A copy that contains certain evidence—an autograph, inscription, marginal comments, or bookplate—of ownership by, or other intimate association with, some famous person— usually the author or someone (including members of author's family) otherwise connected with the book.

AUTHORIZED EDITION. The first legitimate printing of a book, implying that there has already been at least one pirated or illegitimate printing. Often the pirated edition is riddled with error, so that the collector of first editions will be faced with a dilemma concerning which is preferable—the *first* first edition, or the first authorized edition. (The truth is, of course, he will want them both.) This problem flourished most prominently from mid-nineteenth century into the first two or three decades of this century, when the international copyright laws began to have some effect.

BACKSTRIP. The spine of a book.

BESTIARY. A symbolic treatise on fabulous animals, perpetuating many old and curious superstitions. Bestiaries were popular until the Renaissance. They were usually richly illustrated, and are sometimes reprinted in facsimile editions.

BEVELLED EDGES. A decorative bevelling or chamfering of the edges of boards.

BINDING COPY. This term refers to a book whose binding is falling apart. Since it needs rebinding, it might better be designated a "rebinding copy."

BLANK LEAVES. The extra leaves at the front and back that are normally bound in a book. Technically, these are an essential part of the book, but their importance to the collector will vary; if any part of a book has to be missing, there is no more expendable part than a blank at the back or (more serious) at the front.

BLIND STAMP. A designed indentation or impression made upon a binding by means of a plain stamp or tool that does not change the color of the binding in any way.

BLOCK BOOK. Picture books whose pages were printed from single blocks of wood either shortly before or during the infancy of printing as we know it.

BLURB. A publisher's brag or description, or quotation from some distinguished person, providing one of the more evanescent features of the dust jacket.

BOARDS. Generally, that part of the binding that constitutes its hardness (i.e., paperbacks do not have "boards"). Most boards today are made of an especially strong pasteboard or cardboard, and covered with cloth.

BOOKPLATE. A printed label indicating specific ownership and generally attached to the front pastedown or flyleaf of a book. Some bookplates are beautifully designed, and possess something of the charm of a colophon or emblem.

BREAKER (or BREAKING COPY). An illustrated book that is so damaged or incomplete, it can be used only for extracting the plates for framing, or a book—often an atlas—whose value lies solely in its plates, therefore inviting the same sort of fragmentation, sometimes to make a sophisticated copy.

BUCKRAM. A course cotton fabric used as binding cloth, especially popular in the mid-nineteenth century.

CALF. The most common leather binding. Smooth in texture and without apparent grain, it can be dyed almost any color.

CANCEL. Any part of a book that has been replaced by the printer (e.g., a new leaf substituted for an old).

CARTOUCHE. A scroll-like tablet design, often containing an inscription, and usually found on maps, and sometimes on title pages, chapter headings, and so on, in old books.

CATCHWORD. In books printed before 1800, the lower right hand corner of each page contains—isolated from the text—the first word, or sometimes the first syllable (if the word is broken), of that on the next page. This is a *catchword,* and it is a convenience in collating texts, as well as an interesting vestige of old printing.

CHAPBOOK. Small books, generally containing sensationalistic, religious, popular, or juvenile stories and poems, sold by peddlers (once called *chapmen,* hence its name). Usually, these books were very cheaply produced, poorly printed and crudely illustrated.

COLLATION. The verification of a copy's completeness and authenticity according to the best bibliographical criteria, by reference to correct pagination (correct number of pages in correct sequence), number and sequence of plates, chapters, preface or prefaces, and so on.

COLOPHON. An entry, usually at the end of a book, giving information generally about title, author, printer, place and date of printing. Colophons were, in effect, the first title pages; and with the appearance at the front of the book of the title page as we know it (in the sixteenth century) the colophon tended to disappear, although it is still used in some limited editions, private press books, and other books whose design and quality are thought to deserve special reference to such information.

CONJUGATE LEAVES. Leaves formed from a single sheet.

CONTEMPORARY BINDING. A binding of a style and material characteristic of the period in which the book was published. In very old books it is often impossible to determine if a contemporary binding is actually the original binding, in which case the collector must practice serenity, even in uncertainty.

COPYRIGHT PAGE. On the back of the title page, most modern books give essential information about copyright, date of publication, the issue of a particular copy, and so forth. Some publishers conveniently state "First Edition" or "Third Printing" for the edification of the collector.

CROPPED. A book whose leaves have been cut by the binder, usually for the sake of machine binding, is *Cropped.* This can be a serious defect in a book, especially if some of the text is lost or cut into.

CURIOSA. From the Latin *curiosus,* this is a quaint old euphemism for what is more-often-than-not simple pornography, although the term can apply simply to exotic or off-trail material.

DECKLE EDGES. The rough uncut edges characteristic of handmade paper.

DESIDERATA. A list of the titles of books "desired" by a collector or dealer.

DEVICE. A printer's symbol, often included with the colophon at the end of a book. Probably the most famous printer's device is the Aldine dolphin curled about an anchor, which symbolizes the dialectic virtues of flexibility and stability. Other well-known devices are the Elzivir globe, the Estiennes's Tree of Knowledge, and—in modern times—Knopf's famous Borzoi.

DISBOUND. Applied to a book that is no longer in its binding.

DUODECIMO. A small book (about the size of pocket size paperbacks) whose pages are formed by the folding of the sheets into 12 leaves; also printed as both "12mo" and "twelvemo."

DUST JACKET, or DJ (or DUST WRAPPER, or DW). The paper cover that most clothbound books come in. The dust jacket usually carries information about the book (blurbs, design, editorial commentary) that must be considered an important part of the whole book; and since dust jackets are obviously very fragile (much more fragile than what they ostensibly protect), they often have extraordinary value to the collector of modern first editions.

EDITIO PRINCEPS. "First Edition" in Latin.

EDITION. All the books printed from one set of plates. (See also, IMPRESSION, ISSUE, PRINTING, and STATE.)

END PAPERS. The first and last leaves of a bound book, the outer half pasted down upon the inside of the covers. The free endpaper is not pasted down; and the pasted-down part is called the "pastedown," because it is pasted down. All of which is pretty much as it should be.

ENGRAVINGS. Illustrations and other designs made from metal plates or wood blocks.

ERRATA. Misprints and other errors appearing in a printed text. Sometimes when errata are detected in time, their corrections are listed on a tipped-in sheet, called "an errata slip."

EX-LIBRARY (or EX LIBRIS). A copy that has been discarded by a library, after being liberally stamped, chewed, dropped, shoved, pounded, and even read. Most of these old horses are fit only for the glue factory; however a few of them emerge from their stables in virtually mint condition. If library stamps and labels are not too obtrusive, and if the book is sufficiently rare and in good condition, the collector may upon occasions consider it a worthwhile investment. Most ex lib copies must be seriously devalued, however, in terms of collecting.

FACSIMILE. A facsimile edition is an exact reproduction of a book, usually made by offset or some other photocopying process. Many facsimile editions are a boon to collectors, for they make the supremely unattainable rarities attainable in form, if not in body. Facsimile pages are a legitimate resort for the desperate collector who needs to make an incomplete, extremely rare copy whole, and has no other way of achieving his ends.

FIRST EDITION. To collectors, this term usually means the first printing, first state, first issue of a book. Technically, the first edition consists of all copies printed directly from the first set of plates made, and may be comprised of several issues (issues are determined by relatively minor editorial changes in type) and several states (states derive from accidental causes—break in type, correction of an error, addition of an errata slip, and so forth).

FOLIO. A book at its largest and simplest, whose sheets are folded only once. In modern times, folios are pretty much reserved for illustrated and art books.

FOLLOW THE FLAG. This venerable axiom means simply that collectors of first editions "should" seek out the first edition with the author's native country's imprint. Considerable hedging is required, however. While it is true that some of the English editions of Mark Twain preceded the American, and yet prove consistently less valuable (thus vindicating the axiom), there are a number of authors whose careers are not simple in this regard. Kipling resided in America for several years, and some of his first editions are legitimately American. Henry James lived most of his life in England, and priority of some of his first editions is difficult to establish. The principle of following the flag is, in short, only a general one, with many interesting, and sometimes critical, exceptions.

FORE-EDGE PAINTING. A curiosity of book embellishment, in which the edges of a book are tightly fanned so that a scene can be painted upon them; when closed, the scene disappears. In the closed position, they are then gilded.

FORMAT. The sum-total of all the physical features of a book; that is, its shape, size, style, composition of paper, type design, and so forth.

FONT (or FOUNT). The style and size of a letter that distinguishes it

273

from other fonts, or styles. The "type of type," one might say. To printers, font means "A complete set of type of one size and face." (*The American Heritage Dictionary*)

FOXED. A colorful term that is applied to the reddish brown (thus it is a red fox, not a gray that is meant) stains that appear in aged paper because of the rusting of iron in the paper. Slight foxing in a very old book can add to its charm in the eyes of a minority of collectors (I am here); but too much is too bad; and in a modern book, it is strictly not wanted.

FRONTISPIECE. The first illustration in a book that may or may not have other illustrations. The frontispiece is a common feature of older books, and normally appears on the verso (left-hand side) opposite the title page; it is often vulnerable to criminal excision by people who want to make a picture to hang on the wall—therefore, if a copy of an older book does not have a frontispiece, the prudent collector would do well to check a bibliography to see whether that edition simply did not have a frontisipiece, or the frontispiece has been removed.

GATHERING (or QUIRE). The printed sheet after it has been properly folded so as to form the leaves of a book. (The quarto has been folded to make four leaves; the octavo eight; and so on.) Gatherings themselves are gathered together into correct order to make the book.

GILT EDGES. The leaf ends, or edges, are often gilded; thus, gilt edges.

GOTHIC TYPE. An old-fashioned type face—craggy and difficult for the modern eye to read—that is often referred to as Black Letter.

GRANGERIZED. A book that has been embellished by illustrations that were not part of the printed book.

GUARDED. A leaf that has been pasted by its inside edge into a book. Such a leaf is, therefore, not conjugate, not part of a gathering, not sewn in as part of the original book. See also "tipped in."

HALF LEATHER. This refers to a book whose spine and outer-edge triangles are of leather; the remainder cloth. An imprecise term, it may nevertheless be used more-or-less accurately in reference to books whose boards, as seen from above, show an approximate equal division between cloth or paper and leather.

HALF TITLE. The title, often abbreviated (thus "half"), as it sometimes appears on the recto of a leaf before the actual title page.

HEAD-PIECE. A printed ornament that is often used to signal the beginning of a new chapter or section in a book.

HIGH SPOTS. Titles of the best or most desirable collectables, as they are selected and listed by one of a number of enthusiasts who dare to undertake such things.

HINGE. The joint that connects the front and back boards of a book to its spine; thus, that much-trafficked and much-worn part upon which the boards swing. Obviously the most vulnerable part of an old book, the hinges are often found cracked and broken in leather books dating before 1800.

HORAE. Books of Hours, either in manuscript or print, and often lavishly illustrated.

HORN BOOK. Hardly a book at all, the Horn Book is simply a leaf upon which the alphabet, the ten numerals, the Lord's Prayer, and sometimes a few rudiments of spelling have been printed. This leaf is fixed to a sort of paddle and protected by a transparent cover made of horn. Genuine horn books are very old, very rare, and very expensive; Carter mentions that they are often faked.

ILLUMINATED. In early manuscripts and a few very early books initial letters were often magnificently enlarged and designed and decorated in gold and color—thus ILLUMINATED.

IMPRESSION. The copies of an edition printed at one time. This is the term favored in Great Britain; in the United States, the word "printing" is more often used to designate the same fact.

275

IMPRIMATUR. Latin for "let it be printed," the Imprimatur appeared on a separate leaf (called the "Imprimatur Leaf" or "License Leaf") at the very beginning of many sixteenth- and seventeenth-century books. Its purpose was to guard the growing reading public against heresy, error, and false doctrine.

IMPRINT. The listing of those who have produced or published a particular book. The printer's or publisher's imprint.

INSCRIBED COPY. A book inscribed for someone personally by the author. A presentation copy.

INSERTED LEAVES. Leaves tipped into a book (i.e., glued in by the inner edge) after it has been printed.

INTEGRAL. This refers to a leaf that belongs properly to one of the signatures in a book.

ISSUE. A specific printing of a book that can be identified according to certain features of type that distinguish it from all others. All issues after the first are identifiable according to changes in type that are editorially conceived, that is, intended.

LABELS. Made of either very thin leather or paper, labels are glued to the spines (and less often, the covers) of books for purposes of signifying its title, author, and sometimes date, decoratively.

LAID IN. A letter, autograph, errata slip, or some other paper bearing information relevant to the book is said to be laid in when it is *laid in* (i.e., not affixed to the book in any way).

LARGE PAPER COPY. A book that is valued especially because it has been printed upon larger sheets of usually more expensive paper than the trade edition. Often large paper copies constitute a limited edition, and sometimes the true first edition—both of which factors tend to increase its value further.

LEAF. "The basic bibliographical unit." (Carter) It's the whole thing which turns, comprising two pages, one on the front (recto) and one on the back, (verso). The count of leaves is determined by the number of foldings in the printer's sheet.

LIMITED EDITION. A printing and edition (both) consisting of a specific number of copies, which number is significantly smaller than a normal commercial printing. A Limited Edition is usually numbered, for obvious reasons, and often signed by the writer and/or illustrator.

LIMP BINDING. A binding without boards; therefore, soft, limp. Usually such bindings are of cloth, vellum, or some other soft leather or imitation leather.

LOOSE (or LOOSE IN CASE). A clothbound book is termed loose when the binder's glue that holds the inner edge of the paste-down leaf has given up. Also SHAKEN.

MADE UP COPY. A once-incomplete copy that is now complete because of added parts, usually tipped-in pages taken from another imperfect copy. Such a book is also termed a sophisticated copy.

MINT. This refers to a book whose condition is practically as it was upon printing, including (with modern books) a spotless dust jacket, as well. Many try heroically to think of the term as an absolute; however it is not, for paper (especially of modern manufacture) undergoes inevitable changes in time, even when the book and dust jacket are kept in glassine or other airtight wrappers or cases.

MISBOUND. When a plate or signature has been incorrectly placed in a book, the copy is misbound.

MOROCCO. Goatskin tanned with sumac and receptive to almost any color dye. LEVANT, HARD-GRAIN, NIGER are three types of Morocco, classifiable according to the grain and texture of the original skin.

OCTAVO. The most common size of modern books, formed by a sheet being folded into eight (hence its name) leaves, comprising sixteen pages. Most octavos are about 6 by 9 inches. Also written as "8vo."

OFFPRINT. Sometimes a certain number of copies of a section of a larger work, or an individual story, essay, or poem to be published in a magazine, will be run off; these pages will be stapled or glued together, and are often enclosed in paper wrappers, and sometimes even bound. Such an OFFPRINT is usually intended for distribution to friends by the author; and if that author is collectable (or promises to be collectable some day), his offprints may prove very rare, since they come in small numbers, are not offered for sale, and are more vulnerable than books.

OFFSET. An accidental impression (from imperfectly dried ink) upon the adjoining page; many nineteenth-century books come with transparent sheets over the prints to prevent such bleeding. OFFSET also refers (properly PHOTO OFFSET) to a form of photocopying that is relatively inexpensive and widely used.

OUT OF PRINT. (Abbreviation o.p.) When there are no more books in the publisher's warehouse, and no new printing is ordered, the book is o.p. A book may be of collecting interest and still be allowed to go out of print; in which case, the value of the book is immediately nudged higher, consistent with the law of supply and demand.

PARTS. Many Victorian novels were issued periodically, each installment of which had a paper cover that was often illustrated by an artist who was himself famous. These parts were many times collected and bound by individual owners when the series was completed, at about the same time that the novel was commercially bound and published. Since parts were as subject to wear and destruction as dust jackets are today, their bibliophilic value is very high. Sometimes a copy in parts, complete with all covers, illustrations, ads, and so on, will bring several times the price of a good copy of the "real" first edition, bound and sold by the publisher after all the installments were printed.

PASTEDOWN. (leaf) This is the outer half of the end paper, pasted down to the inside of the cover, front and back.

POINT. A clue that reveals the specific edition, issue, or state of a book.

PRELIMS. Abbreviation for preliminary leaves—those which precede the text of a book.

PRESENTATION COPY. A copy of a book the author has presented to someone as a gift, as documented by an inscription.

PRESS BOOK (or PRIVATE PRESS BOOK). Generally, a book that has been printed by a private press, which fact implies that it is conceived and made with a view toward rarity.

PRIVATE PRESS. "A printing house not beholden to publishers," in Eric Quayle's phrase. PRIVATE PRESSES are engaged in the production of those PRESS BOOKS described above.

PRIVATELY PRINTED. A book that is subsidized by the author or some other interested party is, in modern usage, "privately printed." Firms that specialize in such personal subsidy publication are termed "vanity presses," and the pejorative connotation is fully justified in at least 99 out of 100 cases. However, there is always that hundredth case, that rare exception, which exists to tantalize the collector. Some of the greatest and most collectable of authors have, in sheer exasperation at being unpublished, resorted to subsidizing their own books—Stephen Crane (with *Maggie: a Girl of the Streets*) being one of the most famous.

PROOFS. The trial impressions from a set of plates before they are used to make the book. GALLEY PROOFS consist of the complete text as first set up (a sort of "first printing draft"), and often contain a rich harvest of errors. Unlike PAGE PROOFS, GALLEYS are printed on long sheets of cheap paper. PAGE PROOFS represent a "second draft of the printing," on page-size sheets, and should reflect all corrections from galley proofs. (I once found a critical error, in the form of the wrong name of a character, that had survived eight proof readings by the editor, copy editor, and myself. The persistence of human error, as it is reflected in textual errata, is a humbling lesson in human frailty.) Errors that survive all editing to appear in a printed book provide "points" if and when they are discovered and corrected in some subsequent issue or edition.

PROVENANCE. The history or "genealogy" of a book's ownership, and the devolution therein. Autograph signatures, book plates, inscriptions, coats of arms, marginalia and all data for the establishment of provenance.

QUARTER BOUND. This refers to a volume with a leather spine only, and no leather triangles on the corners of the boards.

QUARTO. A book made of sheets folded into four leaves. Sometimes written "4to."

QUIRE. A gathering of printed sheets. Also, 1/20 of a ream of paper.

RAISED BANDS. Lateral ridges on the spine of a book, made by the cords that bind the signatures together. When these ridges are not sunk in grooves, making a flat spine, they protrude; such protrusion is normal with books printed before 1800. Sometimes referred to as "hubs."

REBACKED. Said of a book whose original backstrip or spine has been replaced.

REBOUND. A book whose complete original binding has been replaced is REBOUND.

RECASED. A badly shaken clothbound book may be taken from its covers and then fixed back in (by means of gluing, and usually with new endpapers). The result is a firm, strong copy composed, for the most part, of the book's original components. Often a book will have to be resewed before being recased.

RECTO. That side of a leaf that lies on the right side when a book is opened. Also called the OBVERSE. Its opposite is the VERSO, lying on the left side.

REMBOITAGE. The practice of casing a book in a leather binding made for another; this involves the creation of new labels, along with a careful settling and sewing of the book in its new skins. Naturally, such a practice will serously damage the market value of a book, with the possible exception of casing an extremely rare book, whose cover is missing or shot, in either a duplicate binding, or in an alien binding that is both felicitous and magnificent.

REPRINT. Any new impression made without significant change of type. Sometimes used loosely (and unfortunately) to designate a new edition.

RESET. This term may have one of three meanings: (1) the setting up of new type for a new edition; (2) the gluing of a loosened plate, page, or signature back in its proper place; (3) RECASED.

RUBBED. A descriptive, even self-descriptive, term denoting damage through wear and attrition, rather than from more dramatic trauma, such as scarring, water-staining, tearing, denting, scuffing, and so on.

RUBRIC. Initial capital letters and chapter headings, often enlarged and intricately wrought, designed both to enhance the beauty of the page, as well as signify the textual importance of a new beginning. Although they have always been a feature of the grand style of book-making, RUBRICS go back to the earliest books, and beyond that, to manuscripts. They were characteristically painted red, hence the name.

SCOUT. A book SCOUT is one who seeks out and buys rare books for resale, primarily, to dealers. A successful scout must therefore be knowledgeable in the rare book market, must know current prices, and must have skills and means to buy his stock at a low-enough price to insure a profit.

SCUFFED. A leather-bound book that has had the patina rubbed or peeled off, torn, or gouged is SCUFFED.

SHAKEN. This refers to any clothbound book that is loose in its binding, that wobbles when handled, that is unstable, frightened, worried, that is, in a word, SHAKEN.

281

SHAVED. With the edges of the leaves so drastically cropped by a binder that some part of the print has been SHAVED—without, however, destroying the text.

SHEET. The printer's unit of paper, the whole, unfolded sheet of paper, from which the leaves are formed by folding.

SIGNATURE. A section of a book, determined by the number of foldings so as to make, for example, four leaves, or eight pages (QUARTO), eight leaves, or sixteen pages (OCTAVO), twelve leaves, or twenty-four pages (DUODECIMO), and so on. Properly speaking, SIGNATURE refers to the numeral or letter printed in the tail-margin of the page, indicating for the binder the correct sequence for collecting the gatherings into the book proper.

SILKED. Extremely fragile leaves are sometimes sprayed with a very fine plastic, that hardens on the page, thickening and strengthening it. Such a leaf is said to be SILKED.

SLIP CASE. A protective, tailor-made, tight-fitting cardboard or pasteboard box into which the book for which it has been made may be slipped and kept in security.

SPINE. The backstrip.

STARTED. Said of a signature that has come loose in its threads. Also said of an outer hinge "starting" to break.

STUB. The inner strip of paper that can sometimes be seen protruding from the crease dividing open pages. Sometimes this indicates that a plate has been cut out of the book; sometimes it is a natural vestige of the book's construction. It is always best to collate the book when a stub is detected.

TAIL. The lower margin of a leaf. Also, the foot of the backstrip, or the tail of the spine.

TAIL PIECE. A printed ornament signaling the end of a chapter, or other section of text.

THREE-DECKER. A book published in three volumes. Most of these are Victorian novels.

TIPPED IN. A page or leaf that has been carefully glued by the inner margin into a book.

TITLE. A jazzy abbreviation for Title Page.

TOOLING. Hand-worked impressions in a binding, by means of special metal implements. This is not the same as BLOCKING, which refers to impressions made in the binding by machine.

UNCUT. This refers to leaves with untrimmed edges.

UNOPENED. Some books have not had their leaves separated along those folds that naturally result from the folding of a sheet into its proper signatures. In the past, especially, there was ostentatious pride manifest (on the part of some exotic collectors) in the virginal purity of their still-unopened volumes. To that Reader who should reside at the heart of every Collector, such unread tomes must seem to mock the essential character of the book.

VARIANT. Even out of the mass production of commercial presses, there occur some differences among copies of the same book. Those which do not conform to the generality, are known as VARIANTS. Usually such spots are harmless enough—slight differences in the color of a binding, a slight deviation in the placement of type in a particular signature, different densities in the type, etc. If one of these deviations is repeated sufficiently to form a class, then the VARIANT may be considered a STATE. Priority among VARIANTS is usually as impossible to determine as it is among STATES.

VELLUM. The skin of a calf, usually; but sometimes that of a lamb, sheep, or goat, that has not been tanned, but specially treated so as to remove most of the animal oil. Uterine vellum has been made, as the name suggests, from the embryos of unborn animals. VELLUM can be dyed, but seldom is; it is light in both color and weight; and very durable. It is used for both leaves and bindings.

VERSO. The back, or reverse side of a leaf. The visible or upper side that lies on the left when a book is opened. The copyright page is conventionally on the VERSO.

WASHED. Leaves that have been soaked in water, bleach, or other chemicals, for the purpose of removing stains (usually foxing and water stains) have been WASHED.

WATERMARK. A colorless representation of the papermaker's symbol or initials formed during the manufacturing of sheets of laid paper. They are visible when held up to the light. Often, they are helpful in collating a book.

WRAPPERS. The paper covers of a paperback.

SELECTED LIST

OF BOOKSELLERS

WHO ISSUE CATALOGS

(Note: Most of the following issue catalogues, either on a regular or occasional basis.)

THE UNITED STATES AND CANADA

Acadia Book Store
232 Queen, E.
Toronto, Canada

Acres of Books
633 Main Street
Cincinnati, Ohio 45202

William H. Allen, Bookseller
2031 Walnut Street
Philadelphia, Pa. 19103

Alta California Book Store
1407 Solano Ave.
Albany, Calif. 94706

Antiquités Canadiana
415 Dorchester
Quebec, Canada

Bernard Antmann, Inc.
750 Sherbrooke West
Montreal, Canada

Ark Bookshop
1703 University Ave.
Berkeley, Calif. 97403

Argus Books
P.O. Box 3211
Columbus, Ohio 43210

The Asphodel Book Shop
17192 Ravenna Rd., Rt. 44
Burton,Ohio 44021

Willis C. Baker
301 Hessel Blvd.
Champaign, Ill. 61820

J. N. Bartfield
45 W. 57th St.
New York, N.Y. 10019

Black Sun Books
667 Madison Ave.
New York, N.Y. 10021

Bond's Book Shop
523 Dunsmuir
Vancouver, B. C., Canada

The Bookseller
521 West Exchange St.
Akron, Ohio 44302

The Bookshelf
605 S. Ash Ave.
Tempe, Ariz. 85281

Boyer Gallery
2540 E. 6th St.
Tucson, Ariz. 85716

Brentano's Rare Book Dept.
586 Fifth Ave.
New York, N.Y. 10017

Monk Bretton Books
1 Dale Ave.
Toronto, Ontario M4W 1K2
Canada

The Brick Row Book Shop
251 Post Street
San Francisco, Calif. 94108

Carnegie Book Shop, Inc.
140 East 59th Street
New York, N.Y. 10022

Caveat Emptor
110 S. Indiana Ave.
Bloomington, Indiana 47401

Peggy Christian Bookseller
769 No. La Cienega Blvd.
Los Angeles, Calif. 90069

Ken Crawford Books
2719 E. 16th Ave.
No. St. Paul, Minnesota 55109

The Current Company
PO Box 46
17 Burnside Street
Bristol, R. I. 02809

Dakota Books
505 Main St.
Webster, S.D. 57274

Dawson's Book Shop
535 No. Larchmont Blvd.
Los Angeles, Calif. 90004

Larry Dingman & Associates
1004 Marquette Ave.
Minneapolis, Minn. 55402

Dragon Press, Publishers &
Booksellers
Elizabethtown, N.Y. 12932

Dream House
635 E. High Street
Springfield, Ohio 45505

John F. Fleming
322 E. 57th St.
New York, N.Y. 10022

Alla T. Ford
114 S. Palmway
Lake Worth, Fla. 33460

John Gach Bookservice
3012 Greenmount Ave.
Baltimore, Maryland 21218

The Globe Bookstore
8934 Keith Ave.
Los Angeles, Calif. 90069

Goodspeed's Book Shop
18 Beacon St.
Boston, Mass 02108

Gotham Book Mart
41 W. 47th Street
New York, N.Y. 10036

Gravesend Books
Box 235
Pocono Pines, Pa. 18350

Guidon Books
7177 Main St.
Scottsdale, Ariz. 85251

Charles Hamilton Galleries, Inc.
25 East 77th Street
New York, N.Y. 10021

Lathrop C. Harper
22 E. 40th Street
New York, N.Y. 10016

George Harrington , Bookseller
PO Box 262
Wakefield, Mass. 01880

Robert Hayman
Antiquarian Books
RFD 1
Carey, Ohio 43316

William R. Hecht
Box 67
Scottsdale, Ariz. 85252

Heritage Bookshop
847 North La Cienega Blvd.
Los Angeles, Calif. 90069

House of Books, Ltd.
667 Madison Avenue
New York, N.Y. 10021

House of El Dieff, Inc.
139 East 63rd St.
New York, N.Y. 10021

John Howell, Books
434 Post Street
San Francisco, Calif. 94102

The Invisible Bookman
97 Franciscan Way
Berkeley, Calif. 94707

J & S Rare Books & Graphics
1301 S. Wabash
Chicago, Ill. 60605

Douglas M. Jacobs
PO Box 363
Bethel, Conn. 06801

The Jenkins Co.
Box 2805
Austin, Texas 78767

Joseph The Provider—Books
100 Hawthornden Way
Box 156
Inverness, Calif. 94937

H. P. Kraus
16 East 46th Street
New York, N.Y. 10017

The Lamesa Booksellers, Inc.
PO Box 214
Lamesa, Texas 79331

Edward J. Lefkowicz
PO Box 1017
Taunton, Mass. 02780

Limestone Hills Book Shop
Box 1125
Glen Rose, Texas 76043

The Limited Edition
11 South College
Fort Collins, Colo. 80521

London Book Co.
224 W. Broadway
Glendale, Calif. 91204

M & S Rare Books
Box 311
Weston, Mass. 02193

George S. MacManus Co.
1317 Irving Street
Philadelphia, Pa. 19107

McBlain Books
Box 971
Des Moines, Iowa 50304

Mystery House Books
PO Box 135
Huntingdon Valley, Pa. 19006

Kenneth Nebenzahl, Inc.
333 North Michigan Ave.
Chicago, Ill. 60601

Old New York Book Shop
1069 Juniper St., N.E.
Atlanta, Georgia 30309

Robert A. Paulson
39 Downing Pl.
Harrington Park, N.J. 07640

Phoenix Book Shop
22 Jones St.
New York, N.Y. 10014

Port Folio Books
1952 Queen E.
Toronto, Canada

Paul C. Richards, Autographs
233 Harvard Street
Brookline, Mass. 02146

Richard Owen Roberts,
Bookseller
6167 N. Millbrook Ave.
Fresno, Calif. 93710

Royce et Klaudius
Medicina Clasica
PO Box 1978
Santa Monica, Calif. 90406

William Salloch
Pines Bridge Road
Ossining, N.Y. 10562

William H. Schab
37 W. 57th Street
New York, N.Y. 10019

E. K. Schreiber
PO Box 144
Kingsbridge Station
Bronx, N.Y. 10463

Henry Schuman Rare Books,
Ltd.
2211 Broadway
New York, N.Y. 10024

Serendipity Books
1790 Shattuck Ave.
Berkeley, Calif.

Seven Gables Bookshop
3 W. 46th Street
New York, N.Y. 10036

Stage House II
1936 14th St.
Boulder, Colo. 80302

Henry Stevens, Son & Stiles
Antiquarian Booksellers &
   Publishers
Albee Court,
Larchmont, N.Y.

J.D. Sutter Books
Box 20211
Birmingham, Ala. 35216

W. Thomas Taylor
PO Box 4443
Austin, Texas 78765

Totteridge Book Shop
667 Madison Avenue
New York, N.Y. 10021

Charles E. Tuttle Co., Inc.
Rutland, Vt. 05701

Western Hemisphere, Inc.
1613 Central Street
Stoughton, Mass. 02072

Fred White, Jr.: Bookseller
Box 3698
Bryan, Texas 77801

Karen Wickliff
Rt. 2
Pataskala, Ohio 43062

R. L. Wilbur
Gramercy Book Shop
22 East 17th St.
New York, N.Y. 10003

William P. Wolfe
222 Hospital
Montreal, Canada

Peter Wolff Books
PO Box 778
Barrington, Ill. 60010

Charles B. Wood III Inc.
So. Woodstock, Conn. 06267

Richard S. Wormser
Alfred W. Paine-Books
Wolfpits Road
Bethel, Conn. 06801

Ximenes
120 East 85th St.
New York, N.Y. 10028

The Yesteryear Book Shop
256 E. Paces Ferry Road, N.E.
Atlanta, Georgia 30305

Zeitlin & Ver Brugge
Booksellers
815 N. La Cienega Blvd.
Los Angeles, Calif. 90069

GREAT BRITAIN

Tony Appleton
28 Florence Road
Brighton BNI 6DJ

Henry Bristow Ltd.
105 Southampton Road
Kingwood, Hants. BH 24 IHR

C.K. Broadhurst & Co., Ltd.
5-7 Market Street
Southport PR8 IHD

Bygone Books
The Mount
Ewhurst, Surrey GU6 7PX

Chelsea Rare Books
313 King's Road
SW 3 5 EP

Claude Cox
Old & Rare Books
The White House
Kelsale
Saxmundham
Suffolk, Saxmundham 2786

Crouch & Co.
47A Mornington Rd.
Woodford Green, Essex

Dawson's of Pall Mall
16 Pall Mall
London, SW 1

John Drury
11 E. Stockwell St.
Colchester, Essex C01 ISS

I.D. Edrich
17 Selsdon Rd.
Wanstead
London E11 2QF

E.P. Goldschmidt & Co. Ltd.
64 Drayton Gardens
London SW 10 9SB

R.J. Goulden
15 Cloverdale Garden
Chichester Road
East Croydon

Falkner Greirson & Co. Ltd.
4 Molesworth Place
Dublin 2, Ireland

Paul Grinke
38 Devonshire Place
London WIN IPE

T & L Hannas
33 Farnaby Road
Bromley, Kent 01-460 5702

A.R. Heath
15 Badminton Road
Downend, Bristol BS16 6BB

Hoffman & Freeman
50 London Road
Sevenoaks, Kent

Howes Bookshop
3 Trinity Street
Hastings, Sussex TN 34 IHQ

Anthony W. Laywood
Knipton
Grantham, Lincolnshire

Marlborough Rare Books, Ltd.
35 Old Bond St.
London WIX 4 PT

Peter Murray Hill
35 North Hill
Highgate
London N 6

Winifred A. Myers Ltd.
Suite 52
91 St. Martin's Lane
London WC2

D. Parikian
The Old Rectory
Waterstock, Oxford

Piccadilly Rare Books, Ltd.
London SW 1 01-734 3840

Pickering & Chatto Ltd.
13 Brunswick Centre
Brunswick Square
London WC 1

Potter Books Ltd.
V. Raswell
Loxhill
Godalming, Surrey

Bertram Rota Ltd.
4, 5 & 6 Savile Row
London WIX 2 LN

Sanders of Oxford Ltd.
104 High Street
Oxford

Sevin Seydi
20 Redcliffe Street
London SW10 9DT

Walter T. Spencer
47 Upper Berkeley St.
London W 1

Robert D. Steedman
9 Gray Street
Newcastle Upon Tyne NE1 6EE

Alan G. Thomas
c/o Westminster Bank
300 King's Road
Chelsea, SW 3

G. Walford
186 Upper Street
London N1 1RH

Wheldon and Wesley, Ltd.
Lytton Lodge, Codicote
Hitchen, Herts SG4 8TE

John Wilson
New Yatt
Witney, Oxon

Clare Warrack &
Geoffrey Perkins
Rectory Fram House
Church Enstone
Oxfordshire
OX7 4NL

A BRIEF SAMPLING OF

ESTIMATED PRICE VALUES OF

BOOKS BY CONTEMPORARY AUTHORS

The following list is just what its title says—a *"sampling* of *estimated* prices"; it is based upon twenty recent catalogues put out by dealers in rare books. Please note that the prices given are *retail* prices. Bibliographical information is minimal; for first-issue points consult standard bibliographies, or the catalogues of reputable dealers.

The list is confined to works published by American and English authors now living.

The books listed do not necessarily represent the most valuable works of the authors cited, nor are the works and authors included meant in any way to represent the most collectable of contemporary authors; many who are *not* listed are as "collectable"—in almost any conceivable way that word is defined—as any of those who *are* listed; their works are not represented simply because the particular catalogues I consulted did not list any of them.

All of the copies referred to are first editions, and said to be in fine to mint condition, with dust jackets where called for. The difference between a copy in mint condition with dust jacket and one in merely good or fair condition, without dust jacket, can be as great as that between a bottle of fine vintage wine and a bottle of pop.

Many of the following titles are valuable largely, sometimes primarily, because of the fact they are signed, limited editions.

293

Albee, Edward. *Who's Afraid of Virginia Woolf?* New York, 1962. $35.

Ashbery, John. *Turandot and Other Poems.* One of 300. Illustrated, wrapper, signed. $175.

Auchincloss, Louis. *The Indifferent Children,* by Andrew Lee (published pseudonymously), New York, 1947. $35.

Baldwin, James. *Go Tell It on the Mountain.* New York, 1953. $100.

Barth, John. *The Floating Opera.* New York, 1956. $65.

_____ *The Sot-Weed Factor.* New York, 1960. $50.

Barthelme, Donald. *Come Back, Dr. Caligari.* Boston, 1964. $25.

Beckett, Samuel. *Waiting for Godot.* New York, 1954. (This is the first edition in English, as translated by the author; the *first* edition, *En Attendant Godot,* one of 35 copies, sells in the thousands of dollars.) $75.

_____ *Poems in English.* Signed first edition, one of 100. $150.

_____ *Proust and Three Dialogues.* London, 1965. Signed first edition, one of 100. $125.

Bellow, Saul. *The Adventures of Augie March.* New York, 1953. $25.

Bly, Robert. *The Light Around the Body.* New York, 1967. $20.

Bradbury, Ray. *Dark Carnival.* Sauk City, 1947. $100.

Bukowski, Charles. *At Terror Street and Agony Way.* Los Angeles, 1968, signed first edition, one of 75 with original illustrations by author. $100.

_____ *If We Take.* Los Angeles, 1970. Signed first edition, one of 100. $20.

Bunting, Basil. *Loquitur: Poems.* London, 1965. Signed first edition, one of 26. $75.

_____ *Collected Poems.* London, 1968. Signed first edition, one of 150. $30.

Burroughs, William. *Port of Saints.* London, 1973. One of 200 copies, (unsigned). $35.

———— *Port of Saints.* One of 200 copies (signed). $50.

———— *Naked Lunch.* Paris (1959). $40.

Cheever, John. *The Enormous Radio and Other Stories.* New York, 1953. Author's first book. $25.

Corman, Cid. *All in All.* Origin Press, 1964. $40.

Corso, Gregory. *The Bomb.* San Francisco, 1958. $25.

Creeley, Robert. *The Finger.* Los Angeles. One of 300, wrapper inscribed by author. $25.

Dahlberg, Edward. *Bottom Dogs.* London, 1929. One of 520. $85.

———— *Do These Bones Live?* New York, no date [1941]. $40.

———— *The Flea of Sodom.* Norfolk, 1950. $20.

Dali, Salvador. *The Secret Life of Salvador Dali.* 1942. $50.

deCamp, L. Sprague. *Demons and Dinosaurs.* Sauk City, 1970. $35.

Dickey, James. *Buckdancer's Choice.* Middletown, no date [1965]. $25.

———— *Exchanges.* Bloomfield Hills, 1971. $20.

Didion, Joan. *Play It As It Lays.* New York, 1970. $25.

DiPrima, Diane. *Memoirs of a Beatnik.* New York, 1969, printed wrapper. $15.

Donleavy, J.P. *The Ginger Man.* Paris, no date [1955]. $60.

Dorn, Edward. *The Newly Fallen.* New York, 1961. Printed wrappers. $15.

———— *Slinger (Gunslinger).* Berkeley, 1975. Signed first edition, one of 250. $35.

Duncan, Robert. *Names of People.* Los Angeles, 1968. One of 250. $35.

Durrell, Lawrence. *The Alexandria Quartet.* First collector's edition; signed first edition, one of 500. $75.

———— *A Private Country: Poems.* London, 1943. $40.

Eberhart, Richard. *Brotherhood of Men.* Wrapper, no place, no date [Pawlet, Vermont, 1949]. $100.

Everson, William. *The Springing of the Blade: Poems of Nineteen Forty Seven.* Reno, 1968. Signed first edition, one of 180. $50.

_____ *War Elegies.* Illustrated, wrapper, Waldport, 1944. One of 975. $50.

_____ *Canticle to the Water Birds.* Berkeley 1968. $30.

Farrell, James T. *No Star Is Lost.* New York, 1938. $45.

_____ *Young Lonigan: A Boyhood in Chicago Streets.* New York, 1932. $100.

Ferlinghetti, Lawrence. *Coney Island of the Mind.* New York, 1958. $25.

_____ *The Secret Meaning of Things,* New York, 1969. Signed first edition, one of 150. $30.

Fry, Christopher. *The Firstborn.* Cambridge, 1946. $25.

Gardner, John. *The Wreckage of Agathon.* New York, 1970. $25.

Gass, William. *Omensetter's Luck.* New York, 1966. $15.

Ginsberg, Allen. *Howl.* San Francisco, no date [1956]. (Note: true first edition is mimeographed—a "run" of about 50 copies, one of which brings over $500.) $150.

_____ *Howl.* San Francisco, 1971. Grabhord-Hoyem revised edition, signed first edition, one of 270. $60.

_____ *Wichita Vortex Sutra.* San Francisco, 1966. One of 500, wrapper. $15.

Gold, Herbert. *The Man Who Was Not With It.* Boston, 1956. $20.

_____ *Fathers.* New York, 1966. $25.

Gordon, Caroline. *Aleck Maury, Sportsman.* New York, 1934. $65.

_____ *The Garden of Adonis.* New York, 1937. $20.

Gorey, Edward. *The Bug Book.* New York, 1960. Inscribed by author. $100.

_____ *Amphigorey.* New York, 1972. $25.

Graves, Robert. *Over the Brazier.* No place (Poetry Bookshop), 1916. $200.

_____ *Good-Bye to All That.* London, 1929. Signed. $125.

_____ *Antiqua, Penny, Puce.* Deya, Majorca, 1936. $50.

Greene, Graham. *The Man Within.* London, 1929. $100.

_____ *The Stamboul Train.* London, 1932. $75.

Gunn, Thom. *The Explorers: Poems.* London, 1970. Signed first edition, one of 20, wrapper. $30.

_____ *A Geography.* Iowa City, 1966. Signed first edition, one of 200. $20.

Harris, Mark. *The Southpaw.* Indianapolis, 1953. $15.

Hawkes, John. *The Beetle Leg.* New York, 1951. $25.

_____ *The Lime Twig.* Norfolk, 1961. Signed first edition, one of 100. $50.

_____ *Lunar Landscapes.* New York, 1969. $25.

Himes, Chester. *Lonely Crusade.* New York, 1947. $35.

Hughes, Richard. *A High Wind in Jamaica.* London, 1929. $30.

Hughes, Ted. *Crow.* London, 1970. $15.

_____ *A Crow Hymn.* Frensham, Sceptre, 1970. $15.

_____ *The Hawk in the Rain.* London, no date [1957]. $50.

Jones, Leroi. (Amiri Baraka). *Preface to a Twenty-Volume Suicide Note.* New York, 1961. $25.

Kelly, Robert. *Armed Descent.* New York, 1961. $45.

_____ *Reading Her Notes.* New York, 1972. One of 250. $25.

Kesey, Ken. *One Flew Over the Cuckoo's Nest.* New York, 1962. $35.

Kinnell, Galway. (translator). *Bitter Victory,* by Rene Hardy. Garden City, 1956. $25.

_____ *The Book of Nightmares.* Boston, 1971. $25.

Kinsella, Thomas. *Three Legendary Sonnets.* One of 100, inscribed by author. $35.

Kizer, Carolyn. *The Ungrateful Garden.* Bloomington, Indiana, no date [1961]. $35.

Koch, Kenneth. *When the Sun Tries to Go Down.* Los Angeles, 1969. Signed first edition, one of 200. $30.

Leiber, Fritz. *Night's Black Agents.* Sauk City, 1947. $50.

Lessing, Doris. *The Grass Is Singing.* London, no date [1950]. $20.

Levertov, Denise. *Overland to the Islands.* Highlands, N.C., 1958. Inscribed. $65.

_____ *A Tree Telling of Orpheus.* Los Angeles, 1968. Signed first edition, one of 75. $50.

Lowell, Robert. *Life Studies.* New York, 1959. $20.

_____ *Lord Weary's Castle.* New York, 1946. $55.

_____ *The Mills of the Kavanaughs.* New York, 1951. $35.

MacBeth, George. *Lecture to the Trainees: Poems.* Oxford, 1962. $15.

McClure, Michael. *The Beard.* Berkeley, 1965. First edition, one of 350. $65.

_____ *The Cherub.* Los Angeles, 1970. Signed first edition, one of 250. $50.

_____ *Hail Thee Who Play.* Los Angeles, 1968. Signed first edition, one of 75. $75.

_____ *Mind/Body/Split.* Oakland, no date [1974]. Signed first edition, one of 20. $100.

_____ *Poisoned Wheat.* San Francisco, 1965. Signed first edition, one of 24. $55.

McCord, Howard. *Precise Fragments,* Dublin, 1963. $40.

MacDiarmid, Hugh. *Poems to Paintings by William Johnstone.* Signed first edition, one of 100. $20.

MacDonald, Ross (pseud.) *The Three Roads,* by Kenneth Millar.
New York, 1948. $20.

MacLeish, Archibald. *Conquistador.* Boston, 1932. $50.

———— *An Evening's Journey to Conway, Massachusetts.* Conway,
Massachusetts, 1967. Illustrated by Leonard Baskin, wrapper,
boxed. $25.

———— *Songs for a Summer Day.* No place [New Haven], 1913. $150.

Mailer, Norman. *The Naked and the Dead.* New York, 1948. $30.

Malec, Alexander. *Extrapolasis.* Garden City, 1967. $15.

Merwin, W. S. *The Dancing Bears.* New Haven, 1954. $25.

———— *The Drunk in the Furnace.* London, 1960. $25.

———— *A Mask for Janus.* New Haven, 1952. $55.

———— *Japanese Figures.* Santa Barbara, 1971. Signed first edition,
one of 375. $20.

Miller, Henry. *The Air-Conditioned Nightmare.* No place, no date
[Norfolk, Conn., 1945]. $25.

———— *Order & Chaos Chez Hans Reichel,* New Orleans, 1966.
Signed first edition, one of 26. $60.

———— *Plexus.* Paris, 1953, 2 vols. $150.

Moore, Catherine L. *Judgment Night.* New York, 1952. $15.

Morris, Wright. *The Cat's Meow.* Los Angeles, 1972. Signed first
edition, one of 125. $40.

———— *The Inhabitants.* New York, 1946. $45.

———— *Love Among the Cannibals.* New York, 1957. $25.

———— *War Games,* Los Angeles, 1970. Signed first edition, one of
26. $30.

Murdoch, Iris. *The Bell.* London, 1958. $25.

———— *A Severed Head.* London, 1961. $20.

Nabokov, Vladimir. *Nabokov's Dozen.* Garden City, 1958. $20.

———— *The Real Life of Sebastian Knight.* Norfolk, 1941. $35.

———— (translation) *Three Russian Poets,* translated by Nabokov. Pushkin, Lermontov, and Tytchev. Norfolk, 1944. $35.

Nemerov, Howard. *The Image and the Law.* New York, 1947. $45.

———— *The Painter Dreaming in the Scholar's House.* New York, 1968. Signed first edition, one of 126. $30.

———— *The Salt Garden.* Boston, 1955. $20.

Niedecker, Lorine. *North Central: Poems.* London, 1968. signed first edition, one of 100. $15.

Nin, Anaïs. *A Spy in the House of Love.* New York, 1954. Presentation copy. $20.

———— *The House of Incest.* Paris, 1936. Wrapper, one of 249. $85.

———— *Under a Glass Bell.* New York, 1948. $25.

Oates, Joyce Carol. *By the North Gate.* New York, 1963. $25.

———— *The Girl.* Cambridge, 1974. Signed first edition, one of 50. $35.

———— *The Hostile Sun.* Los Angeles, 1973. Signed first edition, one of 300. $20.

———— *Upon the Sweeping Flood.* New York, 1966. $15.

Patten, Brian. *Atomic Adam: A Poem.* London, 1967. Signed first edition, one of 150. $15.

Percy, Walker. *The Moviegoer.* New York, 1961. $25.

Pinter, Harold. *Five Screen Plays.* London, 1971. Signed first edition, one of 150. $35.

———— *Poems.* London, 1971. Second edition, with additional poems; signed first edition, one of 100. $35.

Porter, Katherine Anne. *Flowering Judas.* New York, 1935. $50.

———— *Noon Wine.* Detroit, 1937. Signed first edition, one of 250. $175.

———— *Pale Horse, Pale Rider.* New York, 1939. $30.

Queen, Ellery. (Frederic Dannay and Manfred B. Lee). *The Chinese Orange Mystery.* New York, 1934. $30.

_____ *The Devil to Pay.* New York, 1938. $30.

Rexroth, Kenneth. *Beyond the Mountains.* Norfolk, Virginia, 1951.
Inscribed. $75.

_____ *The Dragon and the Unicorn.* Norfolk, Virginia, 1952. $15.

Rich, Adrienne Cecile. *A Change of World.* New Haven, Connecticut, 1951. $35.

_____ *The Knight, After Rilke.* San Francisco, 1957. $15.

Roth, Philip. *Goodbye, Columbus.* Boston, 1959. $40.

Sansom, William. *Fireman Flower and Other Stories.* London, 1944. $20.

Saroyan, William. *Inhale & Exhale.* New York, 1936. $30.

Sarton, May. *The Single Hound,* Boston, 1938. $25.

Snyder, Gary. *Fudo Trilogy.* Berkeley, 1973. Signed first edition,
one of 200. $60.

_____ *Regarding Wave.* Iowa City. 1969. Signed first edition, one
of 280. $30.

_____ *Riprap.* Ashland, Mass., 1959. $135.

Spender, Stephen. *Twenty Poems.* Oxford, 1930. Signed first edition, one of 75. $350.

Spicer, Jack. *Billy the Kid.* Stinson Beach, 1959. Wrapper. $15.

_____ *The Heads of the Town up to the Aether.* San Francisco, 1962. $30.

Stafford, William. *That Other Alone.* Mt. Horeb, Wisconsin, 1973.
Signed first edition, one of 120. $40.

_____ *Traveling Through the Dark.* New York, 1962. $25.

_____ *Weather.* Mt. Horeb, Wisconsin, 1969. Wrapper, one of
207. $25.

Stuart, Jesse. *Man with the Bull-Tongue Plow.* New York, 1934. $75.

Tate, Allen. *Jefferson Davis, His Rise and Fall.* New York, 1929. $30.

_____ *Poems 1922–1947.* New York, 1948. $50.

_____ *On the Limits of Poetry.* New York, 1948. $35.

Updike, John. *The Angels.* Pensacola, 1968. Signed first edition, one of 150. $60.

———— *Bech: A Book.* New York, 1970. Signed first edition, one of 500. $35.

———— *The Poorhouse Fair.* New York, 1959. $25.

Vidal, Gore. *Williwaw.* New York, 1946. $35.

Vonnegut, Kurt, Jr. *Canary in a Cat House.* Greenwich, 1961. Wrapper. $20.

———— *Player Piano.* New York, 1952. $35.

Wakoski, Diane. *Black Dream Ditty for Billy "The Kid."* Los Angeles, no date, signed first edition, one of 26. $35.

———— *Dancing on the Grave of a Son of a Bitch.* Los Angeles, 1973. Signed first edition, one of 50. $40.

Warren, Robert Penn. *Audubon: A Vision,* New York, 1969. Signed first edition, one of 300. $25.

———— *Blackberry Winter.* Cummington, Massachusetts, 1946. Signed first edition, one of 280. $50.

———— *Night Rider.* Boston, 1939. $40.

Welty, Eudora. *A Curtain of Green.* Garden City, New York, 1941. $85.

———— *The Golden Apples.* New York, 1949. $30.

———— *The Robber Bridegroom.* Garden City, 1942. $50.

Williams, Tennessee. *Battle of Angels.* Murray, Utah, 1945. Wrapper. $200.

———— *Cat on a Hot Tin Roof.* New York, 1955. $25.

———— *The Glass Menagerie.* New York, 1945. $75.

Wright, James. *The Green Wall.* New Haven, Connecticut, 1957. $30.

Zukofsky, Louis. *5 Statements for Poetry.* Stapled wrappers. Mimeographed work, 58 pp. Blue wrapper. $150.

SELECTED BIBLIOGRAPHY

The book collector's most obviously essential possession is knowledge. Therefore, as many as possible of the following books—or in some cases, others like them—should be either in the possession, or within access, of the private collector. Older biographical and encyclopedic works that may be considered obsolete for many purposes, are often very useful for the collector, since they contain information and often whole entries that have been dropped in later editions, due to the exigencies of space and "relevance."

PRIMARY RESOURCES:

American Authors and Their Books: 1640 to the Present Day. W. J. Burke and Will D. Howe. Revised ed., 1962.

American Book Prices Current. Published annually since 1895, this is a most useful aid to the English as well as American collector (English books sold at English sales are also listed). Older copies are sometimes available for around $10, but of course the prices they record are outdated and the collector is forced to compare and extrapolate on the evidence therein. New copies of recent editions sell for in excess of $40. Special 5-year editions are also issued.

Annals of English Literature 1475–1950. Oxford, 1961.

Basic Reference Sources. By Louis Shores. Chicago, 1954. "Basic" is the word, for this book tells where to look for places *where to look.*

Bibliographer's Manual of English Literature. W. T. Lowndes. 4 vols., London, 1858–1864.

Bibliographia 1750–1900. Ed. by Michael Sadleir. 10 vols. London, 1930–1936.

Book Auction Records. London and New York. Published annually since 1902. Similar to ABPC, but with a stronger emphasis on English books and English sales.

Cambridge Bibliography of English Literature. Ed. F. W. Bateson. 5 vols. Cambridge, 1940–1957.

The Cambridge History of American Literature. 3 vols., New York, 1917–21.

The Cambridge History of English Literature. 15 vols. Cambridge, 1917.

Cassel's Encyclopaedia of English Literature. Ed. S. H. Steinberg. 2 vols. London, 1953.

A Catalogue of the Everett D. Graff Collection of Western Americana. Storm, Colton. Chicago, 1968.

Critical Dictionary of English Literature. S. A. Allibone. 5 vols. Philadelphia, 1859–1891.

Cyclopaedia of American Literature. Evert A. Duyckinck and George L. Duyckinck. 2 vols. New York, 1856. The great usefulness of this work—and others like it in the mid-nineteenth century—is enhanced by careful reproductions of the holograph signatures of many of the authors written about, thus helping one to verify signed and inscribed copies, letters, manuscripts, and so on.

Dictionary of American Biography. New York, 20 vols. 1928–1937.

Dictionary of National Biography. Ed. Leslie Stephen and Sidney Lee. 22 vols. London, 1908–1909. Reprinted in 1950 in 27 vols.

The Encyclopaedia Britannica. Ninth Edition. The American Supplement in 30 vols. Akron, Ohio, 1904. A masterpiece of information and an acknowledged classic. Essential for anyone interested in antiquarian lore, history, the past, or, well, the human fact.

An Encyclopedia of the Book. Geoffrey Ashall Glaister. 1960.

Handbook of Values. Van Allen Bradley. 2nd. Ed., Revised. New York, 1975. A useful, comprehensive price guide for collectors and dealers alike.

An Introduction to Bibliography. Ronald B. McKerrow. Oxford, 1927.

The National Cyclopaedia of American Biography. 10 vols. New York, 1896.

The Oxford Companion to American Literature. James D. Hart. 4th ed. First American printing. New York, 1969.

Short Title Catalogue of Books 1641–1700. Donald Wing. 4 vols. New York, 1945–1955.

Short Title Catalogue of English Books 1475–1640. A. W. Pollard and G. R. Redgrave. Oxford, 1965.

Universal Pronouncing Dictionary of American Biography. 3rd ed., Philadelphia, 1901. This gem gives information about historical and legendary figures that are hard to find elsewhere. A most useful, cumbersome book.

U.S.-iana. Wright Howes. Second ed., New York, 1962. This is the single most useful, most dependable, and most influential book on the collecting and pricing of Americana. Howes' prices have to be updated, of course; but their relative values have endured remarkably. Sometimes Howes, like Homer, nods; but his influence on the collecting of Americana has been enormous.

SECONDARY RESOURCES:

The term "secondary" should not in this context be thought of as pejorative in any way. The following books are not "primary" simply because they do not intend to be minimally factual, but rather entertain such other qualities as judgment, wit, analysis, personal anecdote, and even passion. Booklovers everywhere have a special place in their pantheon for "Books About Books," whose acronymic personification, "Babs," is the most seductive of charmers. Here she is represented in some of her appearances.

Altick, Richard D. *The Art of Literary Research.* 1963.
The Scholar Adventurers. 1966.

Arnold, William Harris. *Ventures in Book Collecting.* 1923.

Bayley, Harold. *A New Light on the Renaissance: Displayed in Contemporary Emblems.* 1909.

Bennett, Paul A. *Books and Printing.* 1951.

Bland, David. *A History of Book Illustration.* 1958.

Burton, John Hill. *The Book-Hunter.* 1862.

Bushnell, George Herbert. *From Bricks to Books.* 1949.

Carter, John. *ABC for Book Collectors.* 1957.
Books and Book Collectors. 1957.
Taste and Technique in Book Collecting. New ed., 1970.

Cobden-Sanderson, T.J. *Cosmic Vision.* 1922.

Cockerell, S. M. *The Repairing of Books.* 1958.

Connolly, Cyril. *The Modern Movement,* 1966.

Diringer, David. *The Alphabet.* Third ed., Revised. 2 vols. 1969.
The Hand-Produced Book. 1953.
The Illuminated Book. 1958.

Everitt, Charles P. *The Adventures of a Treasure Hunter.* 1952

Farrar, Frederick M. *Fred Farrar's Type Book.* 1927.

Frazier, J. L. *Type Lore: Popular Fonts of Today—Their Origin and Use.* 1925.

Hamilton, Charles. *Scribblers & Scoundrels.* New York, 1968.

Haycraft, Howard. *The Art of the Mystery Story.* 1946.

Hunter, Dard. *Papermaking.* 1947.

Jackson, Holbrook. *The Anatomy of Bibliomania.* 1930.
Bookman's Pleasure. 1945.

Johnson, Merle. *American First Editions.* Third ed., 1936.

Kiefer, Monica. *American Children Through their Books, 1700–1835.* 1948.

Lewis, Wilmarth. *Collector's Progress.* New York, 1951.
One Man's Education. 1967.

McMurtrie, Douglas C. *The Golden Book.* 1927.

Madison, Charles A. *Book Publishing in America.* 1966.
The Owl Among Colophons. 1966.

Mahony, Bertha E. and Whitney, Elinor. *Contemporary Illustrators of Children's Books.* 1930.

Meynell, Francis. *Typography.* 1944.
My Lives, 1971.

Morley, Christopher. *Ex Libris Carissimis.* 1932.

Morrison, Stanley. *Modern Fine Printing.* 1925.
On Type Designs, Past & Present. 1962.

Newton, A. Edward. *The Amenities of Book Collecting.* 1918.
A Magnificent Farce and Other Diversions of a Book Collector, 1921.
On Books and Business. 1930.
This Book Collecting Game. 1928.

Orcutt, William Dana. *In Quest of the Perfect Book.* 1926.
The Kingdom of Books. 1927.

Powell, Lawrence Clark. *The Alchemy of Books.* 1954.
  Bookman's Progress. 1965.
  California Classics. 1971.
  A Passion for Books. 1958.

Quayle, Eric. *The Collector's Book of Books.* 1971.

Randall, David A. *Dukedom Large Enough.* 1969.

Rogers, Bruce. *PI: A Hodge-Podge of Letters, Etc.* 1953.

Rosenbach, A. S. W. *Books and Bidders.* 1927.
  Early American Children's Books, 1933.

Sadleir, Michael. *Nineteenth Century Fiction.* 1951.

Sawyer, C. J. and Barton, F. J. H. *English Books 1475–1900.* 2 vols. 1927.

Silver, Rollo G. *The American Printer, 1787–1825.* 1967.
  Typefounding in America, 1787–1825. 1965.

Starrett, Vincent. *Books and Bipeds.* 1947.

Stevens, Henry. *Recollections of James Lenox and the Formation of his Library.* Revised ed. by Victor Hugo Paltsits. 1951.

Targ, William. *Bibliophile in the Nursery.* 1957.
  Bouillabaise for Bibliophiles. 1955.
  Carrousel for Bibliophiles. 1947.

Thomas, Alan G. *Fine Books.* 1967.
  Great Books and Book Collectors. 1975.

Updike, D. B. *Printing Types.* 1922.

Warde, Beatrice. *The Crystal Goblet.* 1956.

Winterich, John T. *Books and Man.* 1930.
  A Primer of Book Collecting. Third ed., revised by David A. Randall. 1966.

Wise, Thomas J. *Letters of Thomas J. Wise to John Henry Wrenn.* 1944.

Wolfe, Edwin and Fleming, John F. *Rosenbach, a Biography.* 1960.

307

INDEX